Liberation and Critic

in Today's Catholic Schools

CRITICAL EDUCATION PRACTICE
VOLUME 11
GARLAND REFERENCE LIBRARY OF SOCIAL SCIENCE
VOLUME 1106

Critical Education Practice

Shirley R. Steinberg and Joseph L. Kincheloe, *Series Editors*

Curriculum Development in the Postmodern Era
by Patrick Slattery

Becoming a Student of Teaching
Methodologies for Exploring Self and School Context
by Robert V. Bullough, Jr. and Andrew D. Gitlin

Occupied Reading
Critical Foundations for an Ecological Theory
by Alan A. Block

Democracy, Multiculturalism, and the Community College
A Critical Perspective
by Robert A. Rhoads and James R. Valadez

Anatomy of a Collaboration
Study of a College of Education/Public School Partnership
by Judith J. Slater

Teaching Mathematics
Toward a Sound Alternative
by Brent Davis

Inner-City Schools, Multiculturalism, and Teacher Education
A Professional Journey
by Frederick L. Yeo

Rethinking Language Arts
Passion and Practice
by Nina Zaragoza

Educational Reform
A Deweyan Perspective
by Douglas J. Simpson and Michael J. B. Jackson

Liberation Theology and Critical Pedagogy in Today's Catholic Schools
Social Justice in Action
by Thomas Oldenski

Liberation Theology and Critical Pedagogy in Today's Catholic Schools

Social Justice in Action

Thomas Oldenski

Routledge
Taylor & Francis Group
New York London

First published by Garland Publishing, Inc.

This edition published 2011 by Routledge:

Routledge
Taylor & Francis Group
711 Third Avenue
New York, NY 10017

Routledge
Taylor & Francis Group
2 Park Square, Milton Park
Abingdon, Oxon OX14 4RN

Library of Congress Cataloging-in-Publication Data

Oldenski, Thomas.
Liberation theology and critical pedagogy in today's Catholic schools : social justice in action / Thomas Oldenski.
p. cm. — (Garland reference library of social science ; vol. 1106. Critical education practice ; vol. 11)
Includes bibliographical references and index.
ISBN 0-8153-2375-1 (pbk. : alk. paper). — ISBN 0-8153-2379-4 (hardcover : alk. paper)
1. Critical pedagogy—United States—Case studies. 2. Liberation theology—Study and teaching (Secondary)—United States—Case studies. 3. Catholic high schools—United States—Case studies. 4. Vincent Gray Alternative High School. I. Title. II. Series: Garland reference library of social science ; v. 1106. III. Series: Garland reference library of social science. Critical education practice ; vol. 11.
LC196.5.U6053 1997
370.11'5—dc21 96-51085
CIP

Paperback cover design by Robert Vankeirsbilck.

I dedicate this book
to Ann and Joe Oldenski,
my first and best teachers

Contents

Acknowledgments

It took the encouragement of a great many friends for me to formalize here my experiences with and conclusions about Catholic education and schooling practices. I am grateful to Peter McLaren, Joe Kincheloe and Shirley Steinberg for their enthusiasm for this project. I am indebted to Dennis Carlson for his friendship and help as I completed my dissertation at Miami University. I also appreciate those professors who introduced me to critical pedagogy, the relationship of critical discourses to schooling, and the value of qualitative research: Henry Giroux, Peter McLaren, Richard Quantz and Richard Hofmann. Thanks also to my colleagues at the University of Dayton for entertaining my interest in Catholic schools and curricula, and in what it means to be a transformative educational leader. I am thankful to the Deans of the School of Education, Ellis Joseph and Patricia First, and to my department chair, William Drury, for the time and support they gave me to ponder and to write.

My special thanks go to the members of my religious community, the Marianists, for allowing me to remain my own recursive project as I work to become an instrument of justice and peace. Thanks to my Mom and Dad, who taught me that being Catholic means showing concern for others; and thanks to my sisters Joanne and Gerry and my brother Rick, who helped make our family a learning community. Also, my friend and fellow doctoral student, Michael Romanowski, continually helps me clarify my thinking in our many conversations.

This book would have been impossible without the cooperation of the students, graduates, teachers and administrators of Vincent Gray Alternative High School in East St. Louis, Illinois. To all of them, I owe an immense debt of gratitude for allowing me into their lives and for helping me discover the value of integrating critical discourses with Catholic schooling practices.

Foreword

Brother Tom Oldenski, a Marianist, is among those cultural workers who are passionately committed to education. Oldenski's book, *Liberation Theology and Critical Pedagogy in Today's Catholic Schools,* attempts to advance the struggle against the dystopian despair of our times. Grounded in the work by liberation theologians, this book considers peace, love and social justice within a democratic curriculum. Love is the primary force of liberation that exfoliates into acts of compassion, understanding, kindness and mercy—all of which are constitutive of an ontological dialectics of desire.

The book is a critical ethnography of Vincent Gray Alternative High School, a Catholic school in East St. Louis, struggling with its own identity as a Catholic institution. Named after the first African American to profess religious vows as a Marianist, the school is described as an arena of "last chances" for high school students "deemed incorrigible by the courts, unteachable by the schools, or lost causes by their won families." Oldenski believes that the critical discourses of liberation theology and critical pedagogy express the qualities and characteristics of a good Catholic education. Further, Oldenski considers the voices of students, administrators, teachers and alumni to both embody and articulate in an implicit manner the critical discourses of liberation theology and critical pedagogy. What Oldenski has discovered is that the diverse voices that fill the school already constitute the nascent elements—the germinating seeds—of what he calls the integrative model of liberation theology and critical pedagogy. This is an important insight and one that critical educators need to acknowledge. One reason that discourses of liberation have been so far-reaching in resisting oppression in all of its guises and in mobilizing consent around the imperatives of peace and love has to do with the fact that they speak to the habits of the heart already present in the lives of ordinary people, those uncommon common folk who fill the classrooms and corridors of our churches and schools.

There is a definite politics of affinity between liberation theology and critical pedagogy. While Oldenski recognizes that critical pedagogy and liberation theology are not subsumable within a single vision of emancipation and self-determination, he explores their connections and overlaps between their respective conceptions of social justice and education.

Without a doubt, Vincent Gray Alternative High School has institutional advantages over other inner-city schools. Its four-to-one student-teacher ratio helps to create a milieu of few discipline problems, no graffiti, no weapons, no beepers, no drugs nor alcohol. But what is truly remarkable about this school is the commitment of its teachers and students to a struggle to change the world in the interests of greater human freedom and social justice.

Oldenski's study is both driven and framed by the following questions: Whom do Catholic schools serve and how are they served? Has the Church abandoned its primary mission of helping the poor? Why are the numbers of poor people growing greater as society continues to embrace the so-called democratic imperative of marketplace capitalism? What does it mean to be a Catholic educator? What does it mean to be a Catholic?

Oldenski discusses how the work of Brazilian educator Paulo Freire has influenced the critical discourses of liberation theology and critical pedagogy through Freire's concern for the wretched of the earth and his attempts at helping economically disenfranchised and marginalized people become critically literate. For Oldenski, liberation theology "starts from action and leads to action" and adopts a philosophy of praxis that operates from the perspective of a faith community. Praxis is both the foundation and the claim of liberation theology, and in a similar fashion, praxis constitutes the dialectical engine of critical pedagogy. Inasmuch as critical pedagogy is able to dialogically secure counterfactual forms of discursive engagement and representational practices, it has the potential (in the sense of Spinoza's idea of *potenza*—a construction within which human production becomes a form of location that possesses subversive power) to transform the culture of schooling into an arena of self-reflection and praxis.

According to Oldenski, the reflexive arch of critical pedagogy in many instances heralds a form of education exemplified by Vincent Gray Alternative High School. Oldenski does not pretend that the praxis of commitment at the school occupies the full range of critical practices that one would expect to see in a school situated under the sign of critical pedagogy. But the lived commitment of the teachers and students to the teachings of Jesus adds to the commitment to social justice and love.

To advocate a preferential option for the poor and dispossessed, as does Oldenski, and to contest the master sin of pride and self-love and the current hucksterism of the spirit found within today's promotional culture, appears almost unnatural in these times. One need only witness the current national climate of renewed racism, corporate greed, Latinophobia, attacks on affirmative action and the hate-filled initiatives of Proposition 187 in California, to feel somewhat hopeless about the future. However, this book is out of synch with postmodernist despair and the fashionable cynicism of current cultural criticism, perhaps even belonging to another time, another age, one in which the use of the word *love* in our high school classrooms would not provoke a shudder of embarrassment or a mocking revulsion. Because this is a decidedly unnatural book, one filled with cautious optimism and hope, I highly recommend it for all those interested in the struggle for peace and social justice.

Peter L. McLaren
University of California–Los Angeles

Liberation Theology and Critical Pedagogy in Today's Catholic Schools

Chapter One

What's "This" All About?

> [Baby Suggs] did not tell them to clean up their lives or to go and sin no more. She did not tell them they were the blessed of the earth, its inheriting meek or its glory bound pure. She told them that the only grace they could have was the grace they could imagine. That if they would not see it, they would not have it.
>
> - Toni Morrison in *Beloved* (1987)

> The Queen remarked, "Now I'll give you something to believe. I'm just one hundred and one, five months and a day." "I can't believe that!" said Alice. "Can't you?" the Queen said in a pitying tone. "Try again: draw a long breath, and shut your eyes." Alice laughed. "There's no use trying," she said; "one can't believe impossible things." "I daresay you haven't had much practice," said the Queen. "When I was your age, I always did it for half an hour a day. Why, sometimes I've believed as many as six impossible things before breakfast."
>
> - Lewis Carroll in *Through the Looking Glass* (1871)

Both quotations encourage me to shut my eyes, to imagine and to believe in different ways of thinking about schools, particularly Catholic schools, and what could be happening in schools differently than what is happening there now. Baby Suggs teaches us to imagine in order to "have it" and the White Queen encourages us to believe in the impossible. My belief in what appears to be impossible stimulates me to ponder many questions. What is it I would like to see in Catholic schools? What would I like to imagine Catholic schools to be like? Could practices in both Catholic and public schools be informed by critical discourses like liberation theology and critical pedagogy? What can these two critical discourses bring to an understanding of Catholic education? Can these critical discourses help us understand what happens in schools and what could be happening in our parochial, private or public schools?

As I ponder these questions and issues, I draw upon my own experiences as a Catholic school teacher and administrator and my current experiences as a professor at a Catholic university. Besides my own experiences, my interest in liberation theology and critical pedagogy influenced my analysis of the relationship between these two critical discourses as well as the relationship of critical discourses to Catholic education. My own interest in the critical discourses of liberation theology and critical pedagogy further prompted me to wonder if and how these appeared in a school committed to teaching and working with some oppressed or marginalized segment of society. My own teaching in Catholic high schools led me to wonder what shape a Catholic school might take if it were committed to such elements and themes of critical discourses as liberation theology and critical pedagogy.

My familiarity with Catholic schools reflects my life within Catholic education. I attended a Catholic grade school, a Catholic high school and a Catholic university. I have spent my adult life as a religious brother in the Marianists, a religious congregation of brothers and priests within the Catholic church, whose history includes an extensive involvement with Catholic schools in our country and others. As a Marianist brother who served as a teacher and an administrator in Catholic schools, I reflected often on what ideals and realities shape these schools in order to help apply the spirit of the Gospels—or in other words, to help promulgate the Kingdom of God. I believe peace, justice and love characterize this Kingdom. Attaining these values in my life and bringing them to the lives of others have been the driving forces in my life, and this is how I want to spend my energies. This is idealistic talk but I find every effort toward this goal is worthwhile.

Meanwhile I have read and pondered many of the liberation theologians of Central and South America. My own experiences of living and working with people in Nigeria, Ireland and Mexico, as well as living and working in Dayton, Kalamazoo and Memphis, brought their words to life. I find hope that many individuals who have become part of my life share these beliefs in the larger community of Christian believers.

After twenty years as a teacher and administrator in Catholic secondary schools, I undertook doctoral studies in educational leadership at Miami University, Ohio. Here I met a new array of educational prophets who criticized our modern schools and suggested possibilities and strategies for improving the lives of the marginalized, silenced and oppressed. These new teachers included Henry Giroux, Dennis Carlson, Peter McLaren and Richard Quantz. I seized the chance to interact with them both as a doctoral student and in informal conversations. They introduced me to critical discourses—namely, critical theory and critical pedagogy. They also introduced me to the work and writings of Paulo Freire and feminist liberation theologians like Sharon Welch and Rebecca Chopp. My excitement grew as I began to discover connections between liberation theology and critical discourses, and saw how these critical discourses helped me to reflect in a different way upon my experiences in Catholic schools.

During his trip to the United States in October of 1995, Pope John Paul II, like Baby Suggs and the White Queen, encouraged us Catholics to imagine and believe in what seems to be impossible. His homilies and other talks during his visit to New York City, Newark and Baltimore focused on what he termed "the new evangelization," which is a deepening of faith in the Gospel as "the power which can transform the world" (1995, p. 13) and which is "a new and vital proclamation of the Gospel aimed at integrating your faith ever more fully into the fabric of your daily lives" (p. 3). It seems to me this new evangelization pertains to those involved with Catholic education. Catholic education has as its very purpose the proclamation of the Gospel and the challenge to help young people integrate faith into their daily lives.

This new evangelization includes both these aspects of the role of faith in life and a new commitment in our culture to celebrate diversity, to be welcoming to new immigrants, and to be concerned for the poor of our own country as part of the proclamation of the transforming power of the Gospel. John Paul expressed these concerns upon his arrival at Newark International Airport where he stated that the United States "has been a haven for generation after generation of new arrivals" and that as a country we need to meet the needs of the poor and the disadvantaged (p. 15). Likewise, in his homily at Giants Stadium, the Pope recalled the words of Emma Lazarus's poem on the Statue of Liberty. He then posed this question: "Is present-day America becoming less sensitive, less caring towards the poor, the weak, the stranger, the needy? It must not! Today as before, the United States is called to be a hospitable society, a welcoming culture" (p. 3).

Once more Catholic educators must evaluate how Catholic schools welcome new arrivals and how Catholic schools express concern for the poor and disadvantaged. How the climate, spirit and practices of Catholic education demonstrate these concerns of diversity and the concerns of the new arrivals, the poor and the disadvantaged? John Paul's recent words animate my desire to enter the dialogue about the identity of Catholic schools and articulate how the critical discourses of liberation theology and critical pedagogy can inform this dialogue.

Melanie Svoboda states that "the essence of all writing is an 'I' hoping to share something with a 'you'" (1995, p. 23). She states my intention here: to share my ideas and my reflections about what I imagine and believe Catholic education can be and the relationship of Catholic education to the critical discourses of liberation theology and critical pedagogy. I believe that one of the ideals of Catholic education is to become and to be a model of critical theory and practice in a liberation theology context. I believe this is possible. Accordingly, I present the case study of Vincent Gray Alternative High School as an example of one school that demonstrates critical theory and practice in a liberation theology context.

As you read this book, you will ideally begin to think of Catholic education in a different way and see some new possibilities. I hope my ideas and reflections will help you to believe in the impossible. As I bring this book to fruition, I share the feelings Svoboda (1995) expresses in her article, "The Eight Beatitudes of Writing." She states that "when we write (as when we really live), we are putting ourselves on the line. In some cases, our necks go on the chopping block. We are proclaiming to the world in big bold letters: 'Look! This Is What I Think! This Is How I Feel! What Do You Think of Me Now?' Is there anything more frightening than that?" (p. 24).

One of my other goals in expressing my ideas and reflections is to help Catholic education improve our world. Svoboda again states that "writing flows from the innate desire to influence (no matter how slightly) people (no matter how few) for the better" (p. 23). Jonathan Kozol, whose works—especially *Savage Inequalities* (1991) and *Amazing Grace* (1995)—have intensified my concern for the poor, also states that he writes "to change the world" (Dreyfous, 1995, p. 19).

My beliefs as a doctoral student encouraged me to focus my dissertation on the relationship between liberation theology and critical pedagogy and the relationship of these two critical discourses to Catholic schools. As I developed my own awareness of such critical discourses as liberation theology, feminist ethics and critical pedagogy, I found myself more concerned about just what actually occurs in Catholic education and whom Catholic schools serve. To what degree do Catholic schools reflect Church documents and Gospel values that urge a concern for the poor? Is it possible to apply the critical discourses of liberation theology and critical pedagogy to Catholic schooling in our country? In light of current discussions within public education of "standards" and "achievement" as well as those proposals involving voucher systems for funding private education, it has become crucial for Catholic schools to struggle with the issue of whom they are serving as well as how they serve. I also find myself asking whether Catholic schools really offer an alternative to public education. Catholic schools like public schools need to confront the reasons for their existence.

In my view, Catholic schools are sites of ethical and social justice. The discourses of liberation theology and critical pedagogy can benefit Catholic education. It is both possible and urgent to understand Catholic schools as political sites in regard to the struggles for social justice, and this conviction led me to identify the site of my research, an alternative Catholic high school in East St. Louis, Illinois.

Subsequently, I focused there on the voices of the students, administrators and teachers of Vincent Gray Alternative High School as I came to know these persons at VGAHS. Their voices express some of the common elements in critical pedagogy and liberation theology and give life to these critical discourses.

A qualitative study focused on the voices of students, teachers and administrators heard in this book became the substance of my dissertation. Likewise, the relationship of the critical discourses of liberation theology and critical pedagogy that led me to develop an integrative model also became a major part of the dissertation. My main thesis became the articulation in these voices of my integrative model of the common elements of the critical discourses in liberation theology and critical pedagogy.

While adjusting now to the life of a university professor, I have been able to focus the implications of this research and my thoughts more on the identity of Catholic schools and how the critical discourses of liberation theology and critical pedagogy can enrich the dialogue of Catholic education. These two discourses can illuminate the current struggle and dialogue over what must become the concerns and focus for a Catholic education of the future. I intend that this discussion encourage those involved with Catholic education who are interested in critical discourses to imagine and believe that what appears to be impossible can become possible.

The students, teachers and administrators of Vincent Gray Alternative High School gave me a way of understanding how critical discourses describe school practices, and their voices helped me start to understand how these two critical discourses can describe, evaluate and influence those practices.

As I ponder the relationship of critical discourse to the identity of Catholic schools, I also struggle to understand modernism and postmodernism, and their effects upon my own thinking in relation to school reform. Patrick Slattery's *Curriculum Development in the Postmodern Era* (1995) helped me understand the relationship postmodernism bears to curriculum development. Slattery focuses on the purposes of schools and the structures schooling takes in reflecting these purposes as affected by the tensions between modernism and postmodernism.

Critical pedagogy must draw upon the best insights of modernism and postmodernism (Giroux, 1991 and 1992), and I have concluded that liberation theology must do the same in regard to modernism and postmodernism. As discourses of critique and possibility, liberation theology and critical pedagogy—in their own practices and self-understandings—actually try to draw upon both modernism and postmodernism.

Briefly stated, modernism offers the ideals of a democratic society —freedom, equity and justice, as well as the notions of individuals' social responsibilities as agents of critique and change. Modernism values the individual as a critical being able to shape his or her own destiny and meaning. Likewise, modernism upholds high culture over popular culture. Knowledge is perceived as totalizing narratives identified with the development of reason, science and technology. Reason, science and technology become sources of power and dominance in establishing the privileged over those who lack them. The only source of this knowledge and power is, however, the metanarratives of the Eurocentric cultures and histories. Thus, schooling becomes a site of transmission of the canon of knowledge and culture, as defined by rationality, science and technology.

Postmodernism, by contrast, expands the concepts of freedom, equity, justice and a democratic society to include an understanding of these phenomena from the perspective of those histories and voices that have been silenced, erased or excluded from the Eurocentric metanarratives of progress and human development. Postmodernism identifies these histories as "dangerous memories" (Taylor, 1990; and Welch, 1990) since they force one to evaluate history as it has been developed and presented from the perspective of the dominant culture and the oppressor. Postmodernism values popular taste and the everyday in the lives of people as vital to shaping and understanding culture. It celebrates diversity and plurality. In regard to knowledge, postmodernism begins to raise questions about how knowledge is constructed, whose interests knowledge serves, and what values and assumptions underlie this knowledge.

Both liberation theology and critical pedagogy integrate these concepts of equity, justice, freedom and a democratic community by according voice to the many others who were and are oppressed by Eurocentric metanarratives. Each of these discourses encourages a reconstruction of history so as to help others understand their own identities and assimilate a democratic society, justice and freedom into their lived experience. Both critical pedagogy and liberation theology echo the questions of postmodernism in regard to the construction and role of knowledge, especially as a source of power and a vehicle for silencing the voices of the poor, the marginalized and the many "others." Both of these discourses value the role of ethics, but this ethics is constructed in response less to ethical demands of power and authority of rationality, science or technology than to solidarity and compassion in creating a juster, more democratic human community. Both draw from modernism a protest against unnecessary human suffering and affirm ethics that reduces human suffering caused by oppression of the marginalized.

My own analysis of critical discourses and their relationship to Catholic education celebrates elements of modernism and postmodernism. Within this tension between modernism and postmodernism, I show how critical discourses can contribute to the dialogue about the identity of Catholic schools. Modernism is reflected in a presentation of the students, teachers and administrators as agents of change in creating a society striving to become more just, equitable and democratic. Presenting the common elements between liberation theology and critical pedagogy, I created a model inductively as I read and coded my first five student interviews. Thus, this model includes some of the integrative elements of these two critical discourses. Then I use this model to analyze the voices of the subsequent students, teachers and administrators. I also present their voices in a structural manner in relation to the integrative model of liberation theology and critical pedagogy.

Elements of postmodernism likewise appear. I focus on an alternative school in a community known as being marginalized by the dominant culture, a predominantly African American city as the result of white flight with a high proportion of its people on social welfare. My study celebrates the voices of diversity: African Americans and whites, the educated and those who have not succeeded in schools, students, teachers and administrators. These voices express a day-to-day existence in one of our poorest cities, and in these voices, one can hear many of the themes from the liberation theology and critical pedagogy texts. The chapters of this book also include my own voice as I interpret the voices of this school and the liberation theology and critical pedagogy texts as they relate to Catholic education.

Vincent Gray Alternative High School currently struggles with its own identity as a Catholic school. The chief administrator had earlier withdrawn VGAHS from the lists of Catholic schools of the local diocese, yet some of the teachers and administrators understand VGAHS as a Catholic school in terms of its values, practices and atmosphere. Moreover, the experiences and practices there demonstrate how Catholic schools can respond to the preference for the poor Catholic doctrine advocates.

I have tried to integrate the best of these discourses—both of modernism and postmodernism, and of liberation theology and critical pedagogy. I emphasize common themes and elements of the critical discourses of liberation theology and critical pedagogy as found in the voices of the students, administrators and teachers. I also focus on the history, the culture and the situation during my time at this school site in attempting to articulate its reasons for being and its vision for introducing justice, empowerment and a democratic community within the African American community of East St. Louis.

Conducting Research at VGAHS

Qualitative research in educational circles has achieved a great deal of sophistication in recent years. It employs a variety of strategies including interviews, participant observations, oral histories, and content analysis of texts, classroom behaviors and school life. Meanwhile, I found my experiences at VGAHS and as an education researcher urging this study from mere qualitative work toward a critical ethnography.

I could hardly separate the site and its practices from theory or from me, myself, as the researcher. This book, therefore, includes the dynamic movements that took place in my own thinking as a result of my on-site experiences in dialogue between my interests in both Catholic schools and public schooling and the viable critical discourses. Both liberation theology and critical pedagogy are viable critical discourses one can productively apply to Catholic education to help our society be a juster and more equitable society than it is now. As a researcher at VGAHS, I have experienced what Richard Quantz (1992) had earlier described: "Those engaged in critical ethnography find any discussion of method outside of theory to be not only sterile but distorted. Method is fully embedded in theory and theory is expressed in method" (p. 449).

As a qualitative researcher, I reasoned inductively as I approached an abundance of interactive data to make sense of what the voices of the participants express (LeCompte and Preissle, 1993; and Schumacher and McMillan, 1993). I also present a model for understanding the commonalities between liberation theology and critical pedagogy for examining the practices of a school to determine if they correlate with these commonalities. This qualitative study reflects my experiences of what Peter McLaren (1992) called research practices in a "critical mode." "Research practices undertaken in a critical mode necessitate recognizing the complexity of social relations and the researcher's own socially determined position within the reality that one is attempting to describe" (p. 84).

Sally Schumacher and James McMillan (1993) observed that "qualitative data analysis is primarily an inductive process of organizing the data into categories and identifying patterns (relationships) among the categories" (p. 479). I strived to code and identify patterns and relationships emerging from the data I obtained, but I did the same in regard to identifying patterns and relationships between the discourses of liberation theology and critical pedagogy. My intent was to develop an integrative model that includes common elements of these two discourses. In approaching the interactive data of the site and continually reflecting upon my experiences there, I used both "emic" and "etic" categories. Schumacher and McMillan (1993) defined these categories as follows:

> Emic categories represent insiders' views such as terms, actions, and explanations that are distinctive to the setting or people. Etic categories represent the outsiders' view of the situation—the researcher's concepts and scientific explanations. . . . Emic categories are explanations of what the phenomenon means to the participants. . . . Etic categories represent what the phenomenon means to the researchers. These categories come from the researcher's personal experiences, his or her academic discipline, or are borrowed from social science literature (pp. 493-494).

I used these etic and emic categories in developing the integrative model of liberation theology and critical pedagogy after reading transcripts of student interviews. I allowed the words of the participants to speak for themselves as I coded the interviews and, as much as possible, when I constructed the integrative model. McLaren (1991 a) characterized critical educational research as an attempt "to situate the construction of meaning within the life worlds of the participants themselves" (p. 18). While reading my interviews, I entered notes in the margins that were certainly influenced by my understanding of the discourses of liberation theology and critical pedagogy as well as the fact that I examined the transcripts sometime after leaving the school site. Then I utilized this integrative model of liberation theology and critical pedagogy to analyze the interviews of the school administrators, teachers and graduates. I also searched for similarities and discrepancies among and between these various groups of persons who are all part of the experience of Vincent Gray Alternative High School.

Almost spontaneously, I moved from the mode of completing qualitative research, or a school ethnography, to conducting critical research. In gathering the data at the site, as well as in reading and pondering the various data obtained from transcripts of interviews, field notes, journal reflections, personal thoughts or other records and documents, I experienced what McLaren described in 1992: "The field researcher needs to share with his or her subjects the discourses at work that are shaping the field site analysis and how the researcher's own personal and intellectual biography is contributing to the process of analysis" (p. 84). According to Quantz and O'Connor (1988), "Ethnography must always be understood as discourse situated in time and place and as authored by humans participating in a discourse of their own" (p. 108).

The participants knew my own interests in completing my work and some of my own history in relation to these discourses and Catholic schooling. Likewise, my own interests in both Catholic schools and the critical discourses of liberation theology and critical pedagogy and my experiences at the site influenced the analysis of the data. McLaren (1991 c) pointed out that "as field researchers, we both actively construct and are constructed by the discourses we embody and the metaphors we enact. We are in effect, both the subject and the object of our research" (p. 152).

Thus, this very book represents some aspects of my own experiences in education as part of a critical ethnography. Quantz (1992) stated that "those engaged in research that might be labeled 'critical ethnography' often have widely varied projects arrived at through unique personal histories." He went on to point out that "any ethnography that claims to be 'critical' must be understood as an utterance in an ongoing 'critical' dialogue" (p. 450). I undertook this project and now present this qualitative study in precisely that spirit, with the hope that I can contribute to an understanding of the critical discourses of liberation theology and critical pedagogy and their feasibility for Catholic schooling. I also intend this book to represent a "risk for knowledge" and a hope for the transformation and emancipation of those currently oppressed by the structures of schooling and society. My description of this qualitative study presents the site, the participants and me in the process of experiencing both the language of critique and the language of possibility of the discourses of liberation theology and critical pedagogy within the context of Catholic schooling. Finally, I hope this study gives life to the following words of McLaren (1991 c) with regard to critical ethnography:

> It is important that field researchers act with the oppressed, not over them or on behalf of them. Critical ethnography must be organic to and not administered upon the plight of struggling peoples. Field researchers should constantly place themselves in relations of "risk of knowledge," which means assuming a stance toward field relations that is not founded on political deceit or moral absolutism. . . . Field relations should be connected to the other such that, in the words of Carol Christ (1987), "the root of our scholarship and research is eros, a passion to connect, the

> desire to understand the experience of another, the desire to deepen our understanding of ourselves and our world, the passion to transform or preserve the world as we understand it more deeply." (p. 58) A politics of field relations must be grounded in eros, in passion, in commitment to transform through a radical connectedness to the self and the other (pp. 162-163).

A year later, McLaren (1992) pointed out that the focus of critical research goes beyond the site and the participants to include the field researchers themselves. "The field site additionally may be considered the site of the researcher's own embodiment in theory and discourse and his or her own disposition as a theorist; within a specific politics of location. . . field workers always are cultural workers who engage not just in the analysis of field sites but in their active production through the discourses used to analyze field relations" (p. 79). Quantz (1992) identified this type of disclosure and value identity as one of the themes of critical ethnography: "[C]ritical ethnographers are occasionally criticized for imposing their values on the group they are studying.... The pointed effort of critical researchers to reveal their own value perspective to the reader may differentiate critical ethnography from other forms and it may be this openness about their values that prompts criticism more than anything else" (p. 471).

Collecting Data at VGAHS

While searching for a site to conduct a qualitative study of the relationship between the critical discourses of liberation theology and critical pedagogy and Catholic schools, I had a conversation with Brother Anthony, the Director of Education of the St. Louis Province of the Marianists, and he suggested Vincent Gray Alternative High School. He also sent me a letter with the name and address of the Executive Director of VGAHS and the Director of the local Marianist community in East St. Louis. I wrote to both of them about the prospects of coming to VGAHS and living with the Marianist community there, and both encouraged me to come.

Then I arranged to spend time in East St. Louis for several weeks during the first semester of the 1992-93 school year. I developed a research plan and a day-to-day calendar for my work at VGAHS and altered some of my activities from each visit to the next. My initial visit, from August 31 through September 4, was also the first time I had been in East St. Louis. The purpose of this visit was introductory for all of us. I was present for the student orientation day at St. Patrick's Campus. I met individually with the Executive Director and the two school principals to elaborate upon my interests and my study. I also met with the faculty of each campus to explain the purpose of my dissertation and with students to observe several classes informally. I also took a tour of East St. Louis with one of the Directors of Operation New Spirit. During this visit I began my collection of various documents and records about East St. Louis and VGAHS, including the student handbook, the faculty handbook, newspaper articles, *Shades of Gray* (the school newspaper), church bulletins, schedules and the school calendar.

My other visits took place during the following dates of 1992: September 14 through 25; October 19 through 30; November 10 through 20; December 2 through 11; and January 21 through 24, 1993. I spent each school day at one of the campuses. My day typically began a few minutes before the first class and lasted well beyond the end of the school day. Some days I ate lunch with the students, particularly when I was on the Downtown Campus. My days included both informal and formal conversations and observations. Moreover, I participated in social activities like monthly birthday celebrations, a Halloween party, and a Monday Special Day sit-down lunch of roast pork.

During the combined faculty meeting of November 20, I was invited to serve as the facilitator of the process for obtaining a recommendation from the faculty to the Board of Trustees with regard to which campus should continue as the site of VGAHS. On this day, my role as an observant researcher changed to the role of an active participant with the faculty. Thus, I used two days of my next visit during December to help the faculty through long sessions with a view toward reaching a consensus on this recommendation. I spent my last visit in January specifically facilitating an all-day faculty meeting which concluded with a consensus statement subsequently presented to the Board of Trustees. I was also present at the January graduation commencement for three graduates I had gotten to know well.

During the other visits, I observed classes of each one of the teachers and followed some students through their school days. I interviewed a few students during each visit and also met and interviewed alumni. The students I interviewed were chosen by the principals. The alumni I interviewed were contacted by the Marianist Brother principal. He also arranged the time and the place for these interviews with the alumni. This initial screening meant that the students and alumni I interviewed represented only the VGAHS success stories. I interviewed no students who were dissatisfied with VGAHS or had left VGAHS. My interview data came, then, from individuals who were experiencing or had experienced VGAHS in a positive vein.

I also interviewed each one of the administrators and each faculty member. I shadowed the Executive Director for a week and also the Sister principal for a week. Each visit added to my document collection. I was present for the weekly all-school meetings of students and faculty and the weekly faculty meetings. My visits also included meetings with social workers and others who worked at other institutions and services in East St. Louis. These included the social workers at De Shields and Griffin Center, with whom I spent three days. I also spent time on several occasions with the teachers and students at the Catholic Day Care Center, across the street from the VGAHS Downtown Campus.

I tape recorded each one of my interviews and several class observations. I kept field notes during each day of my time in East St. Louis as well as a personal journal of my own reflections about the events of each day, including my emotional and rational responses. From this abundance of data I chose to use the words of the students, administrators and teachers expressed during my interviews.

Analyzing This Data

As I read over and analyzed my interviews, I developed a coding process influenced by my knowledge of liberation theology and critical pedagogy. Then I constructed my integrative model of these two discourses. While applying the codes, I focused on how the voices of each of these groups expressed common elements of the critical discourses of liberation theology and critical pedagogy.

I purposely selected certain interviews with students and staff members from each campus, both men and women, representing various lengths of time at VGAHS, and both lay and religious staff people. I chose to focus on six student interviews from the twenty student interviews I had collected. I formally interviewed six alumni and I focused on three of these interviews. I interviewed each of the three administrators and include each one in this study. I interviewed all of the faculty members and in this study, I focus upon six teachers.

During my second visit to the school, I interviewed eight students. As soon as five of these interviews were transcribed, I began the process of coding and analyzing them. This pilot research project would become the foundation for the process of coding and analyzing subsequent interviews with more students, the administrators and teachers. About ten weeks transpired between the time of the actual interviews and the beginning of the coding process. Therefore, I first read through the transcripts of the interviews to recall what was communicated between the students and myself.

During the second reading of each transcript, I began the analysis of the data by reading and rereading the student interviews, and I began to code them using words based upon my own familiarity with the discourses of liberation theology and critical pedagogy. Some of the themes that I utilized from these two discourses were: hope in terms of self, future and the present; oppressed community; presence of violence; community experiences; identifying East St. Louis as a marginalized place; being poor; being African American; voice and awareness; experiencing change; being helped; and so on. These notes began to tell me what these critical discourses meant in the voices of the students.

I then listed the various codes from the first five interviews around common words. For example, the list of initial codes from the first five student transcripts, which developed into the category "*Being Poor or Marginalized or Oppressed,*" included: marginalized people and place; marginalized; being poor, oppressed by the system; oppressed community but living with hope; oppressed by society; being poor, not having money; reality of being oppressed; being oppressed by one's own; and being oppressed as being Black. Through the lists of these initial codes, I identified a pattern and grouped the codes into larger categories, thus identifying conceptual textual segments with these categories. These notes began to tell me what these critical discourses meant in the voices of the students. From the various lists of codes, which I jotted down in the margins of the transcripts, I developed the more general categories or themes. The major key words or categories at this point included: *Hope; Community; Being Poor or Marginalized or Oppressed; Awareness or Voice or Conscientization; Spirituality or Soul; Change; Being Helped or Helping Others.*

Through a "cut and paste" process, I then added the words of the first five transcripts under each of these categories, thus identifying the voices of the students in creating an understanding of liberation theology and critical pedagogy. I then viewed and interpreted the actual texts of the student interviews under each category. These codes and themes became the building blocks of an integrative model accommodating the critical discourses of liberation theology and critical pedagogy. I then concentrated on how this integrative model was expressed in the words of other students, alumni, faculty and administrators.

Through this process, I was able to focus on the three questions I first proposed in formulating my study: (1) To what extent is the integration of liberation theology and critical pedagogy present at this site and how could this integration be developed further? (2) What form does a school take without a conscious understanding of these discourses of liberation theology and critical pedagogy? and (3) What is the best way to make liberation theology and critical pedagogy present in this school or at other sites? These questions raised three associated questions after my experiences of being at the site, and after reflecting on the data, that express the practices of VGAHS. These three new questions became the main focus of the analysis of the data I obtained in my interviews with the students, administrators, teachers and alumni: (1) Can the integrative model of the discourses of liberation theology and critical pedagogy help me to understand what is going on at VGAHS? (2) Can this integrative model, in turn, benefit what is now happening and what could be happening at VGAHS? and (3) Is it possible that both liberation theology and critical pedagogy could benefit other public and Catholic school sites? Presenting the case study from the perspective of the voices of the participants allows me to reveal how the critical discourses of liberation theology and critical pedagogy operate at VGAHS and how both of these critical discourses could benefit Catholic education and other school sites.

I retain the name of the school, Vincent Gray Alternative High School, and the name of the city, East St. Louis, but I have changed the names of the participants. Moreover, the administrators at the site read the draft chapters of the dissertation and offered their suggestions or responses. I took these responses into consideration in my final draft. In the fall of 1994, I returned to VGAHS for four days to share my dissertation, to give them a copy of it, to visit with the administrators and teachers, and to find out what had been happening in the lives of the students who were there while I conducted my research.

An Overview of This Project

This book is, then, the result of my experiences of integrating theory and practice while reconciling the relationship between the critical discourses of liberation theology and critical pedagogy and the relationship between these critical discourses and Catholic education. The book has two major parts: The first part focuses on theory and practices within Catholic schools and the theory of the critical discourses of liberation theology and critical pedagogy. The second part focuses on the integration of theory with the voices of the students, administrators and teachers of VGAHS.

Outlining here in this first chapter my experiences at Vincent Gray Alternative High School as a qualitative researcher, I prepared a reader to understand how theory and practice in a liberation theology context can be possible in a Catholic educational setting. Both of these themes—the liberation theology context and Catholic education—receive specific attention throughout the subsequent chapters.

In Chapter Two, "Catholic Schools: An Identity Crisis," I present my analysis of the current struggle for identity in our Catholic schools. This struggle includes the tension between official ecclesial documents and practices within Catholic schools that accommodate oppressed and marginalized peoples.

The third chapter reviews the recent research from the perspective of whom do Catholic schools serve and how do they serve these constituents. I suggest that there is a need for ethnographic studies with Catholic schools. The chapter concludes with descriptions of two critical ethnographies completed at Catholic schools, one by Peter McLaren and the other by Nancy Lesko.

Chapter Four focuses on the discourses of liberation theology and critical pedagogy, emphasizing the influence of the work and writings of Paulo Freire on the development of these two critical discourses. This chapter concludes with my presentation of the integrative model of liberation theology and critical pedagogy.

Chapter Five centers on the relationship of the critical discourses of liberation theology and critical pedagogy with Catholic education. The second part of this chapter focuses on Vincent Gray Alternative High School, the history and culture of this East St. Louis, Illinois, alternative high school.

The voices of the students and alumni constitute the substance of Chapter Six. This chapter presents the voices of nine students of Vincent Gray Alternative High School and discusses how these voices represent the elements of the integrative model of liberation theology and critical pedagogy. The seventh chapter focuses on the voices of the three administrators and the eighth chapter on the voices of the six teachers, and each of these chapters shows how their voices represent the elements of the integrative model of liberation theology and critical pedagogy.

The final chapter summarizes the voices of the students, administrators and teachers and shows how these voices illuminate the integrative model of liberation theology and critical pedagogy. This chapter also includes my reflections on the significance of this study for understanding education theory and practice in both Catholic and public schools from the perspective of the critical discourses of liberation theology and critical pedagogy. It emphasizes as well the idea that Catholic education needs to be an exemplar of critical theory and practice in a liberation theology context.

Chapter Two

Catholic Schools: An Identity Crisis

> No less than other schools does the Catholic school pursue cultural goals and the human formation of youth. But its proper function is to create for the school community a special atmosphere animated by the Gospel spirit of freedom and charity.
>
> - Second Vatican Council, *Declaration on Christian Education* (1965), p. 12.

> What makes the Catholic school distinct in its religious dimension is (a) the educational climate, (b) the personal development of each student, (c) the relationship between culture and the Gospel, and (d) the illumination of all knowledge in the light of faith.
>
> - Congregation for Catholic Education, *The Religious Dimension in a Catholic School* (1988), p. 3.

I have spent twelve years as a student in elementary and secondary Catholic schools before 1965 and since then, twenty years in Catholic high schools as teacher, counselor and principal. I have benefited immensely from these experiences and am grateful to my teachers and my students. The years I spent in Catholic schools have been years of change and transition both educationally and socially.

I know that Catholic schools produce many positive outcomes, but my concern in this chapter is the question of whether Catholic schools could do more to demonstrate and instill the Gospel values of freedom, love and justice for all—especially in implementing God's preferential love for the poor.

This issue of identity in the chapter title is a struggle Catholic educators experience as they confront the question of what makes a school Catholic or what makes a Catholic school. Beutow (1988) called this one of the most important issues to be confronted by each Catholic school. He emphasized that "today more than ever before, unless a particular Catholic school is considering the principles that give it its Catholic identity and is trying to live by them, it does not deserve to stay in existence" (p. 17). Moreover, he insisted upon this axiom throughout his work on Catholic schools.

The year 1995 was the thirtieth anniversary of the historical Catholic Church Council, Vatican II. The discussions and deliberations during this Council introduced a whole array of changes to the Catholic Church, including theological and ritual changes. Castelli (1995) calls the Second Vatican Council "the central event of Catholic life in the 20th century." Its changes have, indeed, affected the Church throughout the world, influencing both theological doctrine and religious practices. Church documents developed by this Council imbued the Catholic Church with a new social consciousness and a new spirit of community in its interactions with modern cultures. In the United States, these changes have had a radical effect both on the Church and its members and on Catholic schools.

Statistics provide one indicator of how much Catholic schools have changed over the twenty-five years since the Council of Vatican II. Michael Guerra (1991) reported that "at their peak in 1965, 10,879 Catholic elementary schools served 4.5 million students, and 2,413 Catholic secondary schools served 1.1 million students. In 1990 . . . 7,395 Catholic elementary schools are serving 2.0 million students, and 1,324 Catholic secondary schools serve 606,000 students" (p. 5). Various trends account for the declining number of Catholic schools and students attending these schools, but these trends fall outside the scope of this work.

More recently, however, Brigham (1995) states that "in 1994-95, there were 8,293 Catholic schools; of these 6,979 were elementary, 76 were middle, and 1,238 were secondary" (p. 8) The number of students in Catholic schools for 1994-95 was 2,618,567; with 2,021,142 in elementary schools and 597,425 in secondary schools (p. 14). Even though the number of schools has continued to decrease since 1990, the number of students attending these Catholic schools has increased. Still, the number of Catholic schools and students today remains far below that of the 1965 peak year. Nevertheless, students in Catholic schools represent over the last two decades about six percent of the school-age population of the country and half of the total students in private schools.

In addition to the numbers of Catholic schools that existed or now exist, numerous changes have occurred within these schools, changes that reflect the theological and ritual changes in the Catholic Church and thus affect the identity of the schools. For example, a sense of a social consciousness now appears in the curriculum and climate of Catholic schools. Mayock (1979) analyzed the influence of Vatican II on the instructional programs of Catholic elementary and secondary schools and found "clear evidence that the teachings of the Second Vatican Council have had a major impact on Catholic education" (Mayock and Glatthorn, 1980).

Catholic schools are also influenced by cultural developments within society. O'Gorman (1987) stated that since Vatican II, "traditional beliefs have been shattered and Catholics differ radically on the nature of their commitment [to Church doctrine]. As a consequence, educational direction [policy] is wavering. To put it simply, we cannot formulate educational policy if we cannot agree on what it means to be a Catholic. If identity changes, then that change is reflected in education both as a cause and effect" (p. 5).

Similarly, Shimabukuro (1993) indicated that both society and the Church have experienced a paradigm shift that affects Catholic schools. She stated that "this shift in emphasis in the Catholic school from institutional observances and hierarchy to individual formation in the context of the community reflects philosophical developments in the larger world" (p. 7). Slattery (1995) points out that "there has been a loss of identity in parochial schools brought on by the ravages of modernity" (p. 90).

John Meyers (1994) reflecting on his twelve years as the President of the National Catholic Educational Association observed that the issues of viability and academics were only part of the problem with Catholic schools during his 1974-1986 tenure. The issue of the identity of the Catholic schools was the other part of the problem:

> Catholic schools also had to be just that: *Catholic!* What would make them so? Surely not just the religious habit of the teacher. Not just the crucifix on the wall or the holy water font by the door. Not just the religion text or the religion teacher. What then? The search was on for a modern philosophy of Catholic education (p. 62).

The history of Catholic schools since Vatican II has yet to be written, but this epoch will certainly be characterized as one of change and conflict in dialogue with a long cultural history, and as a time of struggling with issues of how to restructure the process of education in Catholic schools. John J. Convey (1992) attempted to present this history in a book that includes a summary of the major research conducted with Catholic schools between 1965 and 1990. This is one useful perspective on the history of Catholic schools since Vatican II, but we need many other perspectives.

The issue of the identity of Catholic schools arose long before Vatican II. Current discussions continue to echo such questions from the history of Catholic schools as: What is the relationship of Catholic schools to public education? What textbooks should be used in Catholic schools? What is the role of vowed religious and the laity in Catholic schools both as teachers and administrators? How autonomous is each Catholic school from other Catholic schools? and What characterizes a Catholic teacher, a Catholic school, a Catholic curriculum and a Catholic education? For the most part, the identity of American Catholic schools throughout their history has reflected the identity of the Catholic culture in our country (Beutow, 1970; Burns, 1912a, 1912b, 1917; Burns and Kohlbrenner, 1937; and Dolan, 1992). As the Catholic community struggles with the issue of what it means to be Catholic, so do Catholic schools (Beutow, 1988; Bryk, Lee, and Holland, 1993; Kelly, 1991; and O'Gorman, 1987).

Church Documents and Catholic Schools

Any discussion of the identity of Catholic schools must take into account the ecclesial documents on Catholic schools developed since the Vatican II Council. These documents include *To Teach As Jesus Did* (National Conference of Catholic Bishops, 1972), and the Congregation of Catholic Education's *The Catholic School* (1977), *Lay Catholics in Schools: Witnesses to Faith* (1982), and *The Religious Dimension of Education in a Catholic School* (1988). Each of these documents addresses the issue of what makes a school Catholic. Each has its own perspective on this issue, but they include some common themes. Moreover, each document is concerned about the quality of schooling and the transmission of the Catholic faith in light of the Gospel values of living a moral life, characterized by justice and a concern for the poor. A brief quotation from each of these documents illustrates some of the aspects of the various articulations of the issue of Catholic school identity:

> This integration of religious truth and values with life distinguishes the Catholic school from other schools. . . . Racial and ethnic tensions and conflicts reflect an absence of local and national community. War and the exploitation of poor nations by the rich dramatize the same tragic lack of community on the international level. Today's Catholic school must respond to these challenges by developing in its students a commitment to community and the social skills and virtues needed to achieve it (*To Teach As Jesus Did*, pp. 29-30).

> Catholic schools must be seen as meeting places for those who express Christian values in education. The Catholic school, far more than any other, must be a community whose aim is the transmission of values for living (*The Catholic School*, pp. 22-23).

> Critical transmission also involves the presentation of a set of values and counter-values. These must be judged within the context of an appropriate concept of life and of the human person. Examples of such attitudes would be these: a freedom which includes respect for others; conscientious responsibility; a sincere and constant search for truth; a calm and peaceful critical spirit; a spirit of solidarity with and service toward all other persons; a sensitivity for justice; a special awareness of being called to be positive agents of change in a society that is undergoing continuous transformation (*Lay Catholics in Schools: Witnesses to Faith*, p. 18).

> The Catholic school finds its true justification in the mission of the Church; it is based on an educational philosophy in which faith, culture and life are brought into harmony. . . . Therefore a Catholic school should be sensitive to and help to promulgate Church appeals for peace, justice, freedom, progress for all peoples and assistance for countries in need (*The Religious Dimension of Education in a Catholic School*, pp. 19 -23).

Those involved with Catholic schools find a familiarity with and a dialogue on each of these documents necessary to the ongoing development of the response to the issue of the Catholic school identity. In one sense, the response to the question of what this identity is depends upon one's understanding of these documents applied to the reality of what is happening in Catholic schools. These documents, like most other ecclesial documents, use theological language and offer the Catholic community an ideal. The struggle for those involved in Catholic schools comes in determining what these documents mean in the realm of schooling practices and climates.

The most recent document, *The Religious Dimension of Education in a Catholic School* (1988), presents various characteristics of a Catholic school and its climate. It states that the Catholic school is more than "a place where lessons are taught" (p. 15), as a matter of fact "classes and lessons are only a small part of school life" (p. 24). The climate of the school is characterized by the "Gospel spirit" and is "an example of simplicity and evangelical poverty" (pp. 16-17). The Catholic school exists as an educational and religious community, characterized by a Christian "love for all that excludes no one because of religion, nationality or race" and includes "a preferential option for the less fortunate, the sick, the poor, the handicapped, the lonely" (p. 39). The document also specifies those conditions which are favorable for the religious dimension of the school climate:

> Some of the conditions for creating a positive and supportive climate are the following: that everyone agree with the educational goals and cooperate in achieving them; that interpersonal relationships be based on love and Christian freedom; that each individual, in daily life, be a witness to the Gospel values; that every student be challenged to strive for the highest possible level of formation, both human and Christian. In addition the climate must be one in which families are welcomed, the local Church is an active participant, and civil society—local, national, and international— is included (pp. 45-46).

Moreover, the document indicates those conditions unfavorable to fostering the religious dimension of the climate of Catholic schools:

> Strong determination is needed to do everything possible to eliminate the conditions which threaten the health of the school climate. Some examples of potential problems are these: the educational goals are either not defined or defined badly; those responsible for the school are not sufficiently trained; concern for academic achievement is excessive; relations between teachers and students are cold and impersonal; teachers are antagonistic toward one another; discipline is imposed from on high without any participation or cooperation from the students; relationships with families are formal or even strained, and families are not involved in helping to determine the educational goals; some within the school community are giving a negative witness; individuals are unwilling to work together for the common good; the school is isolated from the local Church; there is no interest in or concern for the problems of society; religious instruction is routine (p. 46).

One might use these two lists as criteria for evaluating what transpires in Catholic schools. Is the school characterized by those elements favorable or unfavorable for developing a climate that fosters the religious identity of the Catholic school? One can also wonder if these lists are unique to Catholic schools or if some of these conditions could characterize every type of school.

Gini Shimabukuro (1993, 1994) focused her research on the identity of the Catholic school from the perspective of its teachers, and she raised these questions about the identity of Catholic school teachers: "What distinguishes me, a Catholic school teacher from my public school colleagues, many of whom I admire deeply? How do I as a Catholic school teacher weave the faith dimension into the curriculum—into math, history and language arts?" (1994, p. 23). She answered these questions by performing a text analysis on eight ecclesial documents pertaining to Catholic education to develop an ideal profile of the teacher in Catholic schools. Then she suggested that these "documents offer us an opportunity to clarify our identity" (p. 23).

Five major themes emerged from Shimabukuro's text analysis, and "these themes compositely distinguished the Catholic school teacher as (1) forming the Christian spirituality of the students, (2) being vocationally prepared, (3) being a builder of community, (4) forming the humanity of students, and (5) being professionally prepared" (1993;

p. 142). Her closing remarks related her focus upon teachers in Catholic schools with the issue of the identity of Catholic schools:

> This time in the history of Catholic education is characterized by a dramatic shift from religious to lay teachers. Coupled with the pressures and confusion of a world preoccupied with materialism and beleaguered by a host of global threats, it is no wonder that individuals in Catholic school classrooms are questioning their identity as Catholic educators (p. 147).

Other Expressions of This Identity Crisis

The discussion of the identity of the Catholic schools extends beyond Church documents and their analysis. The issue is frequently discussed by many Catholic school faculties as they struggle to formulate vision and mission statements for their schools. Teachers seriously struggle with the question of what it means for their schools to be Catholic schools in their particular locations and serving their particular students. As in most other schools, these teachers wonder how they can bring vision and mission statements to life in their classroom practices. They wonder as well how these statements affect the policies and practices of a school. Like Gini Shimabukuro, many teachers in Catholic schools wonder about how their teaching of an academic subject differs from the instruction in public schools or other private schools. How do the student handbook and faculty handbook reflect the unique visions and missions of Catholic schools as articulated and challenged by ecclesial documents?

Others have contributed publicly to this discussion of Catholic school identity (Kelly, 1991; McDermott, 1986; and numerous publications of the National Catholic Educational Association). For example, McDermott (1986) articulated his understanding of the "distinct qualities" of Catholic schools in a short publication issued by the National Catholic Education Association (NCEA). His reflections appear rooted in the Church documents as well as the historical development of Catholic schools. McDermott emphasized a Catholic education as the right of parents and the Church. He traced Catholic schools to the teachings of Jesus and presented Jesus as teacher (a title applied to Jesus forty-one times in Scripture) as a major motivation for the existence of Catholic schools. He stated that "the Catholic school is unique because it is a religious community within an academic community" (p. 11).

Beutow (1988) developed many of McDermott's ideas and added his own on the issue of Catholic school identity in his major volume, *The Catholic School: Its Roots, Identity and Future.* In his introduction, Beutow stated that "to explore the identity of the Catholic school is the purpose of this book." He further observed that "one of the ways that Catholic schools could be made truly Catholic and more effective, their worth discovered, and their future made more secure, is to obtain renewed insights from a reconsideration of their identity. The material of this book is intended to aid this task, and will help do so if it is reflected upon, discussed, and lived" (p. 18).

While Beutow's works (1970, 1988) represent significant contributions to the understandings of the identity of Catholic schools, both historically and currently, most readers find his writing laborious. But Beutow's density should not detract from his contributions and the need for those involved in Catholic schools to reflect on and discuss how Beutow guides our own attempts to formulate the identity of a Catholic school.

Kelly (1991) edited an NCEA publication that includes several papers delivered and discussed at an Institute on "What Makes a School Catholic?" held in 1988 at the University of Dayton with 180 Catholic school educators. As Kelly wrote in the introduction, obviously this issue is "ever more urgent" for those involved and concerned about Catholic schools.

The current situation revolving around the identity of Catholic schools influences each school. How this identity is articulated can vary from school to school. The school I focus on in this book, Vincent Gray Alternative High School, struggled with its identity and began to build its foundation in response to the alternative forms a Catholic school might take. The Catholic identity of VGAHS remains at issue. The school was originally recognized as an "official" Catholic High School in its diocese. When I was there, the chief administrator asked to have the school's diocesan connections severed, even though it continued to maintain its identity as part of the Catholic ministries to the people of East St. Louis. In my conversations with teachers, I found the concern for the VGAHS identity as a Catholic school a lively issue engendering an array of opinions.

Whether or not VGAHS articulates its own identity as an official Catholic school, it definitely shares in the usual expressions of what makes a school Catholic—for example, crucifixes in the classrooms and other religious symbols in the building, times set aside for prayer and reflection and a concern for the individuals in the school community and for developing a community spirit among both the faculty members and the students. Even though, VGAHS offered no formal religion classes, the faculty set aside time each week for focusing upon one's personal moral and value development as an individual and as part of the school community. In addition to these, the atmosphere and practices at VGAHS resemble those qualities expressed in Church documents since Vatican II, especially in terms of being a community concerned with serving the poor. The faculty includes many religious teachers, more than most other Catholic schools can claim, and along with the other teachers at VGAHS, they continue to proclaim by their lives and ministry in East St. Louis their belief in a Christ with a preferential love for the poor, the marginalized and the oppressed.

This identity conflict at VGAHS recalls the sentiments of Carleen Reck (1991) that the identity of Catholic schools includes more than merely occupying a place on the bishop's list of approved schools:

> More essential to the identity of the Catholic school is its involvement in the mission of the Church, the religious formation of its students, the inclusion of Gospel values, the building of a faith community, its distinctive climate, its commitment to service, and its global concern (p. 37).

Certainly, the history and experiences of Vincent Gray Alternative High School's students, administrators and teachers reflect the identity conflict of a Catholic school within modern culture and society, but also its struggle for the meaning of Catholic education and the restructuring of Catholic schools to embody that meaning.

Whom Do Catholic Schools Serve?

The key issue for me here is this: Is it possible to apply the critical theory languages of critique and possibility—namely, the discourses of liberation theology and critical pedagogy—to Catholic education in the United States? Can these two critical discourses benefit Catholic education now and in the future as Catholic educators plan for Catholic schools and struggle with their identity crisis? Can my experiences at VGAHS supply knowledge for those eager to understand how critical theory in a liberation theology context can illuminate the discussion of Catholic school identity?

My experience in Catholic secondary schools in the years since Vatican II also lead me to wrestle with these questions: Whom do Catholic schools serve and how are they served? To what degree have we made real the words of those Church documents that address Catholic schools? How do Catholic schools exist as communities permeated by the Gospel spirit of freedom and love?

Similar questions were raised at the 1992 National Catholic Education Association Conference in St. Louis. In her presentation on the National Congress for Catholic Schools, which took place in November, 1991, in Washington, D.C., Sister Mary Ann Eckhoff (1992) asked "Whom do we educate?" The Congress never quite reached a consensus. She also asked, "What does it mean to prefer the poor?" And later in her talk, she observed, "We need to move the directions [of the Congress] into a plan of action. The question whom do we educate needs to be resolved."

In his presentation at the same convention, Father John Kavanaugh (1992) suggested that "we are afraid of the preferential option for the poor." Brother Robert Hoatson (1992) echoed the same themes in his presentation on "Serving the Poor—Exploring the Options." He stated that "Catholic education began in order to educate the poor. Have we abandoned our primary mission?" Hoatson also asked, "Are we now part of the oppression? Why are we not daring to do the same for the new set of immigrants as done for the Euro-immigrants of the past? and Why are there more poor people today?"

As I familiarized myself with the critical discourses of liberation theology and critical pedagogy, I found myself increasingly concerned with what actually transpires in Catholic education and whom we serve. In light of current public discussions of school standards and achievement as well as those ubiquitous proposals of voucher systems for funding private education, it seems crucial for Catholic schools to address the issue of precisely whom they serve as well as how they serve this constituency. I also find myself asking if Catholic schools really offer an alternative to public education? Catholic schools, like public education, need to confront their reasons for being. All of these concerns lend another perspective to the issue of the identity of Catholic schools today and in the future.

Bryk, Lee and Holland (1993) expressed similar sentiments about the current and future possibilities for both Catholic and public education:

> The problems of education in large cities have never been greater. The sweeping economic and social changes over the last two decades have left the poor heavily concentrated in cities, creating a new class of truly disadvantaged. At a time when the link between quality education and economic advancement, both individual and societal, appears stronger than ever, urban institutions appear overwhelmed, unable to cope with the enormity of the demands and the accumulated constraints under which they work. Earlier in this century, Catholic schools played a major role in the education of urban immigrants. Catholic school systems in archdioceses such as Boston, New York, and Chicago once rivaled the corresponding public school systems in size. Social gospel Protestants were also a vital force in the cities. With their own sense of religious understandings, they too brought personal concern and a willingness to commit effort on the behalf of others. These individuals and institutions had drawbacks, but they were an active humanitarian force. Such a force is in very short supply today. At a time when the problems are more pervasive and the needs more expansive, there are fewer societal resources to draw upon (p. 342).

The discourses of liberation theology and critical pedagogy can help Catholic schools formulate and evaluate their reasons for being. Vincent Gray Alternative High School is an example of an alternative Catholic school in which teachers and administrators struggled with what it means to exercise a preference for the poor and how best to serve the poor educationally.

Since Vatican II, Church documents have echoed the plea of liberation theology for a preferential option for the poor and marginalized peoples. This same commitment exists as a characteristic of critical pedagogy. Meanwhile, a concern for the poor and disadvantaged has always been a hallmark of the Christian tradition. It is impossible to follow the Gospel of Jesus without being moved with compassion for the poor. Once again I quote directly from several Church documents on this point. The Third Synod of Bishops held in

Rome, 1971, focused upon justice in the world. The document this synod produced, *Justice in the World*, is a theological justification for the church's concern for justice as well as the need for education for justice:

> But education demands a renewal of heart, a renewal based on the recognition of sin in its individual and social manifestations. It will also inculcate a truly and entirely human way of life in justice, love and simplicity. It will likewise awaken a critical sense, which will lead us to reflect in the society in which we live and on its values; it will make men ready to renounce these values when they cease to promote justice for all men (Roman Synod, p. 279).

Members of the National Conference of Catholic Bishops echoed this plea in their 1972 pastoral letter, *To Teach As Jesus Did.* This document is more familiar than other Church documents to many within Catholic education, but some of its ideas remain as vital now as they were when they first appeared twenty-three years ago:

> The unfinished business on the agenda of Catholic schools, like many other schools, also includes the task of providing quality education for the poor and disadvantaged of our nation. Generous, sustained sacrifice is demanded of those whom God favored in order to make available educational programs which meet the need of the poor to be self-determining, free persons in all areas of individual and social life (p. 34).

The bishops publicly expressed their support for Càtholic schools in their pastoral statement of 1976, *Teach Them*, and again in 1990, *In Support of Catholic Elementary and Secondary Schools.* Both of these documents express hope for ways to help minorities and the poor attend Catholic schools and value their importance:

> In a special way there is a need for careful identification of the facts, both quantitative and qualitative, concerning the Catholic school's role in educating those who have suffered economic deprivation, or experienced discrimination because of racial, cultural or linguistic differences. This will help both to demonstrate the contribution now being made in this way by

> Catholic schools to American society generally and to foster the formulation of proposals for further steps to maintain and strengthen this commitment, including the possibility of some form of nationwide action (*Teach Them*, p. 9).
>
> In *To Teach As Jesus Did,* we called upon parents, educators, and pastors to ensure the continuance and improvement of Catholic schools. And we pointed to specific areas of concern: greater fiscal responsibility, quality education for the disadvantaged, and the need to look at alternative models. Much progress has been made. More needs to be done (*In Support of Catholic Elementary and Secondary Schools*, p. 4).

More recently, in their pastoral letter, *Catholic Schools: Heritage and Legacy*, the Catholic Bishops of Ohio (1990) continued to urge that Catholic schools concentrate on educating the poor:

> We wish to find ways to continue our schools where they serve the poor. Our tradition and our faith demand that we show preferential love for those who are less fortunate. Our service to the poor is based upon their dignity as human beings and upon our responsibility to live in solidarity with our brothers and sisters of the human family. By educating the children of the poor, Catholic schools help families break the cycle of poverty and give those families a future. Through Catholic schools, the Church helped marginated immigrants, whatever their ethnic origin, to move to the center of American society. In Catholic schools, especially of the inner cities and rural communities, we strive to continue this tradition (p. 5).

The African American Catholic Bishops also emphasized the need and role of Catholic schools in regard to serving minority peoples. Writing in their 1984 pastoral letter, *What We Have Seen and Heard*:

> Today the Catholic school still represents for many in the Black community, especially in the urban areas, an opportunity for quality education and character development. It also represents—and this is no less important—a sign of stability in an environment of chaos and flux. . . . The Catholic school has

> been and remains one of the chief vehicles of evangelization within the Black community (p. 28).

In 1986, the National Catholic Education Association (NCEA) published a study (Benson, Peter, et al.), *Catholic High Schools: Their Impact on Low-Income Students*, concerned with the impact of Catholic schools on low-income families. Its introduction includes a brief history of Catholic schools in the United States, emphasizing how these schools were developed to serve the great influx of immigrants from Ireland and southern and eastern Europe. This history also mentions the similar service of Catholic schools among Black inner city youth and Native Americans. It states that "between 1890 and 1917, seventy-six schools for inner-city Blacks were opened [and] by 1890, there were 48 boarding schools and 17 day schools enrolling Native Americans" (p. 4). This introduction presents the mission of Catholic schools as part of the Catholic Church's commitment to the poor:

> Catholic schools represent one of the long-standing efforts of the Church to build a more just and loving human community that combats the destructive human consequences of poverty. An important part of the school's mission is to offer students from all socio-economic, racial, and ethnic backgrounds a community that cares and challenges and an education that empowers and liberates (p. 3).

The Beliefs and Directions Statement of the National Congress on Catholic Schools for the twenty-first century shows that the Congress members discussed both the identity of Catholic schools and whom Catholic schools serve. Responses to these issues became part of the official statement. I quote some of these statements from the executive summary (Guerra, Haney, and Kealey, 1992; and *Momentum*, May, 1995). The statements I chose shed further light on the discussion of Catholic school identity from the perspective of whom Catholic schools now serve and might possibly serve in the next century:

> The Catholic school creates a supportive and challenging climate which affirms the dignity of all persons within the school community (p. 17).

> We will welcome and support a diverse cultural and economic population as a hallmark of our Catholic identity (p. 18).
>
> Catholic schools are committed to educate students of diverse economic, cultural, religious, racial and ethnic backgrounds. Catholic schools are called to be catalysts for social change based on Gospel values (p. 21).
>
> We will aggressively recruit and prepare leaders who reflect the church's multicultural, multiracial and multiethnic populations. We will open new schools and design alternative school models to reflect the changing needs of family, church and society (p. 22).
>
> Leadership in and on behalf of Catholic schools is deeply spiritual, servant-like, prophetic, visionary and empowering (p. 29).

Thus the Church documents and the Beliefs and Directions Statement of the National Congress on Catholic Schools agree that Catholic schools should serve the poor and disadvantaged and the minority communities. But do they? The question whom do Catholic schools serve and how do they serve remain to be answered in the current school system that includes a range of schools deployed among people from various income levels and racial and ethnic backgrounds.

It is all too easy today to become a private school system catering to those able to afford private education, and Catholic schools in many areas find themselves comfortably serving the white populations of suburbia, while the inner-city Catholic schools, focused on serving African Americans and Latinos and new immigrants, struggle to keep their doors open.

The Church documents clearly call those of us who are involved with Catholic schools to confront our own beliefs about whom Catholic schools serve and how we serve them, particularly if we aspire to heed the Gospel call of preferential service for the poor. Some within the Catholic community consider this Gospel summons to a preferential love for the poor mandatory rather than optional. Such an adamant stance should force us to consider schooling practices and structures as having become permeated by the words of the Church documents that address both the identity of Catholic schools and their rightful constituency.

This challenge is difficult but meeting it would produce an understanding of and familiarity with such theories as the discourses of critical pedagogy and liberation theology. The official ecclesial statements on Catholic education and critical discourse can be integrated with the evaluation of practices in Catholic schools, and this process could become a source of hope for new structures and practices designed to transform Catholic schools into communities where justice and preferential service for the poor exist. This is more than just the dream of an ideal. Schools like VGAHS demonstrate to Catholic educators that critical theories can become part of schooling practices and part of a way of understanding what transpires in schools and what could happen there.

The value of any theory, discourse or theology is that it becomes part of the experiences of a people and influences the practices of a culture, including the culture of schools. It is too easy to applaud ourselves for the contributions Catholic schools have made to the waves of immigrants and the poor of the past. We in Catholic education must now challenge ourselves to accommodate new immigrants and the growing population of the poor today. This challenge confronts those involved with Catholic education and all educators as well.

CHAPTER THREE

What the Research Reveals About Catholic Schools

> Despite the dramatic increase in the number of studies dealing with Catholic schools during the past twenty-five years, the research agenda on Catholic schools is far from complete. A coordinated research effort is needed that will enable researchers, policy makers, and consumers to understand Catholic schools better, monitor their quality, and continue to identify those factors that contribute to their effectiveness.
>
> - John J. Convey in "Priorities for Research on Catholic Schools" (1994)

The current research on Catholic schools provides yet another perspective on these schools. It describes how large this parochial system is and helps measure its effectiveness. It also provides additional insights, beyond those elaborated in the last chapter, into the issues of the identity of Catholic schools and whom Catholic schools serve.

Several studies addressing Catholic schools have taken place since Vatican II, twenty-five years ago. Between 1976 and 1987, a total of 989 doctoral dissertations focused on the general subject though only 7 dealt with ethnic, multicultural or minority concerns (Traviss, 1989). Convey (1992) presented an overview on Catholic school research published between 1965 and 1991. He reported that "the major studies between 1965 and 1980 examined the effects of Catholic schools on the religious development and attitudes of their students. . . . [And] after 1980, the research achieved national prominence and had an important impact on educational policy, both in the Catholic and public sectors" (p. 1). The major studies in the 1980s include those of Coleman, Hoffer (*Public and Private High Schools: The Impact of Communities,* 1987) and with Kilgore (*High School Achievement: Public, Catholic, and Private Schools Compared*, 1982); Greeley (*Catholic High Schools and Minority Students,* 1982); and the research sponsored by the NCEA (Bryk et al., *Effective Catholic Schools: An Exploration,* 1984; Yeager et al., *The Catholic High School: A National Portrait,* 1985; and Benson et al., *Catholic High Schools: Their Impact on Low-Income Students,* 1986).

Traditional Academic Research on Catholic Schools

Almost all of the research concerned with Catholic schools over the past thirty years has used the standard methodology. Convey (1992) stated that "most studies are descriptive and employ simple statistics, such as means, standard deviations, percentages, and correlations" (p. 5).

James Coleman's research with Sally Kilgore and Thomas Hoffer (1982, 1987) reported that 90 percent of the schools in the United States are public schools; the other 10 percent are private schools, with 6 percent of these being Catholic. Surveying the total student population, Guerra (1991) stated that Catholic schools have 2.6 million, other private schools have 2.6 million, and the public schools have 45 million. The size of the Catholic school system is, therefore, much smaller than one tends to think.

Frederick Brigham (1990) indicated that Catholic schools constitute 38.6 percent of all private schools; however, student enrollment in Catholic schools is half of the enrollment in all private schools. More recently, Brigham (1995) points out that in 1994-95, 1,238 Catholic secondary schools enrolled 614,957 students, a decrease of 106 schools and an increase of 8,594 students since his 1989 study. We also find an increase in the number of non-Catholic students in Catholic schools. Brigham found a 14.3 percent non-Catholic enrollment in secondary schools for 1989-90 and 16.6 percent in 1994-95.

The table below, following Brigham's two studies, presents the ethnic background of the student enrollment of Catholic secondary schools for the academic years of 1989-90 and 1994-95. This table provides one profile of whom Catholic schools serve:

	1989-90	**1994-95**
African Americans	49,652 - 8.2%	46,931 - 7.6%
Hispanic Americans	59,467 - 9.8%	64,594 - 10.5%
Asian Americans	22,960 - 3.8%	25,843 - 4.2%
Native Americans	2,524 - .4%	2,632 - .4%
All others	471,354 - 77.8%	474,571 - 76.3%

Concerning the increase of minority enrollment in Catholic schools, Guerra (1991) stated that

> Minority enrollment has increased from 11 percent in 1970 to 23 percent in 1989. Of that 23 percent, 10 percent are Hispanic Americans, 9 percent are African Americans, 4 percent are Asian Americans. While 97 percent of the Hispanic students are Catholic, about two-thirds of the Black students in Catholic schools are non-Catholic. The percentage of non-Catholic students in Catholic schools has grown slowly in recent years, and stood at 12.5 percent in 1990 (p. 6).

Comparing his data with public schools, Bruno Manno (1985) reported that "Catholic schools have a larger percentage of Hispanic students (8.9 versus 8 percent) and Asian Americans (2.4 versus 1.9 percent) [but] 8.6 percent Blacks compared with over 16 percent in public schools, and fewer American Indians (.3 versus .8 percent)."

In addition, the 1990 Census Bureau figures as reported in the *Cincinnati Enquirer* (1991) reveal that "Blacks are about 12 percent of the population, Hispanic people are about 9 percent, Asians about 3 percent" (Section A, p. 1). The ethnic diversity figures for 1989-90 and for 1994-95 Catholic secondary school enrollment are slightly above the national percentage for Hispanics and Asians, but continue to be below that for African Americans.

Coleman, Hoffer and Kilgore (1982) conducted a comparative study of the achievement of high school students in public, Catholic and private schools. They presented a draft report entitled, *Public and Private Schools,* through the National Center of Educational Statistics in April, 1981. In 1991, Guerra observed that "[Coleman and his colleagues] compared academic achievement in public, Catholic and other private schools, and found Catholic schools produced significantly higher achievement than public schools among students of comparable backgrounds" (p. 10). Chapter 3 of the Coleman study addresses the student composition of public and private schools, and one can read the data here as a partial answer to whom Catholic schools serve. The ethnic distribution of students in public and Catholic schools Coleman found in 1980 follows:

	Public Schools	**Catholic Schools**
White	78%	85.4%
Black	12.2%	5.5%
Hispanic	6.3%	6.7%
Other	3.6%	2.5%

Analyzing this data, Coleman and his colleagues concluded that "for Hispanics, there is very little difference between the public and private sectors, either with respect to the proportions of Hispanics in each sector, or in the internal distribution of Hispanics within the schools of each sector. . . . There is a substantially smaller proportion of Blacks in the private sector than in the public sector—less than half as high a proportion in the Catholic schools" (p. 36).

Further into this study, Coleman et al. reported on the percentage of the population of ethnic groups that are Catholic: "about 9 percent of Blacks, about 35 percent of Whites, and over 65 percent of Hispanics " (p. 55). Thus the actual number of Catholics of a specific group influences the number of those from an ethnic group enrolled in Catholic schools.

Concerning students with disabilities, they pointed out that "in the public sector the average percentage of the student body that is handicapped is more than double that in the non-Catholic private schools, and over four times that in the Catholic schools" (p. 46).

Concluding their study by addressing the issue of student composition, Coleman, et al. stated that

> Blacks and whites are less segregated within Catholic schools than are Blacks and whites in public schools. Note that this does not mean that Catholic schools make a positive contribution to school integration, because they have only about half as high a proportion of Black students as do the public schools. . . . Catholic schools have about the same proportion of Hispanics as do the public schools, and they are somewhat more integrated than the public schools, though not by a great amount (p. 194).

In an interview Manno (1982) held with Coleman, Hoffer and Kilgore concerning this research, *Public and Private Schools*, he asked them to respond to the question, What types of students attend these schools?

> About 86 percent in the private sector are non-Hispanic white, compared with 76 percent in the public sector. Hispanics are equally represented in both sectors: approximately 7 percent in the public sector and 6 percent in the private sector. Blacks are under represented in the private sector: approximately 14 percent in the public school sector compared with 5 percent in the private sector. When compared with the non-Catholic private sector, the Catholic sector enrolls double the proportion of minority students (p. 5).

Coleman's team concluded the interview by emphasizing these four findings: "(1) on average, Catholic schools are more effective than public schools; (2) Catholic schools are especially beneficial to students from less advantaged backgrounds; (3) their strong demands account in large part for the differences between the sectors' average levels of achievement; and (4) Catholic schools do not have a racially segregating effect beyond that which already exists in public schools" (p. 7).

Andrew Greeley's research (1982) focused on minority students in Catholic high schools. He characterized his work as the first study of Catholic secondary schools and minorities, contending that a wasteland of literature had already accumulated on the effect of Catholic secondary schools, "to say nothing of a literature on the effect of such education on minority students" (p. 8). He drew upon the work of Coleman et al. and went on to point out that "Catholic schools are somewhat less ethnically and racially segregated than public schools (on a national average), and a Black or Hispanic who attends Catholic school is more likely to have white schoolmates than a Black or Hispanic who attends public secondary schools" (p. 10).

Greeley concerned himself with the family background and economic differences of minority students in Catholic high schools and recognized some of the differences between minorities in public schools and their counterparts in Catholic schools. He described Black and Hispanic minorities in Catholic high schools as being less "affluent than white Catholic school students, but they are more affluent than their minority counterparts in public schools and their parents" (p. 16). He also found them to be the children of "the more affluent, better educated, and more successful minority group members" (p. 19). Greely continued to contrast the minorities in Catholic schools with those in public schools:

> Catholic school minority students then tend to come from affluent, well-educated families with powerful college aspirations and a physical environment conducive to academic success. Differences on all these measures are so striking that one would be inclined to believe that they measure very critical differences in the family background of public school and Catholic school minority young people (p. 24).

Greeley then presented data reflecting the academic achievement of minority students in Catholic high schools, and his conclusions resemble those of the Coleman, Hoffer and Kilgore report. Greeley's disagreement with their report is that the family background of minority students in Catholic high schools and the ownership of some Catholic schools by religious communities strongly affect the academic and disciplinary environments in Catholic schools (pp. 57-58).

In comparing Catholic schools with public schools, Greeley stated that "in an astonishing turn of the tables, it would appear that instead of the public schools being the great assimilators, they are the most successful with the affluent, while Catholic schools are most successful with the poor" (p. 84). On the upward mobility of students in Catholic schools, Greeley discussed the poor white students there:

> The apparent effect of Catholic schools discussed in this book seems to be as true of lower-class Whites as it is of lower-class

> minority students. . . . It would appear that the Catholic school effect is "ethnic" and "social class" rather than specifically racial . . . these schools have been especially successful with upwardly mobile "ethnic immigrants" and still are, whether the "ethnics" be black, brown or white (pp. 86-87).

Anthony Bryk, Peter Holland, Valerie Lee and Reuben Carriedo (1984) set out "to identify the factors associated with the effectiveness of [Catholic] schools through a broad exploration of their academic and social organization" (p. 3). Their study focused on seven different "types" of Catholic high schools, but they report hardly anything about the minority composition of these schools. They stated that "about 15 percent of Catholic secondary students are minority and 12 percent are non-Catholic," and on that thin basis, they concluded that "on the one hand, students in Catholic secondary schools are diverse in race, social class, religious practice, and family background" (p. 24). They neglected, however, to develop these assertions beyond merely stating them.

In regard to diversity and achievement of various social classes within Catholic high schools, they agreed with the conclusions of Coleman et al. and those of Greeley:

> [S]ocial class is less predictive of achievement in Catholic than in public schools. We conclude academic policy is a key factor in this regard. In particular, since Catholic schools generally require a substantial core of academic courses for all students, a major source of variation that often perpetuates social class effect is removed. Social class does influence choice of school attended. Once inside, though, its influence is substantially reduced (p. 64).

Bryk, Lee and Holland (1993) revisited their 1984 study on the effectiveness of Catholic schools in order "to offer a portrait of Catholic high schools [and] to examine the distinctive features of Catholic high schools and the ways in which these features combine to form supportive social environments that promote academic achievement for a broad cross section of students" (Preface). They updated their earlier account of the history and development of the seven Catholic high schools their first study focused on, and this more recent work became a vehicle for presenting their NCEA-sponsored research to a wider audience than Catholic school circles. The last two sections of this newer study suggest the implications of their work for other schools and for the future of Catholic schools.

In 1985, the NCEA sponsored a research project addressing Catholic high schools in response to two troubling national reports, *A Nation at Risk* (1983) and *High School: A Report on Secondary Education in America* (1983). Researchers Robert Yeager, Peter Benson, Michael Guerra and Bruno Manno (1985) observed that

> The time is right for a comprehensive study of Catholic high schools. The 1980s represent a crucial decade as Catholic high schools try to come to terms with hard financial realities, the increasing presence of laity in administrative and teaching positions, and a rapidly changing society that has led some to question the mission and purpose of educational institutions. It is also a decade in which federal and state policies toward non-public education are being reviewed. Tuition tax credits, vouchers, and government aid for non-public school programs are currently under debate in a number of legislative agencies. It is a time of decision-making for leaders inside the Catholic community as well as for those outside it—decision-making that requires a systematic understanding of the nature and scope of Catholic high schools (p. 1).

In their study, Yeager et al. stressed the differences among three distinct types of Catholic high schools:

> First, while most schools, for example, emphasize a rigorous academic curriculum, some have a special mission to provide a general or vocational education for non-college-bound students. While most schools have primarily Catholic teachers serving Catholic students, some have a majority of non-Catholic teachers. A few schools (about 3 percent of the total) have a majority of non-Catholic students. . . . Second, many Catholic high schools also adopt a special mission to serve a particular kind of student. Out of the 910 schools in this project, there are: five schools in which a majority of students are Asian, three schools in which a majority of students are Native American, 36 schools in which a majority of students are Black. In four of these, all students are

> Black; in 46 schools a majority is Hispanic; and in 24 schools a majority of students comes from families whose income is below the federal poverty line. Third, diversity among Catholic high schools is reflected predominantly in the characteristics in which there is more variation than commonality. These characteristics can be grouped into the areas of teachers, students, governance, social context, programs, and development and finance (p. 16).

On the question of whom Catholic high schools serve, Yeager, et al. found that in regard to minorities "57 percent of high schools have a student body that is racially homogeneous; 10 percent or less of their students are members of a minority. Some 25 percent of the schools have a student body that is more than 20 percent minority" (p. 16). They also found that "the average percentage of minority students in a Catholic high school is 18.8. . . . The largest minority in the average Catholic high school is Hispanic (8.3 percent). Five percent of Catholic high schools report having no minority students" (p. 22). Comparing the percentage of minority students in Catholic high schools, Yeager et al. agreed with the research reported by Coleman et al.

On the gender composition of the students of Catholic high schools, Yeager and his colleagues found that "56 percent of the schools are co-educational; 26 percent enroll girls only; and 18 percent enroll boys only" (p. 16). Moreover, "[of this 44 percent of gender-specific schools] 52 percent of Catholic high schools are female, 48 percent are male" (p. 19).

Concerning students from low-income families, Yeager et al. stated that "to a great extent, the income of the families of Catholic high school students parallels the income distribution found nationally. Catholic students' families are not, on the average, poorer—nor are they wealthier" (p. 25). And appraising how hard Catholic Schools strive to serve low-income families, they stated that "most Catholic high schools (82 percent) have some students whose family incomes are below the federal income line; and 8 percent of the schools enroll more than 20 percent of their students from low-income families. Eighteen percent of the schools have no low-income families" (p. 139).

Yeager et al. proceeded to emphasize the differences among Catholic high schools and the wide range of those students Catholic high schools serve. They concluded that "nearly the same percentage of minority students are enrolled in Catholic high schools as in public schools" and that "Catholic high schools serve a range of students, from below poverty level to high income" (p. 35).

The following year, the NCEA published the work of Peter Benson, Robert Yeager, Philip Wood, Michael Guerra, and Bruno Manno (1986), which focused on the impact of Catholic high schools on low-income families. Building upon the work of Coleman et al. and Greeley and Yeager et al., Benson and his colleagues focused on five diverse Catholic high schools serving mainly low-income families. This study emphasized the "Catholic school effect," which Coleman et al. had earlier described as part of the reason for higher achievement scores in Catholic school students. Benson et al. described the school climate of Catholic schools that serve low-income families, emphasizing faith, community, morale, academics and discipline.

Though restrained in tone, this research raised some critical questions within Catholic circles. The chairperson of the United States Catholic Conference Committee on Education, Bishop William Hughes (1986), commended the study but asked "What can the schools do to strengthen the already vibrant ministry to the poor? . . . What is the fairest way to allocate scarce resources? . . . How can those who are blessed with abundance effectively help with the systemic and structural problems of the poor?" (p. 7)

Christine Vladimiroff (1986) considered the study only the beginning of a long dialogue about the future of Catholic schools, and she raised the following questions: "Should we, can we, stay in the [urban] schools? How long will we survive there?" (p. 15) She urged that "[Catholic schools] look at the attitudes and behaviors that we teach regarding race and minority groups in American society. Do we model the mutuality of male and female? How can we serve the non-Catholic and still teach and celebrate in our tradition?" (p. 16)

With regard to educating Hispanics, Ricardo Jimenez (1986) wondered whether Catholic schools are "providing the best opportunity possible for Hispanic students to learn in such a way so as not to trade in the richness of their ethnic culture for equal access to predetermined academic resources developed with predetermined educational goals and outcomes" (p. 9).

Concerned for Catholic inner city high schools, William Harkins (1987) asked "What are the implications of these statistics for the Catholic high school with a large minority population?" (p. 15) He also challenged Catholic high schools to reflect on how they welcome minority students. "Perhaps the lead question on climate questionnaires distributed to Black students in Catholic high schools should be 'Does this school receive you as you think Jesus Christ would receive you?'" (p. 16).

This type of questioning persists today among those involved with those Catholic schools that serve minorities in the inner cities. For example, at the National Congress on Catholic Schools (1992), the late James Lyke, who was the Archbishop of Atlanta, stated that "today's challenge demands that Catholic schools, especially in poor communities, be aggressively supported. The reality? So many are forced to close!" (p. 47). Clarence Waldon (1994), the pastor of a parish accommodating a Catholic school in an inner city, stated that "inner city parishes with schools are like financial problem children. . . . Many Catholics and even some pastors and diocesan leaders question the existence of Catholic inner city schools" (p. 21-22). Thus, an ongoing concern exists over the ways in which Catholic schools serve the poor and minorities and for making Catholic schools more accessible to these students.

In 1987, Coleman and Hoffer published yet another research project, *Public and Private High Schools: The Impact of Communities.* Guerra's (1991) words to describe it: "[T]his extraordinary study goes well beyond their earlier review of academic achievement in high school to look at dropouts, college placement, employment and earnings" (p. 21). Coleman and Hoffer attributed the effectiveness of Catholic schools to community support and involvement in these schools. They further developed their concept of the "Catholic school effect" into a concept of the "effect of the Catholic community." Their second chapter describes the race and ethnicity of the students in the schools they studied:

> Catholic schools enroll a smaller proportion of Blacks (6 percent) but a comparable proportion of Hispanics (10 percent). Blacks are very sparsely represented in the other private schools (2 percent) and Hispanics are also underrepresented, though to a lesser extent (8 percent). Minorities thus constitute a sizable part of Catholic school enrollments, though not of other private school enrollments. While Blacks are the most under-represented group in the Catholic schools, the 6 percent figure is striking when one considers that relatively few Blacks are Catholics (pp. 31-32).

Throughout this study, Coleman and Hoffer emphasized the achievement benefits Catholic school attendance offers those who are either economically disadvantaged or are Black or Hispanic.

Focusing on African Americans in both Catholic schools and other private schools, Dianna Slaughter and Deborah Johnson (1988) largely confirmed the findings of Coleman, et al., Greeley and the line of research sponsored by the NCEA.

Then a recent study by Michael Guerra, Michael Donahue and Peter Benson (1990) compared the effect of schooling on Catholics in public schools with Catholics in Catholic schools. Interestingly, gender, class and race play no role in this study, except in the observation that "due to the relatively small number of minority students in the samples, no separate analyses by race or ethnic group were performed" (p. 17). This study did, however, emphasize and identify the major areas of differences between public and Catholic high schools: school "climate," parental involvement, teacher commitment, leadership and autonomy, the functional community and the academic curriculum.

From this review of the principal studies of Catholic schools, one might conclude that the issue of whom Catholic schools serve went unaddressed, except perhaps statistically. One does get a sense, however, of the complexity and diversity of the Catholic school system which, after all serves only 6 percent of the overall school population. But a definite answer to the question awaits future research responding to the challenges presented by contemporary society and modern theological, philosophical and educational discourses.

The typical research approach is evident in our discussion here. The empirical question of whom Catholic schools serve becomes a matter for the statistician, and the conclusions suggest that Catholic schools do an adequate job of serving minorities and the poor. Meanwhile, functioning in the real world, Catholic educators and Church leaders and ministers challenge this complacent conclusion, and use the research to rally other Catholic educators satisfied with the status quo.

The results from the statistical data do sketch general norms for Catholic schools throughout the United States. But the current way of serving minorities and low-income students appears to be inadequate, both from the perspective of the numbers of minorities and poor served by Catholic schools and how these students are served. Catholic schools must consider how more of them can follow their implicit mission.

Most of the research draws upon the discourses of human capital and an economic rationale to measure effectiveness and success. From this understanding of effective schools, one can easily compare Catholic schools with public schools, which tend to accept these same discourses and tend to measure effectiveness the same way (Bryk, Lee and Holland, 1993). Yet Catholic schools must be more than just academically and economically effective. They must judge effectiveness from the perspective of how well they teach social justice as both theory and practice. Likewise, they must consider how to make concrete the challenges of the ecclesial documents as well as Gospel teachings and values.

Moreover, Catholic schools must invest more effort in the disadvantaged populations, minority groups and the poor, and they need to rely on more than the current discourse of school effectiveness in serving these populations. Catholic schools must involve themselves in the struggles of disadvantaged peoples and their communities. These challenges imply a new curriculum built upon social justice as theory and practice. They imply, in fact, an alternative system as Catholic schools were at their own inception (Beutow, 1970, 1988; Burns, 1912a, 1912b; Dolan, 1992; and O'Gorman, 1987).

Ethnographic Research Focused on Catholic Schools

Convey (1992) pointed out that most of the relevant research over the past 25 years addressed Catholic school effectiveness. Concluding his account of Catholic school research, he urged further research on the uniqueness and identity of Catholic schools and their religious outcomes. He also advocated a change in its methodology since "a majority of the major studies are descriptive or comparative studies that employ a survey research methodology." He went on to note that ethnographic studies in Catholic schools would be beneficial and "particularly useful," and he cited Nancy Lesko's (1988) study of a Catholic high school as an "excellent example of an ethnographic study involving Catholic schools " (p. 183).

While Convey neglected to mention Peter McLaren's (1986) ethnographic study of a Catholic junior high school, David Purpel (1988), Karen-Ann Watson-Gegeo (1987), Colin Lankshear (1989), Eileen Tway (1988) and Geoffrey Coward (1989) praised McLaren's work as (for example) a "scholarly contribution to theory development" (Lankshear, p. 144). Each acknowledged the value of critical ethnographic research in schools and affirmed the challenges McLaren presented. McLaren's work has, in short, been extolled as an outstanding ethnography, as an adept treatment of ritology and the integration of this theory with the practices of schooling, and as a work likely to affect any serious educator's thinking about the need for a critical approach to schooling procedures.

Before describing my own research at Vincent Gray Alternative High School, I will review the ethnographic studies of McLaren (1986) and Lesko (1988). My interests in McLaren's ethnography at a Catholic junior high school centers on the critical perspective he brought to his data understanding rituals within schooling to produce an ethical and political project. McLaren focused on a culture oppressed by others and a Catholic school that offered hope through some religious rituals and some of its classes and activities. My own study of VGAHS focused as well on an oppressed group with the idea that what happens within this alternative high school would be both critical of society and a source of hope in making social justice attainable.

My interest in Lesko's ethnography lies with its focus on life in a coeducational Catholic high school. Lesko (1988) emphasized that school ethnographies tend "to fail to understand, probe, and translate the participants' views" (p. 30) and are also "overly rational" (p. 32). She located her ethnographic study of "St. Anne's" in relation to McLaren's study of "St. Ryan's" in regard to the development of critical ethnography this way:

> McLaren's study (1986) of the physical dimensions of education does move away from the overly rational and arid school descriptions to an investigation of the somatic manifestations of educational control. The present study combats the literal and rational approach to educational research by focusing upon the symbolic and metaphorical dimensions of school meaning as well as upon ritual and story-telling in the school as a whole (p. 32).

Lesko told the story of "St. Anne's" from the perspective of schooling as meaning-making and identity-creating, and in so doing, she influenced my own interest in and concern for what transpires at a Catholic alternative high school. Lesko both interpreted her story of "St. Anne's" from the perspective of the actors and challenged further research and practice "to conceive of schools as creations of human actions with meaning and potential beyond the surface. We must interpret schools, not just report surface characteristics, and we must view aspects of school in relation to other aspects, and in relation to social and cultural configurations" (p. 147).

McLaren's (1986) ethnographic study, *Schooling As a Ritual Performance*, focused on how one could understand student life from the perspective of domination and resistance. He presented day-to-day life at "St. Ryan's" as ritual making among both students and teachers. McLaren stated the purpose of his research at the very outset: "This book will argue the primacy of understanding schooling from the perspectives of culture and performance. The major themes which inform this investigation have grown out of an empirical application of the concept of ritual to school settings, particularly the events and conditions which provide the context for classroom instruction" (p. 1). He repeated his purpose near the conclusion of his study as "an exploration of the symbolic interstices of meaning and action in the instructional rituals of schooling" (p. 243).

McLaren moved educational research into a mode of critical ethnography and presented an insightful story about Catholic education. His focus was on junior high school students at "St. Ryan's School" in Toronto. He describes "St. Ryan's" as

> a relatively modern school and quite pleasant in appearance. The grounds are clean and attractively landscaped. The well-kept appearance of the school contrasts sharply with the dingy smokestacks of the surrounding factories, the broken windows of the abandoned warehouses and the deserted lots full of debris which were once used to store sheet metal and auto parts. The interior of the school is also kept in good condition (p. 67).

The majority of the students, the key protagonists in McLaren's story, at "St. Ryan's" were sons and daughters of Portuguese (from the Azores) and Italian immigrants. He attempted a "novel critique of school life through an interrogation of its symbol systems, ethoses, pervading myths and root paradigms" (p. 6). Later in his study, McLaren identified these root paradigms as "being a Catholic" and "being a worker," and he identified his own position "as a Catholic and an educator" (p. 13) explicating the rituals operating at "St. Ryan's."

McLaren described these daily rituals from five perspectives. The first is the micro ritual consisting "of the individual lessons that took place on a day-to-day basis." The second, the macro ritual, consisted of "the aggregate of classroom lessons over a single school day." The third, rituals of revitalization, McLaren characterized as "a processual event that functions to inject a renewal of commitment into the motivations and values of the ritual participants." Fourth, the rituals of intensification, unified a group of teachers or students or both within a classroom. Fifth, the rituals of resistance, McLaren understood as rituals of conflict and destructuring (pp. 79-80). He also developed an array of critical questions in regard to these rituals (pp. 82-83). For example, who benefits most from the ritual structures remaining as they are? Who is marginalized as a result? How are power and control invested and mediated through the ritual symbols, ritual paradigms and ritual codes?

Throughout this work, McLaren interpolated his insights and conclusions about life at this Catholic school. Over and over again he referred to the role of the religion class as an avenue for students becoming critical and expressing resistance to domination in an organized and informed way. McLaren also noted characteristics of resistant behavior on the part of the students in terms of the different languages or rituals performed as part of the various cultures in which the students located themselves, for example, the street culture, the neighborhood culture and the Church culture.

McLaren pointed out that Catholic schooling at "St. Ryan's" did "show flashes of progressivism and emancipation in its religious teachings" (p. 227). Likewise, he noted that the fight for social equality was hardly new in the teachings of the Catholic Church (pp. 228-229). He also identified the task of schooling for Catholic schools as a political and ethical project and he urged that public schooling become a political and ethical project at achieving social justice:

> Not only must we dream a better world but we must muster the civic courage which requires us to act as if we are living in a democratic society. Within the tensions and conflicts that exist between radical critiques of schooling and Catholic education I am confident that, in the long run, a vision of social justice and emancipation can be won. More important, I am confident that

> educators will begin to take a more active role in the fight for equality and liberation (p. 254).

Some of McLaren's conclusions and recommendations focused on the all-to-apparent inequality in schools. He pointed out that "forms of instruction and teaching practices generally constituted an inadvertent ritualized reaffirmation of ethnic stereotypes and the daily ritual remaking and reconfirmation of class division" (p. 224). He also concluded that even the religion classes and religious rituals and values conveyed a subservience to the powers of the institutional Church. McLaren summarized his conclusions this way on page 229:

> What is of ultimate importance with respect to the instructional rite is how they are put into effect, predicated or bodied forth, and how well their missions are carried out and made relevant for the youth of today. We must discern just how pedagogical rituals are affecting students. To what extent are they alienating and anxiety producing? To what extent do they muffle communities and reproduce the division of labor in the wider society?

The recommendations of McLaren's study challenge educators to strengthen the link between the role of ritual and the student body, on the one hand, and instructional methods, on the other. Likewise, McLaren recommended that an understanding of both the ritual and culture of the students would enhance both curriculum and instruction.

More specifically in regard to "St. Ryan" and Catholic schools, McLaren affirmed "the achievements of Catholic schooling, which have been outstanding, particularly with regard to preserving an enclave for the exercise of care and compassion in an often indifferent society" (p. 248). But he also suggested that a "new approach to schooling is required that refuses to humanize inhumanity or spiritualize injustice" (p. 248). We need, he said, to "act on the moral imperative of creating a pedagogy for the opposition" (p. 254).

Like Peter McLaren, I approached my own ethnographic study as a Catholic and an educator. I share his hopes for a world that is characterized by social justice. Having spent many years in Catholic schools, I agree with McLaren that religious education has always provided an avenue for resistance to be broached as both part of the biblical prophetic tradition and the Church's social teachings. As I said,

McLaren's study challenges those involved in Catholic schools to reflect and assess what they accomplish in light of the prophetic aspirations for a more equal and just world. In his last paragraph, McLaren returned to this challenge specifically aimed at Catholic schools:

> In conclusion, it remains the task of Catholic schooling to decry the mythological abuse (in Barthes' sense of the term) that has rendered working-class students as inferior beings in the minds of many educators. If Catholic schooling persists in remaining tributary to the political project of social justice by holding at arm's length critical social analysis and practice, history may one day record this quietistic detachment as a deep moral stain in the Christian soul. Schools must begin to give measurable shape to our dreams for a more just society by becoming not only laboratories for critique, but also strongholds for purposeful and life-giving symbols (p. 256).

I found myself challenged and inspired by McLaren's work, the first to my knowledge to apply a critical ethnography in a Catholic school. McLaren described incidents and situations similar to my own Catholic school experiences. He also articulated a theory that helps identify current schooling practices, and he proposes a project for schools that responds to what Catholic Church documents proposed as the central mission, namely, the development of a community from the perspective of the Gospel values of equity and justice. McLaren's work is, in short, the starting point for my own interest in conducting a critical ethnography on a Catholic alternative school for African Americans, and his work serves as a model for future ethnographies on a variety of Catholic school settings.

Another important ethnographic study of Catholic schools is the work of Nancy Lesko (1988), *Symbolizing Society: Stories, Rites and Structure in a Catholic High School*, already mentioned. As Michael Perko (1990) noted "[O]ne of the most understudied sectors of the American educational landscape was that occupied by Catholic K-12 schooling" (p. 98), and with Convey, he acclaimed Lesko's work as a "work of considerable merit . . . [because] *Symbolizing Society* breaks ground in its thoughtful, clear and elegant examination of the 'inner life' of a typical Catholic secondary school" (p. 102).

Lesko chose a Catholic school because "the current spotlight on parochial education provides an opportunity to examine closely an alternative system that puts greater emphasis on developing interdependence and cooperation among students and teachers" (p. 3). She further observed that "contemporary Catholic schools thus exhibit tensions between an emphasis on education in skills and self-interested achievement and a religious-based education emphasizing character and morals" (p. 19).

Lesko focused her ethnographic study more specifically on the conflicts between individualism and community as experienced at "St. Anne's High School," emphasizing the need "to penetrate further into basic assumptions of schools to explore what the web of meaning is, and how that particular web of meaning is produced" (p. 15). She presented the life at "St. Anne's" as the "symbolic aspects of schooling . . . as a site of meaning-making and identity creation, rather than merely as a training or contest site" (p. 146).

Lesko found this tension between the individual and community present in most Catholic schools today and in public schools as well. She proposed that the cult of individualism is prevalent in secondary school practices and structures, and she identified seven practices of schooling that contribute to radical individualism:

> (1) preeminence of a definition of education as skills acquisition,
> (2) a strong emphasis on individual competition,
> (3) specialization among teachers,
> (4) a therapeutic model of school discipline,
> (5) legalistic, bureaucratic school organization,
> (6) an official value-neutrality, and
> (7) continuous present moment with a neglect of past and future (p. 14).

She went on to assert that "a religious-based school may illuminate how individualism can be tempered and collective orientations fostered, as well as how the sacred status of radical individualism in other types of schools erects barricades for many young men and women" (p. 16). From this perspective, then, Lesko told the story of "St. Anne's," stating that the myth of "St. Anne's" is "that individual and community, private and public are integrally related and complementary. The school's 'fun' and 'love' were intended to convince participants that the social group—exemplified as the school, the church, society—was a necessary component of a quality life for each person" (p. 144).

Lesko used this theme of the individual versus community in some of her other work, notably, her research with cheerleaders (1988) and earlier articles that dealt with her research at "St. Anne's High School" (1983, 1986).

The students of "St. Anne's," a coeducational Catholic secondary school, are Lesko's main protagonists. Throughout her study, Lesko remained faithful to her conviction that "the present study gives highest priority to students' experiences in school, while analyzing those events from a perspective of social integration, identity, and system of thought" (p. 31). She identified two predominant themes as she listened to and observed the "St. Anne's" staff members and students. The first theme "centered on the nice 'feel' of the school, its warmth and unity. People care about one another at St. Anne's" (p. 37). The second theme revolved around "the limits of harmony and caring . . . intense competitions and favoritism, the widespread lack of objectivity in the treatment of different students" (p. 37). She pursued these two themes with a thorough "examination of freshmen orientation, an annual ritual that serves to reestablish school traditions and values for returning staff members and students, as well as to induct freshmen" (p. 43).

She continued the story of "St. Anne's" focusing on friends and student groups. Here the main actors were young women in their junior year placed in three distinct groups: the rich and populars, the burnouts and the apathetic. She presented how the members of each group conceived of themselves and what they had to say about the other groups. She concluded that the students' talk about peers "evidenced a preoccupation with the issues of belonging and treating others decently, making something of oneself, and defining a good member, or citizen, of the school" (p. 96).

Lesko concluded that "the school's impact on the differences among groups" invites one to isolate "some of the unifying times and some of the separating times to examine the process and impacts involved in the connections and the fragmentations among students" (p. 101). Assuming this perspective, Lesko then focused upon homecoming—or more precisely, the homecoming spirit assembly and an all-school mass. In analyzing these two events, Lesko found that "these two assemblies involved 'fun' and 'love'" (p. 115). Likewise, these two assemblies contextualized students in relation to others by:

> (1) being all together as a school (both assemblies);
> (2) cheering together as a school class (spirit assembly);
> (3) seeing oneself as a "senior" in relation to juniors (spirit assembly);
> (4) seeing all participants as having equal importance (both assemblies); and
> (5) connecting the present students with the school's past (spirit assembly) (p. 115).

Lesko continued the story of "St. Anne's" by examining "several students' constructions of identities that combine aspects of the cultural themes of caring and contest in very different ways" (p. 119). She focused on popular students, referring to them as "the queens," and also the unpopular students, calling them the "social outcasts." Then she demonstrated from the perspective of these students "a range of identities constructed from the tension between caring and contest." She concluded that "the queens demonstrated 'public' selves that combined caring and contest and connected peers with one another and with the school. The social outcasts created identities that were largely private and which emphasized the fragmentation, autonomy, and objectivity of the contest view of school and of society" (p. 137).

Lesko ended her study by reminding readers that she presented "the culture of St. Anne's High School as a myth, told in words and actions. The subject of the myth is the conflict between two codes of conduct, caring and contest, each of which embodies a distinct way of thinking about, seeing, and acting in school" (p. 139). She urged that each school "develop and project a unique identifiable character" (p. 145), and she proposed that "this study of St. Anne's informs future research and theorizing about schools. Schools need to be discussed in symbolic, communal terms, as public sites, as well as in terms of training for individuals" (p. 147).

Lesko's final paragraph exhorts educators to think in new ways as ethnographers and as interpretative researchers. Her final paragraph recalls the hopes and exhortations of McLaren's study of "St. Ryan's," and this paragraph too heightened my own interests in researching Catholic schools:

> At each level of research and practice, we must strive to conceive of schools as creations of human actions with meaning and potential beyond the surface. We must interpret schools, not just report surface characteristics, and we must view aspects of school in relation to other aspects, and in relation to social and cultural configurations. The many layers of meaning and conflicting meaning must be examined. We must consider schools as sites of identity-creation as well as of training and competition. We should try on the interpretive and relational thought processes as ways to reestablish that approach to viewing education. Both the contest and caring views of schools need to be preserved; the tension between them is productive, just as is the tension between public and private welfare. Those are the lessons of St. Anne's private school for public education and scholarship on schooling (pp. 147-148).

The challenges of McLaren's and Lesko's critical ethnographies with Catholic schools informed my own work on the discourses of critical pedagogy and liberation theology in the context of Catholic schools. Is it possible that these critical discourses have already become part of the process of Catholic schooling? How can they influence the shape of what happens at Catholic schools? Can critical discourses assist those involved in Catholic education to reflect upon the poor and the minorities they serve?

By marshaling the actors and events of a Catholic alternative high school, I resolved to continue the investigation into the schooling process McLaren and Lesko had begun. Peter McLaren (1992) stated that "ethnography can serve both as a practical ethics and an ethics of practice that is never far removed from the frontiers of hope sought by those who still choose to struggle and to dream" (p. 90). Ideally, my analysis and interpretation of the voices of the students, administrators and teachers of Vincent Gray Alternative High School would add an understanding of the ritual and symbolic parts of the schooling process as a critical and ethical project, rooted in the educational discourse of critical pedagogy and in the theological discourse of liberation theology.

CHAPTER FOUR

Critical Discourses of Liberation Theology and Critical Pedagogy

> One of the most exciting theoretical accomplishments that has emerged in critical social theory is the development of a discourse that links certain strands of radical feminist theory with selected aspects of liberation theology.
>
> \- Henry Giroux in *Schooling and the Struggle for Public Life* (1988, p. 92)

> [Postmodernism] posits instead a faith in forms of social transformation that are attentive to the historical, structural, and ideological limits that shape the possibility for self-reflection and action. It points to solidarity, community, and compassion as essential aspects of how we develop and understand the capacities we have for how we experience the world and ourselves in a meaningful way.
>
> \- Henry Giroux in *Border Crossings* (1992, p. 123)

The preceding two chapters focused on the issue of the Catholic school identity and the recent research into Catholic education, with an emphasis on the ethnographic studies of Peter McLaren and Nancy Lesko. This chapter turns to the discourses of liberation theology and critical pedagogy and explores the relationship of the themes common to these two discourses, while acknowledging their many differences. My goal is to show how these discourses can contribute to the discussion Catholic school identity and to show how these discourses can help Catholic schools serve the poor and minorities.

Immersed in the literature of the discourse of critical pedagogy, one at first wonders whether this could be the language of an educational or theological discourse like liberation theology. One is continually reminded that both critical pedagogy and liberation theology provide a language of possibility and transformation, and both have implications for what transpires in schools and what purposes schools serve. Both discourses challenge the current practices in most schools, both public and Catholic. Pamela Smith (1989) concluded her work on democratic education in public schools by stating that "a discussion of democratic education could be strengthened by a clear, theoretical explication of hope and how it can be supported by reconceptualized understandings of power and voice. Liberation theology might be a focal point in this area" (p. 254).

While these critical discourses share similarities, however, each continues to maintain its uniqueness. Critical pedagogy has evolved from the democratic discourses in education originally articulated by John Dewey, George Counts, Harold Rugg and other social reconstructionists, by neo-Marxist discourses of liberation and transformation, and by the Frankfurt school of critical theory. Liberation theology is rooted in the Christian Scriptures and has evolved from a political-critical theology. While drawing from a variety of different sources, the two come together in the work and writings of the renowned Brazilian educator, Paulo Freire.

I intend to elaborate on Freire's "pedagogy of conscientization" as a common source for liberation theology and critical pedagogy, along with the theory and method of liberation theology as articulated by Latin American theologians, Leonardo Boff and his brother Clodovis, feminist theologians, Sharon Welch and Rebecca Chopp, and the discourse of critical pedagogy associated with Henry Giroux and Peter McLaren. I conclude this chapter by presenting a generalizable model of the common themes or elements of the discourses of liberation theology and critical pedagogy that posits liberation theology and critical pedagogy as discourses of praxis and transformation.

I developed this model as the result of synthesizing these two discourses, and I intend that it be understood less as a reified or static model of what liberation theology or critical pedagogy is than as a heuristic model helpful in understanding the similarities between these two discourses. One can also use this model to determine whether elements of these two critical discourses characterize the climate and practices at Vincent Gray Alternative High School, or for that matter any other school. In subsequent chapters, I analyze how these critical discourses and practices emerge in the voices of the students, administrators and teachers of VGAHS, incorporating elements of my integrative model of liberation theology and critical pedagogy.

Paulo Freire's Influence on Liberation Theology and Critical Pedagogy

Paulo Freire wrote his classic work, *Pedagogy of the Oppressed*, in 1968 and it first appeared in English and Spanish in 1970. John Medcalf (1995) claims that "no book on the philosophy of education has received so many garlands" and that "the pages devoted to the importance of dialogue deserve unreserved support" (p. 801). Patrick Slattery (1995) points out that Freire's classic work is "an important early example of critical theory in practice" (p. 198). Certainly Freire's work has inspired "hundreds of scholars worldwide to link literacy, culture and politics" (Pinar, Reynolds, Slattery and Taubman, 1995, p. 230). Gadotti (1994) called *Pedagogy of the Oppressed* "Freire's most important and extensive work" (p. 43).

In *Pedagogy of the Oppressed* (1989), Freire begins the development of his pedagogy by acknowledging that humanity's central problem is achieving humanization, since the effort leads to the recognition of dehumanization. In his view, "the great humanistic and historical task of the oppressed is to liberate themselves and their oppressors as well" (p. 28). He presented the pedagogy of the oppressed as

> a pedagogy which must be forged with, not for, the oppressed (whether individuals or peoples) in the incessant struggle to regain their humanity. This pedagogy makes oppression and its causes objects of reflection by the oppressed, and from that reflection will come their necessary engagement on the struggle for their liberation. And in the struggle this pedagogy will be made and remade (p. 33).

This pedagogy produces a solidarity with the oppressed and then the oppressed with each other. This solidarity—this entering into the experience of the oppressed—is a radical posture, defined as "fighting at their side to transform the objective reality which has made them 'beings for another'" (p. 34). It is an act of love, existential and praxis, a "reflection and action upon the world to transform it" (p. 36).

The method of this pedagogy is dialogue or problem posing as opposed to a "banking" methodology; it values the voices and experiences of the students in the process of developing knowledge.

This process of dialogue is also characterized as an act of love and commitment to other persons; as intense faith in humanity's "power to make and remake, to create and re-create, faith in its vocation to be more fully human" (p. 79); and also as mutual trust between persons and hope for the "encounter of seeking to be more fully human" (p. 80).

Critical reflection on one's situation of being oppressed begins the dialogue. By "critical thinking" Freire meant "a thinking which discerns an indivisible solidarity between the world and people and admits of no dichotomy between them—thinking which perceives reality as process, as transformation, rather than as a static entity—thinking which does not separate itself from action, but constantly immerses itself in temporality without fear of the risks involved" (p. 81).

In *Education for Critical Consciousness* (1990), first published in 1978, Freire continued these themes but developed the concepts of the process of human agency and "conscientization." He is clear there that "to be human is to engage in relationships with others and with the world. . . . [and that] people relate to their world in a critical way" (p. 3). Education is the process that helps individuals understand themselves and their world with a view toward transforming it. Freire stated that "the important thing is to help men and nations help themselves, to place them in consciously critical confrontation with their problems, to make them agents of their own recuperation" (p. 16). Education then helps people "reflect on themselves, their responsibilities, and their role in a new cultural climate—indeed to reflect on their very power of reflection" (p. 16).

Freire identified this process of critical awareness "conscientization." It involves the process of dialogue and " a critical education which could help to form critical attitudes" (p. 32). Thus, education becomes an act of love and courage, since education "cannot fear the analysis of reality or, under pain of revealing itself as a farce, avoid creative discussion" (p. 38).

In some of his later essays, Freire (1985) described the process of conscientization as acts of denunciation and annunciation in a specific historical context (pp. 58-59). He identified it with theological language as an experience of Easter (pp. 122-123) and as the role of the prophetic Church (pp. 137-140). He also defined conscientization as "the effort to enlighten men about the obstacles preventing them from a clear perception of reality. In this role, conscientization effects the ejection of cultural myths that confuse people's awareness and make them ambiguous beings" (p. 89). Concerning the process of conscientization,

Freire stated that

> The word "conscientization," the process by which human beings participate critically in a transforming action, should not be understood as an idealist manipulation. Even if our vision in conscientization is dialogical, not subjective or mechanistic, we cannot attribute to this consciousness a role it does not have, that of transforming reality. Yet we also must not reduce consciousness to a mere reflection of reality. One of the important points in conscientization is to provoke recognition of the world, not as a "given" world, but as a world dynamically "in the making." . . . It is precisely this creation of a new reality, prefigured in the revolutionary criticism of the old one, that cannot exhaust the conscientization process, a process as permanent as any real revolution (pp. 106-107).

Freire (1989) continued to expand on his pedagogy of the oppressed, putting it into practice as head of the Education Department of the World Council of Churches and with adult literacy programs in Guinea-Bissau and Sao Tome. In 1987, Freire began to speak of his own work and pedagogy as an "emancipatory and critical pedagogy." In their 1987 conversation, Paulo Freire and Ira Shor identified Freire's pedagogy of the oppressed as potentially a viable pedagogy for the United States. Freire understood the process of schooling to involve the development of a critical awareness of one's world and the injustices and oppressions that exist in that world, and he hoped this critical awareness could lead to political actions that would help to transform it.

Peter McLaren and Tomaz Tadeu da Silva (1993) offered this brief summary of Freire's pedagogy as well as the effects of Freire's work:

> Freire's move away from the pseudo-equality of liberal pluralism is evident in his challenge to deepen our understanding of how individuals can gain a greater purchase on social agency through a critical narrativization of their desire, through the naming of their own histories, and through claiming the necessary power to resist their imposed subalternity and the deforming effects of social power. For nearly two decades, Freire's work has been employed by teachers, social workers, literacy workers, theologians, and others to construct an educational vision in which self-development and social transformation go hand in hand in the

struggle for social justice (p. 52).

Freire's experiences as Secretary of Education of Sao Paulo informed his *Pedagogy of the City* (1993). Beyond narrating these experiences, Freire expressed the need to integrate theory with practice as a teacher and educational leader, amid hopes for what schools could be. "We must," he said, "change the face of schools" (p. 32). This progressive struggle requires a vision of schools that generate happiness rather than torpor. Freire characterized the new face of schools as "serious, competent, fair, joyous, and curious—a school system that transforms the space where children, rich or poor, are able to learn, to create, to take risks, to question, and to grow" (p. 37).

Freire went on to characterize the teacher in this new school as integrating theory with practice. He stated that "one of the indispensable virtues of a progressive educator has to do with the coherence between discourse and practice" (p. 119). In addition, Freire observed that the role of the teacher is "to testify constantly to his or her students his or her competence, love, political clarity, the coherence between what he or she says and does, his or her tolerance, his or her ability to live with the different to fight against the antagonistic" (p. 50). He urged that teachers discover education as possibility and a source of liberation.

Again, Freire affirmed the pedagogy of dialogue rather than the pedagogy of banking; his school is "one where there is great emphasis on the critical apprehension of meaningful knowledge through the dialogical relation. It is the school that stimulates the student to ask questions to critique, to create" (p. 77).

Meanwhile, Freire shared some of his hopes for a democratic school with the interests of underprivileged children at heart. As he said, "[T]he utopian dream that always served as the impetus for all my political and pedagogical adventures . . . has to do with a society that is less unjust, less cruel, more democratic, less discriminatory, less racist, less sexist" (p. 115).

Recently, Paulo Freire (1994) augmented his classic work with *Pedagogy of Hope: Reliving Pedagogy of the Oppressed*, in which he focused less upon what he had previously written and more on the need for hope. Guided by his own considerable experience, Freire nevertheless stated that "I do not intend to wallow in nostalgia. Instead, my reencounter with *Pedagogy of the Oppressed* will have the tone of one who speaks not of what has been, but of what is" (p. 11).

As Freire explained the context in which he wrote his classic work and those that followed, he reemphasized the principles of his pedagogy of dialogue and conscientization, as well as the necessity of confidence in this process. "Things have not changed a great deal between 1973 and 1994," Freire observed, "when it comes to an all but systematic refusal on the part of the antiracist and antisexist movements . . . and the same is true for the struggle against the thesis of unity in diversity" (p. 158).

Concerning hope, he makes it clear that "without a minimum of hope, we cannot so much as start the struggle"; and that "the progressive educator, through a serious and correct political analysis, can unveil opportunities for hope, no matter what the obstacles may be" (p. 9). This element of hope lives at the heart of critical discourses as one becomes more and more concerned with the poor and the oppressed. Hope offers a way of coping with the discouraging situations that exist in today's schools and world. Progressive educators cannot afford to abandon efforts to change school practices or the world.

Freire also emphasized dialogue and conscientization as the key elements of his educational pedagogy, suggesting that "teaching is a creative act, a critical act" in conveying hope. He reaffirmed that "one of the tasks of democratic popular education, a pedagogy of hope, [is] that of enabling the popular classes to develop their own language—which, emerges from and returns upon their own reality, sketches out the conjectures, the designs, the anticipations of their new world" (p. 39). Freire could not "resist repeating [that] teaching is not the pure mechanical transfer of the contour of a content from the teacher to passive, docile students" (p. 69), and he emphasized that the role of the progressive educator "is to bring out the fact that there are other readings of the world, different from the one being offered as the educator's own, and at times antagonistic to it" (p. 112). This process of teaching and learning through dialogue would "while respecting the educands' understanding of the world, challenge them to think critically, [then] refuse to separate the teaching of content from the teaching of thinking precisely" (p. 169).

Freire continued to describe the process as a pedagogy of both denunciation and annunciation:

> There is no authentic utopia apart from the tension between the denunciation of a present becoming more and more intolerable, and the annunciation, announcement, of a future to be created, built—politically, esthetically, and ethically—by us women and

> men. Utopia implies the denunciation and proclamation, but it does not permit the tension between the two to die away with the production of the future previously announced (p. 91).

I have already suggested the indebtedness of both liberation theology and critical pedagogy to Freire's work, and Medcalf (1995) points out that liberation theology was "influenced by [Freire's] thought and in turn influenced him" (p. 801). Freire rooted his pedagogy of the oppressed and liberation theology in Brazilian experiences of the 1960s. As Freire developed the practice and theory of a liberating pedagogy while instilling literacy among the poor of Brazil, numerous Church leaders in Brazil were developing the pedagogy of Christian-based communities. Freire based his articulation of a pedagogy of the oppressed upon what he saw happening in his own work with indigenous people. At the same time, liberation theologians began to articulate what was happening among these same people from a theological and spiritual perspective.

Henry Giroux (1988a) acknowledged Freire's relationship with liberation theology as well as his influence upon liberation theology this way:

> Freire's own philosophy of hope and struggle is rooted in a language of possibility that draws extensively from the tradition of liberation theology. It is from the merging of these two traditions that Freire has produced a discourse that not only gives meaning and theoretical coherence to his work, but also provides the basis for a more comprehensive and critical theory of pedagogical struggle. . . . Freire's opposition to all forms of oppression, his call to link ideology critique with collective action, and the prophetic vision central to his politics are heavily indebted to the spirit and the ideological dynamics that have both informed and characterized the Liberation Theology Movement that has emerged primarily out of Latin America (pp. 110-113).

Alfred Hennelly (1990) began his documentary history of liberation theology with a talk that Freire delivered in Rome in 1970. He noted that the Church appeared to follow something resembling "conscientization" in Latin America (p. 2) and similar principles informed the discussions and documents of the 1968 Medellin Conference of Latin American Bishops (pp. 103-105).

The Medellin Documents represent the first official Catholic Church articulation of, and commitment to, liberation theology; in fact, they "serve as the founding documents of Latin American liberation theology; they determine, as well, a direction of solidarity and liberation through the creation of grassroot communities" (Chopp, p. 15).

Anticipating Hennelly, Rebecca Chopp (1989) acknowledged Freire's influence upon and relationship with liberation theology: "Latin American liberation theology draws upon the resources of Paulo Freire, Marxism, and modern theology to demand that theology be grounded in a concrete praxis of commitment to social justice" (p. 5). Chopp argued that liberation theologians had borrowed Freire's concept and method and that "Latin American liberation theologians revise conscientization to name the activity of faith: becoming human in solidarity with God and with the poor" (p. 21).

Still earlier, Leonardo Boff and Clodovis Boff (1984, 1989) also noted that liberation theology borrows from Freire's conscientization. They presented the strategy of liberation as "the oppressed come together, come to understand their situation through the process of conscientization, discover the causes of their oppression, organize themselves into movements, and act in a coordinated fashion" (1989, p. 5).

Clodovis Boff (1987) mentioned Freire's influences upon his own understanding of theology as a dialectic of theory and praxis similar to Freire's development of conscience and revolution. He also related his development of relevant themes of theology to Freire's use of generative themes as part of the process of popular education.

According to Leonardo Boff (1991a), the popular pedagogy of liberation theology "extensively uses the contributions of Brazilian educator, Paulo Freire." He went on to describe this pedagogy as helping people "to discover the pathways of their own liberation—techniques that begin with their values, culture and practices" (p. 68). The influence of Freire, moreover, extends beyond liberation theology to a whole new sense of evangelization. Boff (1991b) described this new evangelization as a "new way of being church" and employing

> new methods, along the lines of the pedagogy of the oppressed, and of education as a practice of freedom, of the famous Christian educator Paulo Freire, according to whom educand and educator, catechized and catechist, enter into a process of mutual apprenticeship and exchange of learning, on the basis of accumulated experience, which is criticized and broadened in an

> integral perspective that attends to the various dimensions of personal, social, intellectual, affective, cultural and religious human existence (pp. 116-117).

Freire (1985), himself, developed a sense of the relationship between the role of theologians and the Church and the role of education. He wrote of the Church as a prophetic institution that understands itself as having a political and an emancipatory project, involved with education as an "instrument of transforming action." In regard to liberation theology as a part of his process of transformation, involving both critique and possibility, Freire (1985) observed that

> This prophetic attitude, which emerges in the praxis of numerous Christians in the challenging historical situation of Latin America, is accompanied by a rich and a very necessary theological reflection. The theology of so-called development gives way to the theology of liberation—a prophetic, utopian theology, full of hope. Little does it matter that this theology is not yet well systematized. Its content arises from the hopeless situation of dependent, exploited, invaded societies. It is stimulated by the need to rise above the contradictions that explain and produce that dependence. Since it is prophetic, this theology of liberation cannot attempt to reconcile the irreconcilable (p. 139).

Freire is clearly familiar with liberation theology and recognizes its relationship with his own work and writings, and this relationship between his discourse of a liberatory or critical pedagogy and liberation theology gains continual recognition. Stanley Aronowitz (1993) found Freire's pedagogy "grounded in a fully developed philosophical anthropology, that is, a theory of human nature, one might say a secular liberation theology" (p. 12).

Carlos Torres (1993) described Freire's early involvement with the Catholic Church in Brazil, concentrating on the development and influence of liberation theology. In so doing, he observed that "one of the main reasons for Freire's success was the close relation between Freire's early philosophy of education and Catholic thinking. [In 1963], Freire's method of literacy was given official approval by the National Bishop's Conference in Brazil and was adopted by the Movement of Education from the Bases as its own method of attaining literacy" (pp. 121-122). Freire's thought influenced the document on education among the Documents of Medellin that emerged from the Latin American Bishops Conference in 1968. Moreover, since Freire's return to Brazil, he maintains close contact with liberation theology and the Catholic Church in Brazil. Torres also described some of Freire's activities in Brazil since 1980; among these he mentioned that Freire is a Professor in the Faculty of Education at the Catholic University of Sao Paulo and that he remains involved in a project of popular education sponsored by the Archdiocese of Sao Paulo (pp. 136, 142).

Freire's work and writing developed in dialogue with liberation theology, and his contributions to the discourse of critical pedagogy continue in dialogue with liberation theology. Liberation theologians acknowledge that Freire influenced both their theology and their praxis of liberation, and he both provides a source for liberation theology and critical pedagogy and demonstrates the communality between these two critical discourses.

Educational theorists also acknowledge the relationship between critical pedagogy and Freire's work and they acknowledge as well that Freire has become a reliable reference for the critical discourses of schooling (Bennett and LeCompte, 1990; Pinar, Reynolds, Slattery and Taubman, 1995; Slattery, 1995; and Spring, 1991). In his book on urban school reform and the teachers' work in these schools, Dennis Carlson (1992) acknowledged that "critical pedagogy, as Giroux and others have developed it within an American context, owes much to the work of the Brazilian educator, Paulo Freire" (p. 274). David Purpel (1989) advocated that educators in public schools become aware of Freire's writing and start to analyze schooling from his perspective. He also admitted that "the writings and life of Paulo Freire have had a profound influence on [my] ideas" (p. 156), in that they address "a cultural, political, and moral crisis and hence, ipso facto, an educational crisis" (p. 1). Freire and Giroux jointly contributed the introduction to Purpel's book.

Repeatedly, Giroux (1981a, 1983, 1988a, 1988b, 1992) acknowledged the relationship between his development of the discourse of critical pedagogy and Freire's work, and Aronowitz and Giroux (1985) dedicated their book, *Education Under Siege,* to him: "This book is dedicated to Paulo Freire who is a living embodiment of the principle that underlies this work: that pedagogy should become more political and that the political should become more pedagogical."

Freire wrote the foreword to Giroux's *Theory and Resistance in Education: A Pedagogy for the Opposition* (1983) and Giroux also included Freire in his dedication. The mutual admiration continued: Freire wrote the introduction to *Teachers As Intellectuals: Toward a Critical Pedagogy of Learning* (1988), and Giroux wrote the introduction for two of Freire's books (1985, 1987). Within these forewords and introductions, Freire and Giroux acknowledged their influence and thought upon each other. In Giroux (1992), moreover, David Trend acknowledged Freire's influence upon critical pedagogy in the introduction of his interview with Giroux: "Giroux has emerged as one of the most outspoken proponents of the 'critical pedagogy' movement, an amalgam of educational philosophies that first gained wide public recognition in the 1960s through the writings of Brazilian expatriate Paulo Freire" (p. 149).

A decade before, Giroux (1981b) wrote that he was already "indebted to Paulo Freire for the insight he provides and the courage he displays in fighting for social justice." Giroux proceeded to develop Freire's approach to radical educational theory and practice, and with regard to Freire's pedagogy being utilized by educators, Giroux stated that

> Freire's work demonstrates that the dynamic of progressive change stems, in part, from working with people rather than on them. It is in the latter spirit of respect for human struggle and hope, that an emancipatory pedagogy can be forged, one in which radical educators can consolidate and use the insights of Freire within the context of our own historical experience in order to give new shape to the meaning of radical praxis (p. 139).

Giroux (1983) next developed Freire's concept of critical literacy as a radical theory of literacy and pedagogy. He pointed out that when addressing literacy, "Freire moves from critique to cultural production to social action linking these notions of culture and power within the context of a radically informed pedagogy" (p. 226).

Freire's model of emancipatory literacy, his conception of cultural politics, and his languages of critique and possibility helped him develop critical pedagogy, and Giroux (1988a) declared that Freire "has provided one of the few practical models upon which to develop a radical philosophy of literacy and pedagogy" (p. 153). About Freire's work and influence on critical pedagogy, Giroux (1988b) stated that

> Freire's work provides a view of pedagogy and praxis that is partisan to its core; in its origins and intentions it is for "choosing life." Moreover, Freire demonstrates once again that he is not only a man of the present, he is also a man of the future. His speech, actions, warmth, and vision represent a way of acknowledging and criticizing a world that lives perilously close to destruction. In one sense, Freire's presence is there to remind us not simply about what we are but also to suggest what we might become (p. 120).

Meanwhile, over and over again, Peter McLaren (1986a, 1986b, 1987, 1989, 1991a, 1993a, 1993b, 1994, 1995) has acknowledged Freire's influence upon his work with the discourse of critical pedagogy. McLaren's book on critical pedagogy, *Life in Schools: An Introduction to Critical Pedagogy in the Foundations of Education* (1989), identified Freire as a critical educator and presented his writing as an important part of critical pedagogy. McLaren observed there that "the work of Brazilian educator Paulo Freire places him in the front ranks of that 'dying class' of educational revolutionaries who march behind the banner of liberation to fight for social justice and educational reform" (p. 194).

McLaren further pointed out that "Freire's work, cited by educators throughout the world, constitutes an important contribution to critical pedagogy not simply because of its theoretical refinement, but because of Freire's success at putting theory into practice" (p. 194). Likewise, throughout his 1989 book, McLaren included Freire and Giroux as sources for his discussion of critical pedagogy: "This book draws primarily on radical perspectives exemplified in the works of such theorists as Paulo Freire and Henry Giroux, who make an important distinction between schooling and education" (p. 165). These same sentiments appear in the second edition of *Life in Schools* (1994).

Peter McLaren and Peter Leonard (1993) introduced their edition of the book, *Paulo Freire: A Critical Encounter*, celebrating Freire's contribution to critical pedagogy, this way:

> This volume of chapters on the work of Paulo Freire is an intellectual contribution to the central political project of our time: how to struggle for the social transformation of our post-modern and postcolonial world in the interests of the liberation of subordinate populations and cultures from the structures and

> ideologies which dominate them. . . . Today Freire's influence extends far beyond the area of literacy and includes developments in social work education, economics, sociology, liberation theology, participatory research, and critical pedagogy, developments of concern to the authors of this book (pp. 1-2).

In the foreword, Freire wrote that "more than a testament to my work alone, however, this volume attempts to grapple with a number of pivotal issues currently engaged by critical scholars who have set out to refine and develop a critical pedagogy attentive to the changing face of social, cultural, gender and global relations" (p. ix).

In *Politics of Liberation: Paths from Freire* (1994), Peter McLaren and Colin Lankshear collected essays that reflect Freire's influences on educational practices in both developed and developing countries. In his Afterword, Joe Kincheloe observed that "this book is a testament to Freire's critical pedagogy—it is an example of what happens when students are empowered" (p. 216).

Thus, one can easily see Freire's influence upon the development of critical pedagogy, and his work still influences critical pedagogy as it conducts a dialogue with such current theoretical discourses as feminism, postmodernism and postcolonialism. Particularly, Freire's concept of conscientization—of valuing the voices and experiences of the poor, the marginalized, and the "other"—has influenced critical pedagogy from the beginning. Critical pedagogy aims to apply Freire's concepts to schooling in our own country, and Giroux and McLaren have expanded his concept of literacy in relationship to curricular issues and pedagogical practices.

I have shown here how Paulo Freire's work influences the critical discourses of liberation theology and critical pedagogy because Freire's influences account for the fact that these two discourses share themes and elements. Both begin with a concern for the amelioration of society and focus upon the economically poor and marginalized. Now I turn to a description of each of these critical discourses, and an explanation of their importance.

Liberation Theology: A Critical Discourse and Method

Liberation theology appears at first to be Freire's process of conscientization expressed in the language of religion. But it is more than that, since liberation theologians require that liberation take place before theology begins. They view liberation theology less as a theological movement and more as a theology within a movement.

One can understand the link between liberation theology and the pedagogy of the oppressed from the perspective of Robert Ackermann's understanding of religion as criticism. As Purpel (1989) pointed out, "Ackermann's position is that religion has played an important role in providing critical criteria for judging the moral adequacy of a culture, in participating in the active change of protest and organization, and in offering a set of alternatives. Ackermann goes on to assert that only those religions that engage in social and cultural criticism can retain their legitimacy and vitality" (p. 79).

Like Freire's conscientization, liberation theology begins with reflection upon experience. It is also a consequential ethics, its aims being part of the process itself. Its goal includes the amelioration of society, especially for those who experience oppressions like classism, racism and sexism. Boff and Boff (1989) stated that

> [L]iberation theology is far from being an inclusive theology. It starts from action and leads to action, a journey wholly impregnated by and bound up with the atmosphere of faith. From analysis of the reality of the oppressed, it passes through the word of God to arrive finally at a specific action. "Back to action" is a characteristic call of this theology. It seeks to be a militant, committed and liberating theology (p. 39).

Liberation theology attempts to integrate both theory and praxis from the perspective of a faith community. Like Freire's pedagogy of the oppressed, it is more than simply aid or reformism: It is a process of seeing, judging and acting. Boff and Boff define liberation theology as "reflecting on the basis of practice, within the ambit of the vast efforts made by the poor and their allies, seeking inspiration in faith and the Gospel for commitment to fight against poverty and for integral liberation of all persons and the whole person" (p. 8).

Sharon Welch (1985) noted that the integration of theory and praxis of liberation theology also includes an integration of the political with the spiritual: "Liberating communities of faith show no separation between the spiritual and the political. The worth of human life is undivided; spiritual transformation is inextricably tied to social and political transformation. These claims are radical; the practice they reflect and enhance is revolutionary" (p. 51).

Liberation theology has its roots in the experiences and the actions of those who resist oppression in the attempt to integrate theory with praxis. Welch saw that the uniqueness of liberation theology is "its reconceptualization of theology in light of a particular experience of the relation between theory and practice" (p. 25).

In 1990, Welch (1990) set forth a feminist ethic of risk in dialogue with liberation theology and in opposition to a patriarchal ethic of control. In developing the ethic of risk, Welch used the voices of African American women (Paule Marshall, Toni Morrison, Mildred Taylor and Toni Cade Bambara) as expressed in their novels to develop a sense of memory and accountability. These African American writers, she perceived are the bearers of "dangerous memories" and demonstrate an ethic of risk in action; they present a "rich heritage of empowerment, resistance and renewal, offering models of how Euro-Americans who resist oppression can find courage to face the long struggle for justice" (p. 19).

The feminist ethic of risk is a communicative ethic "characterized by three elements: (1) a redefinition of responsible action, (2) a grounding in community, and (3) strategic risk taking" (p. 20). Significantly, Welch developed this ethic as part of the discourse of liberation theology:

> In the past twenty-five years many theologians have turned to an analysis of the theological dimensions of movements for political liberation. Liberation theologians (African American, feminist, and Third World), join poets and singers in a celebrative retelling of stories of solidarity and defiance. We name the divinity at work in our people's histories. . . . A critical theology of liberation can do much to motivate and sustain us in our work for social transformation. Communicative ethics can lead to a critical theology of liberation, a theology that begins with an acknowledgment of the cultural and the political matrix of our thought as well as our particular location within a tradition (pp. 155-156).

One immediately notices elements in the feminist ethic of risk and an ethic of liberation theology. In developing her feminist ethics of risk, Welch demonstrated how liberation theology represents an integration of theory and praxis based upon the experiences of those marginalized or silenced by dominant others.

Liberation theology also demands a radical commitment of the victims of oppression while it gives a voice to the oppressed. It is not a theology conducted by others for others; it rallies the victims of oppression, and points them toward "the transformation of present society in the direction of a new society characterized by widespread participation, a better and more just balance among social classes and more worthy ways of life" (Boff and Boff, p. 5). It also demands of those who are poor and oppressed a commitment of solidarity. As Gustavo Gutierrez, one of the leaders of liberation theology, said "We will have an authentic theology of liberation only when the oppressed themselves can freely raise their voice and express themselves directly and creatively in society" (cited in Welch, 1985, p. 44).

Boff and Boff (1989) are adamant about this commitment to and solidarity with the poor as main characteristics of liberation theology, and they formulated this commitment to the poor as existing at three distinct levels: visiting the poor, conducting scholarly work in regard to the poor, and to living permanently among the poor. Even the pre-theological stage, Boff and Boff insisted, demands an effective solidarity with the oppressed and their liberation: "One point is paramount. Anyone who wants to elaborate relevant liberation theology must be prepared to go into the 'examination hall' of the poor. Only after sitting on the benches of the humble will he or she be entitled to enter a school of higher learning" (p. 24).

Chopp (1989) also understands liberation theology as an ethical discourse of theory and praxis—a discourse, which like Freire's conscientization, includes critical reflection, action, and solidarity with the oppressed. She compared the work of such Latin American liberation theologians as Gustavo Gutierrez (a Roman Catholic from Peru) and Jose Miguez Bonino (a United Methodist from Argentina) with the German political theology developed by Johann Metz (a Roman Catholic) and Jurgen Moltmann (a Lutheran). She called these theologies "two distinct voices within the paradigm of liberation theology" (p. 4). Utilizing the work of these four theologians, Chopp constructed two models: "Christ Liberating Culture" and "Toward Praxis: A Method for Liberation Theology":

> The first model of Christ liberating culture considers the fundamental claims of liberation theology to relocate human existence in praxis and to reinterpret Christianity as a praxis of solidarity with those who suffer. . . . The second model, a model

> of critical praxis correlation, investigates the methodological claims of liberation theology. Through the identification of six theses, this formal model sketches the new nature and process of theological reflection through the use of practical hermeneutics, ideology critique, and social theory (p. 6).

The six theses of liberation theology Chopp developed are as follow:

> (1) The two sources for Liberation Theology are human existence and Christian tradition.
> (2) Liberation Theology interprets the source of human existence politically, using, among other disciplines, the social sciences to reflect on the full concreteness of historical existence.
> (3) Theology employs a hermeneutics of liberation, including a project of deideologization in relation to the source of Christian tradition.
> (4) The method of Liberation Theology can be characterized as a critical praxis correlation, wherein praxis is both the foundation and the aim of theological hermeneutics.
> (5) Liberation Theology's method of critical praxis correlation is, by its nature, a form of ideology critique.
> (6) Liberation Theology must develop an adequate social theory to attend to the full meaning of praxis (pp. 134-148).

I (Oldenski, 1995) suggested that liberation theology—as developed by Boff and Boff, Chopp, and Welch—appears to be the religious version of the language of critique and possibility of critical pedagogy, or the language of denunciation and annunciation in Freire's process of conscientization. Liberation theologians acknowledge Christian faith and human experiences as its two sources; however, they realize that liberation through critique and possibility must first take place before they can construct a theology. Liberation theology is not just a new theology or a new theory or metanarrative; it is, to repeat, a theology in movement characterized by praxis and a commitment to the oppressed and the marginalized. Like critical pedagogy, its main project is ethical and political, and that project aims to develop a more just and democratic society for all. But liberation theology views and understands this ethical and political project as being integrated with the practices of one's religious faith and commitment.

Understanding theology as a source of knowledge thus leads liberation theology, like critical pedagogy, to raise similar critical questions (Clodovis Boff, 1987; and Segundo, 1976, 1992). Whose God is known in this knowledge? Whose interests does this theological knowledge serve? What values and assumptions form the foundation for such theological knowledge? Who are the marginalized and silenced people excluded from these theological discourses? Why do they continue to be excluded?

Liberation theology moves directly into a language of possibility by offering a radical commitment to the poor, the oppressed, and the silenced (Boff and Boff, 1984, 1989; Gutierrez, 1988, 1991). Liberation theology values the memories and everyday experiences of these "others" as the source of a new theology: a new way of constructing an understanding of and relationship with God. Liberation theology rejects the dominating theological discourses of a pervasively Eurocentric cultural experience of religion, spirituality, and even church, in attempting to reconstruct these theological concepts and religious practices.

Liberation theology criticizes how the Eurocentric churches historically used and currently use power. It sees how this history can perpetuate the oppression and marginalization of those who have been excluded from the Eurocentric metanarratives. Liberation theology aims to convey power to the people whose histories and situations include them among the victims of poverty or other forms of oppression. Liberation theology values their everyday experiences as a source of power, theology and spirituality. Liberation theology is also a process of conscientization of individual identities, rights and freedoms so as to rid society of social injustice.

Liberation theology presents a new understanding of what it means to be Christian in a transformative way. It suggests that the act of believing in Jesus includes a belief in social justice as a prime virtue and in the reality of evil as the social injustice that dominates and marginalizes oppressed people. One exercises Christian faith by participating in the transformation of society toward a more just and democratic society and establishing a solidarity with other people, including a commitment to the poor, and the victims of gender, class and race oppression. Liberation theology understands theology in a multicultural perspective and values diversity as opposed to mono-cultural religious practices and theological discourse.

Boff (1991) characterized one of the results of liberation theology as a new understanding of evangelization which he called "popular Catholicism." He supposed that this new evangelization requires the Church to relinquish any "option but the option for the cultures of the oppressed and the marginalized, with a view to their liberation" (p. 116).

Boff further characterized this new evangelization as

> based on the Gospel rather than on the pure and simple propagation of church doctrine. . . . [I]ts principal subject and agent are the poor themselves. . . . [I]t has new addresses such as popular culture and piety, Blacks, marginalized women, street children, the chronically sick, the landless, the homeless, slum dwellers, and so on. It is new in that it employs new methods, along the lines of the pedagogy of the oppressed, and of education as a practice of freedom, of the famous Christian educator Paulo Freire . . . . [I]t communicates a new content, derived from an interrelationship between the discourse of faith and the discourse of the world of the oppressed. . . . [I]t inaugurates a new way of being Church . . . . [I]t generates a new spirituality, which appears in celebrations not only of the mysteries of faith, but of the struggles and joys of community. It appears in the manner of its political commitment to collective causes concerned with the poor and outcast. . . . [I]t forges a new relation of church to world (pp. 116 -117).

Thus, liberation theology echoes the pedagogy of the oppressed of Paulo Freire as a process of conscientization which leads to transformation. Seeing in liberation faith themes and language similar to those which Freire used, Welch (1985) concluded that

> Liberation faith is conversion to the other, the resistance to oppression, the attempt to live as though the lives of others matter. . . . To live honestly and believe as universal the imperative of love and freedom is to hope that suffering can be ended, to hope that all lives without liberation in history were not meaningless, but it is to work for this hope without the guarantee that such meaning is possible (p. 87).

Meanwhile, we can find this process of transformation and hope echoed in critical pedagogy.

Critical Pedagogy: A Discourse of Critique and Possibility

Many individuals working in diverse fields have become associated with the discourse of critical pedagogy—for example, Michael Apple, Ira Shor, Patti Lather, Jennifer Gore and Carmen Luke. In developing an understanding of critical pedagogy, however, I chose to focus on the work of McLaren and Giroux, who have directly influenced my own thinking and understanding of critical pedagogy.

While a doctoral student at Miami University during the Fall semester of 1991, I heard Giroux elaborate on the development of critical pedagogy through four stages. Giroux noted that critical pedagogy has entered its fourth stage of development, which is its relationship with the discourses of postmodernism and postcolonialism.

He located the origin of critical pedagogy in the work of the social reconstructionists of the 1930s and 1940s, and particularly the work of John Dewey and George Counts, both of whom sought to assimilate democracy into education so as "to redefine the meaning and purpose of schooling around an emancipatory view of citizenship" (Giroux, 1988, p. 8).

Giroux's second stage of the development of critical pedagogy is characterized by "the categories of social and cultural critique" developed by the Frankfurt School as critical pedagogy meets reproduction theory (Giroux, 1983, p. 42). Reproduction theory is based upon "the theories of social reproduction of Louis Althusser (1969, 1971) and Bowles and Gintis (1976, 1980) and the theories of cultural production of Pierre Bourdieu (1977a, 1977b) and Basil Bernstein (1977, 1981)" (Giroux, 1983, p. 78).

These neo-Marxist theorists focused on the role of "cultural capital" and the idea that schools and forms of knowledge exist in the interests of dominant power blocs or classes to maintain a skilled and unskilled labor force. Bowles and Gintis developed a correspondence theory which "posits that the hierarchically structured patterns of values, norms, and skills that characterize the work force and the dynamics of class interaction under capitalism are mirrored in the social dynamics of the daily classroom encounter" (Giroux, 1983, p. 84).

These social and cultural reproduction theories provide a valuable commentary on what transpires in schools. But critical pedagogy struggled both with how schools reproduce cultural capital and with how schools resolve the contradictions between class, race and gender that exist within the dominant culture. Critical pedagogy suggests a need exists for understanding schools as political sites that produce meaning in opposition to dominant cultural values and practices while understanding students and teachers as social agents of change.

One can associate the third stage of the development of critical pedagogy with the influence of the theories of conflict and resistance as expressed in such ethnographic studies as Willis's *Learning to Labour* (1977). These theories of resistance acknowledge that students produce and act as agents within the process of schooling and within the wider society. Students insert themselves into school and do resist if they do not like what they experience. Resistance theories helped students use their experiences as impetus for change.

While recognizing the contributions of resistance theories, critical pedagogy began to focus on the relationship between the hidden curriculum on the one hand, and, on the other, social classes and gender, the voices of oppressed men and women, and the role of student resistance as political action aimed at creating a new public sphere, which "represents a critical category that redefines literacy and citizenship as central elements in the struggle for self and social emancipation" (Giroux, 1983, p. 116).

The current stage of critical pedagogy, as we saw, juxtaposes it with various discourses of postmodernism and postcolonialism. Critical pedagogy is now viewed as a form of border pedagogy (Aronowitz and Giroux, 1991; Giroux, 1991, 1992; and Giroux and McLaren, 1994). As a critical discourse, it presents schooling less in a language of reproduction and resistance and more in terms of different ways of articulating one's identity from the perspective of social class, gender, race, and sexual preference, and in terms of developing a language of meaning as teachers and students address together the issues and struggles of critique and possibility. Issues of power and identity construction receive productive consideration in a language of the self and the other, acknowledging and accommodating differences with the hope of transforming society. The discourses of schooling and pedagogy derive from social and literary theories and various forms of popular culture that characterize present-day postmodernism.

McLaren (1989) presented critical pedagogy as both a new theory and a sociology of education, and he noted that "critical pedagogy examines schools both in their historical context and as part of the existing social and political fabric that characterizes the dominant society" (p. 159). In *Life in Schools: An Introduction to Critical Pedagogy in the Foundations of Education*, McLaren presented both the major themes of critical pedagogy and some examples of its relevant educators, their work and their thinking: Jonathan Kozol, Paulo Freire, John Dewey, Michael Apple and Henry Giroux. Kathleen Bennett and Margaret LeCompte (1990) discussed the historical roots of the work of Apple and Giroux, emphasizing not only the theories of reproduction and correspondence, but also the "Frankfurt School of critical theory, the writings of Italian Marxist Antonio Gramsci, and the work of Brazilian educator Paulo Freire" (p. 24).

Giroux (1988a, 1988b, 1991, 1992, 1993) and McLaren (1986, 1987, 1989, 1991a, 1993) continue to develop critical pedagogy as a discourse for schooling responsive to the situation of today's educational practices. Giroux has written that "the over-riding goal of education is to create the conditions for student self-empowerment and the self-constitution of students as political subjects" (1988b, p. 167). In the foreword to Giroux's *Teachers As Intellectuals* (1988b), McLaren commented that "the major objective of critical pedagogy is to empower students to intervene in their own self-formation and to transform the oppressive features of the wider society that make such an intervention necessary" (p. xi).

Thus the goal of critical pedagogy is to free students from those practices that now oppress them in their schooling. Giroux (1988b) concluded that the central question for schooling is "How can we make schooling meaningful so as to make it critical and how can we make it critical so as to make it emancipatory?" (p. 2). Students and teachers require mutual solidarity to resist those traditional elements that oppress them and deny their dignity as human persons with valued lives and experiences. Meanwhile, schooling itself becomes a site for struggle leading to a structured transformation. Giroux (1993) pointed out that central to critical pedagogy is "the need to rewrite the relationship among cultural and pedagogical production as part of a broader vision that extends the principles and practices of human dignity, liberty and social justice" (p. 79).

Giroux (1988a) also concluded that "radical educational theory needs to develop a moral discourse and theory of ethics [and that] educators should link a theory of ethics and morality to a politics in which community, difference, remembrance, and historical consciousness become foundational" (p. 58). He envisioned this radical theory of ethics productive of emancipatory schooling as "based on norms of solidarity, sympathy, caring, friendship and love." In this regard, he drew upon both feminist theory and liberation theology "in order to redefine how authority and ethics can be formulated in order to reconstruct the role that teachers might play as intellectuals engaged in criticizing and transforming both the schools and wider society" (p. 73).

Giroux acknowledged the contributions of both liberation theology and a feminist ethic of risk to the discourse of critical social theory:

> What is important to recognize here is that both feminists and religious critics have increasingly contributed to developing a new language of critique, and uncovering forms of knowledge generally removed from the dominant public sphere; moreover, they have begun to redefine in critical and emancipatory terms the language of ethics, experience and community (1988 a, p. 92).

Like John Dewey, Giroux (1988a, 1988b) presented teachers as transformative intellectuals with the task of defining "schools as public spheres where the dynamics of popular engagement and democratic politics can be cultivated as part of a struggle for a radical democratic society" (1988a, p. 32). Teachers would thus take the responsibility for making the pedagogical more political. Teachers as transformative intellectuals must "speak out against economic, political and social injustices both within and outside of schools . . . must work to create the conditions that give students the opportunity to become citizens who have the knowledge and the courage to struggle in order to make despair unconvincing and hope practical" (1988b, p. 128). Giroux went further:

> As transformative intellectuals, educators can serve to uncover and excavate those forms of historical and subjugated knowledges that point to experiences of suffering, conflict, and collective struggle. In this sense, teachers as intellectuals can begin to link the notion of historical understanding to elements of critique and hope. Such memories keep alive the horror of needless exploitation as well as the constant need to intervene and to struggle collectively to eliminate the conditions that produce it (p. 220).

He went on to develop an emancipatory curriculum that would provide a critical understanding of social reality and individual experience. This transformative curriculum

> would be developed around knowledge forms that challenge and critically appropriate dominant ideologies, rather than simply rejecting them outright; it would also take the historical and social particularities of students' experiences as a starting point for developing a critical classroom pedagogy; that is, it would begin with popular experiences so as to make them meaningful in order to engage them critically (p. 184).

Thus, the curriculum would focus on democratic empowerment and provide a language of possibility as well as a pedagogical basis "for teaching democracy while making schooling more democratic." This curriculum would include both basic skills for work and adult life and "knowledge about the social forms through which human beings live, become conscious, and sustain themselves, particularly with respect to the social and political demands of democratic citizenship." The starting point for such a curriculum would be the problems and needs of the students, and it would provide them "with a language through which they can analyze their own lived relations and experiences in a manner that is both affirmative and critical" (pp. 102-103).

As you recall, the previous chapter presented McLaren's (1986) ethnography, which recommends an emancipatory curriculum that would "help to render problematic the meanings embedded in the cultural forms and content of the classroom instruction" (p. 253). McLaren also identified schooling rituals as "shap[ing] the discourses of critique and possibility. Seen in this light, rituals are no less than means to cultural power" (p. 253).

McLaren (1989, 1994) developed, in one sense, a primer on critical pedagogy. As his preface stated, "This book represents an approach to schooling that is committed to the imperatives of empowering students and transforming the larger social order in the interests of justice and equality" (p. vii). He described there the current situation in public education as well as excerpts from his journal and field notes on his experience teaching in a suburban ghetto. He also developed the major concepts of critical pedagogy and summarized the thinking of the educators who had guided his thought. Its major concepts urge an attention to issues of hegemony and resistance; cultural capital and the reproduction of social capital; the construction and forms of knowledge, power and culture and the influence of race, class and gender.

Critical pedagogy as formulated by Freire, McLaren and Giroux subverts the canon of knowledge and the neutrality this knowledge claims. It pushes the purpose of schooling beyond the transmission of the knowledge and culture of Eurocentric metanarratives. It questions how knowledge is constructed, whose interests knowledge serves, whom knowledge excludes or silences and what values and assumptions inform knowledge. Critical pedagogy draws upon postmodernism in rejecting the totalizing narratives of reason, science and technology that emerged from the Enlightenment. Critical pedagogy values popular culture as part of understanding the milieu and rejects the positioning of high culture over and opposed to popular culture. Thus critical pedagogy includes the memories and voices of those who have been rejected and marginalized by monocultural Eurocentrism.

Likewise, critical pedagogy questions the use of power from a base of knowledge and reason. The voices of those who have been silenced and excluded through the exercise of power must be included in reconstructing knowledge and in the process of schooling. This inclusion requires valuing the experiences of students, the marginalized and the oppressed. Critical pedagogy begins with their experiences as a source of knowledge, including their everyday culture expressed in a variety of contemporary and familiar forms. Thus schooling becomes less a "banking" process and more a process of "conscientization" as developed in the works of Freire and expanded by McLaren and Giroux.

Meanwhile, classroom teachers pass beyond performing as instruments of technical rationality or serving as sources of power and knowledge. This traditional expectation keeps them deskilled and driven by hegemonic mandates shaped by standardized testing, prepackaged curriculum units, a "national curriculum" and the like. Critical pedagogy, in short, cries out against how society understands and how universities prepare teachers—that is, subservient to the hegemonic controls of government and business. Instead, teachers must become transformative intellectuals and schools of education must prepare them for this new role.

In this new role, teachers must know how to act against social injustices and create conditions to help transform society, including changing their own working conditions. As teachers begin to realize that schooling includes the reality of being linked to society in a wider context of developing a just and democratic society, they become aware of social injustices created by monoculturalism, the current cynical structures of schooling like tracking and sorting students, and the authentic purpose of schooling as the transmission of culture and knowledge. Teachers must develop new belief systems in regard to themselves, their students and the purposes of schooling, and they must realize that the curriculum itself bears changing and reconstructing once self, students and "the others" of society become empowered.

Henry Giroux (1992) developed nine principles for recasting "the relationship between the pedagogical and the political as central to any social movement that attempts to effect emancipatory struggles and social transformations" (p. 73). These nine principles echo some of the earlier themes and elements of critical pedagogy, but Giroux casts them in light of postmodern and feminist discourses:

(1) Education needs to be reformulated so as to give as much attention to pedagogy as to traditional and alternative notions of scholarship.
(2) Ethics must be seen as a central concern to critical pedagogy.
(3) Critical pedagogy must focus on the issue of difference in an ethically challenging and politically transformative way.
(4) Critical pedagogy needs a language that accommodates competing solidarities and political vocabularies that do not reduce the issues of power, justice, struggle, and inequality to a single script, a master narrative that rejects the contingent, the historical, and the everyday as serious objects of study.
(5) Critical pedagogy must create new forms of knowledge through its emphasis on breaking down disciplinary boundaries and creating new spheres in which knowledge can be produced. In this sense, critical pedagogy must be reclaimed as a cultural politics and a form of social memory.
(6) The Enlightenment notion of reason must be reformulated within a critical pedagogy.
(7) Critical pedagogy must regain a sense of alternatives by combining a language of critique and possibility.
(8) Critical pedagogy must posit educators and cultural workers as transformative intellectuals who occupy specific political and social locations.
(9) Central to the notion of critical pedagogy is a politics of voice that combines a postmodern notion of difference with a feminist emphasis on the primacy of the political. To engage

> issues regarding the construction of the self is to address questions of history, culture, community, language, gender, race, and class (pp. 73-80).

Giroux continues to view pedagogy as a "technology of power, language, and practice that produces and legitimates forms of moral and political regulation, which construct and offer human beings particular views of themselves and the world" (p. 81). This pedagogy invites attempts "to negotiate, accommodate, and transform the world in which we find ourselves" (p. 81).

Since the early 1980s, Giroux and McLaren have expanded the discourse of critical pedagogy and refined their own thinking about this pedagogy. They are both influenced by Freire and one can easily recognize Freire's ideas in the language of critical pedagogy Giroux and McLaren adopt. Critical pedagogy continues to challenge schools and educators to embrace an agenda of transformation and hope as a strategy to ameliorate the lives of students and society. Moreover, the demands and challenges of this discourse resemble those called for in liberation theology in that both are discourses of critique and possibility with the hope of transforming the lives of individuals and their worlds.

An Integrative Model of Liberation Theology and Critical Pedagogy

The similarity between liberation theology and critical pedagogy just noted is hardly accidental, both discourses being strongly influenced by Paulo Freire. Thus, one naturally wonders whether their common elements could be developed into a model or a "constructed theory." As I struggled to explain the two discourses to my undergraduate students and my colleagues, who were unfamiliar with them, I found myself naturally talking in terms of models. Finally, the idea of an integrative model of liberation theology and critical pedagogy presented itself explicitly as I reviewed my experiences and my interviews with students, teachers and administrators of Vincent Gray Alternative High School, and even more so as I coded the transcripts of those interviews. At this point, therefore, I present the model formulated as I attempted to explain the elements these two critical discourses share. In subsequent chapters, I use this model to demonstrate how their common elements and themes appeared first in the voices of the students of VGAHS and then in the voices of the administrators and teachers.

Both liberation theology and critical pedagogy address any situation or anyone's experience so as to describe what is happening. One can call this reality "my present world"—that is, the worlds in which people find themselves, the living situation in which they now exist. As critical discourses, liberation theology and critical pedagogy assume that all is not well with the way things are and have been. These discourses animate individuals to identify and describe the precise problems with the hope of reducing them. Thus, an individual acknowledges that something is wrong with "my world" as I now perceive it to be. Freire identified this process as "conscientization" —that is, becoming aware of my world and my life in a whole new way and gaining a new perspective on it.

As an individual acknowledges that something is wrong with "my world," the critical discourses of liberation theology and critical pedagogy both urge that individual toward the realization that "I want to make my world better." The individual now takes the position that he or she does not want to go on experiencing reality as it is. He or she wants to make it different, to be an "agent of change." Thus, the individual takes on a political role. Both discourses encourage that individual to make his or her world more caring and just, and thus eliminate or lessen that which oppresses or keeps the world from accommodating the individual and others in the same "state of existence." Drawing upon the ideas of Paulo Freire, therefore, critical pedagogy and liberation theology share the same model as critical discourses and discourses of possibility.

In liberation theology, however, becoming more humane and just through political action aimed at eliminating oppression also derives from the tradition of justice as expressed in the Scriptures, certain aspects of this tradition receiving emphasis in the struggle to affect a better, more caring and just world. Some of these emphasized aspects include the prophetic tradition implicitly promising justice, the Book of Exodus and its themes of freedom and overcoming slavery, the teachings of Jesus about the Kingdom of God, the universal community as demonstrated by caring for others and sharing one's goods with others, and the writings of the apostles who stress the themes of justice and generosity. This sense of willing self-sacrifice and love is presented as the Christian ideal known as *agape*. This love feast tradition specifies the Kingdom of God as the place where one enjoys justice, freedom, peace and love. Explicitly or by implication, all liberation theologians acknowledge the Christian Scriptures as the starting point of their critiques. These Scriptures also provide a language of longing to make the world better, different, and more caring and just.

Critical pedagogy draws from various critical discourses for its sources, and these sources reside in "feminist literature, in literary theory and in liberation theology" (Giroux, 1992, p. 13). Giroux recognized that his "referent is how we make this country a real critical democracy" (p. 18). Schooling becomes the site of struggle for critical pedagogy, which proposes to make the world of schooling more humane and equitable and, in turn, make the world more humane and equitable. Giroux sees schooling in terms of "educating students for public life" (p. 18). We have already seen these ideas expressed repeatedly throughout Giroux's and McLaren's writings on critical pedagogy.

The Scriptures define being human as being a member (as a son or daughter of God and as a brother or sister to each other) of the community of the Kingdom of God. This membership subsumes the realities of this secular world, and one gains rights and privileges simply by becoming a member.

Sometimes, the liberation theologians draw apart from those who neglect to acknowledge their membership in the Kingdom, behavior that presents a challenge to liberation theology both as a practice and as a discourse. How does this apartness affect those who are resolutely non-Christian or those who belong to different Christian communities from one's own? Can we extend our understanding of what it means to "be human" to include those who do not believe in the Christ or those who express their belief in the Christ differently? Thus, the challenge of making our world more humane and just also challenges liberation theology to espouse inclusivity for those beyond the Christian beliefs. This challenge requires the application of Christ's words as recorded in Scripture to the world as it now is.

The critical discourses of liberation theology and critical pedagogy provide a three-step method—that is, a way to change the reality of what is to what it can be. The practices one can infer from these discourses provide a methodology for changing "my world" and constructing "my new world." This methodology includes, first of all, becoming aware of those conditions that sicken the current world and, therefore, require treatment or cure. This part of the method I call "critical reflection upon my world."

The second part of the methodology involves proposing solutions for curing my current world. These solutions may include either large or modest efforts at improving or righting the current reality. Proposing solutions is also part of critical reflection, including as it does the realization that "what can be" emerges from "what is" and need not involve creating something totally new.

Third, this methodology includes implementing the proposed solutions—that is, putting into practice the products of reflection. These three steps together constitute praxis: the integration of critical reflection with practice and then continuing the process of critically reflecting upon the present practices always with a view of improving world conditions.

Employing this methodology, both liberation theologians and critical pedagogues engage in a political and ethical discourse because each attempts to change the systems and establishments of political power or those realities that either afflict my world or oppress someone else.

The critical discourses of liberation theology and critical pedagogy start with a concern for the poor or oppressed, specifically those individuals or groups that have been dominated in one way or another by those in power. This concern evolves into a commitment to the poor and oppressed to help them change their world through political action. One demonstrates this commitment in solidarity with the poor and oppressed and in helping to form a more humane community. Sometimes this commitment requires one to enter into experiences far different from one's own.

Hope and transformation are characteristics of both critical pedagogy and liberation theology and significant elements of each. Both imply that a "my new world" does, in fact exist, is in fact possible. This hope also presumes each person can be an agent of change, making a significant contribution to the construction of a new world better than the old.

Changes in how individuals see themselves and their worlds are also part of the hope and transformation these two discourses promote. The accompanying change in the language of theology develops as a process of conversion or transformation, a "change of heart" in the scriptural tradition. This personal change is also characterized by hope. In critical pedagogy, it also demands a personal transformation and an understanding of self as an agent of change.

Meanwhile, liberation theology and critical pedagogy are both recursive—that is, they are ongoing and perpetuate themselves with change, modification and refinement by repeating the steps of the methodology, an ongoing praxis of reflection and action. Thus, both discourses offer a methodology for change that is constantly in process itself. So in one sense—as discourse in praxis—both liberation theology and critical pedagogy remain unsatisfied with what is now and continually long for "more": a more just and caring world, a better world, a world different than it is now.

Might the critical discourses of critical pedagogy and liberation theology be influencing those schooling practices that include the best of these two discourses as a language of critique and possibility during the learning process? Could the discourses of liberation theology and critical pedagogy benefit Catholic education in the United States? Can an integrative model of these two discourses help one to understand what occurs at a specific school site—a site, for example, like VGAHS? Can this integrative model, in turn, benefit what occurs at VGAHS? My responses to these questions demonstrate that both liberation theology and critical pedagogy provide viable discourses for understanding schools like VGAHS, and many more besides. These two critical discourses appear to me to offer much in the dialogue on the identity of Catholic schools, and the need for Catholic schools to emphasize a concern for the poor and marginalized peoples. These two critical discourses help establish meaning in the lives of students. The challenge before these two discourses is to start guiding school practices, thus making a more humane and just society, in which all people enjoy democracy and emancipation.

This chapter concludes with an outline of this integrative model of liberation theology and critical pedagogy. The intention is not to simplify the common elements and themes of the discourses of liberation theology and critical pedagogy. Nor do I contend that this model presents either a complete depiction of the contradictions within and between these discourses or the ongoing implications of these critical discourses as they meet other critical discourses and new social and cultural experiences. Rather, the model merely synopsizes schematically the main points of the foregoing discussion and illustrates the nature of the analysis to follow.

An Integrative Model of Liberation Theology and Critical Pedagogy

A. CRITICAL DISCOURSE describing my "present" world and its problems
  (1) Something is wrong with my world.
  (2) I want to make it
    a. better,
    b. different, and
    c. more caring than it now is, thus more humane and just.

B. METHOD producing change
  (1) A methodology for changing "my current world" to "my new world" would
    a. develop an awareness of those conditions that spoil my current world and therefore require change, and
    b. propose solutions that could transform my current world.
  (2) That methodology would also suggest implementation for creating my new world.

C. Both Liberation Theology and Critical Pedagogy offer these benefits. They
  (1) begin with a concern for the poor and the oppressed,
  (2) encourage solidarity with the poor and oppressed in developing a humane and just community,
  (3) offer hope,
  (4) offer change in how I see myself and my world, and
  (5) perpetuate themselves even as they achieve change.

CHAPTER FIVE

Catholic School: A Home for Critical Discourses

> Multicultural education and critical pedagogy bring into the arena of schooling insurgent, resistant, and insurrectional modes of interpretation and classroom practices which set out to imperil the familiar, to contest the legitimating norms of mainstream cultural life, and to render problematic the common discursive frames and regimes upon which "proper" behavior, comportment, and social interactions are premised. Together, they analyze extant power configurations and unsettle them when such configurations serve to reproduce social relations of domination. Critical and multicultural pedagogy defamiliarize and make remarkable what is often passed off as the ordinary, the mundane, the routine, and the banal.
>
> - Christine Sleeter and Peter McLaren, *Multicultural Education, Critical Pedagogy, and the Politics of Difference* (1995, p. 7)

Catholic schools and critical discourses share a natural kinship, and the description of critical pedagogy and multicultural education Sleeter and McLaren provide here could easily apply to descriptions of the history and the identity of Catholic schools. The previous chapter demonstrated that liberation theology and critical pedagogy share elements and themes and, in fact, coexist in a unique relationship. It showed how educators like Paulo Freire, Henry Giroux and Peter McLaren relate the elements and themes of liberation theology to the school context. This chapter turns specifically to how Catholic schools and critical discourses relate to each other.

Chapter Two established that recent documents of the Catholic church concerning education urge Catholic schools to focus on how these schools serve the poor and other marginalized populations. Beyond these formal ecclesial statements, the history of Catholic schools in the United States has continually demonstrated this commitment.

Catholic schools evolved to provide a sound education with a religious orientation to the younger members of the Catholic community (Beutow, 1988). They increased rapidly as Catholics struggled to maintain their identity in response to the use of the King James Version of the Bible and both overt and covert anti-Catholic sentiments in the public schools. Thus, Catholic schools became a separatist response to the public school movement, a response strengthened at the elementary and secondary level, by the influx of immigrants from southern and eastern European countries.

The Catholic Church, like the United States, itself is no stranger to cultural pluralism and ethnic diversity, and both the Catholic schools and the American Catholic Church became identified with populations marginalized by the dominant culture of the country at various historical times. Catholic schools then naturally focused on educating students to keep and grow in their faith, while keeping their cultural identities even as they entered the mainstream of the dominant culture and becoming successful by the standards of the dominant culture (Obidinski, 1984; Ryan, 1992). Even though ethnic Catholic parishes and schools insisted on their own languages and customs, their goals were to help Catholic immigrants become American (Keely, 1989). Thus Catholic schools developed partly in resistance to the dominant culture and its public schools, and partly to accommodate large numbers of Catholic immigrants (Beutow, 1970; Burns, 1912a, 1912b, 1917; Burns and Kohlbrenner, 1937; and Dolan, 1992).

We see here a critical discourse occurring but aimed at what is the possibility of starting something new. This process of critique and possibility amounts to an act of resistance to what is expressed and practiced in the dominant culture. This act of resistance also provides hope to an oppressed and marginalized group. The discourses of liberation theology and critical pedagogy, as we have seen, both begin with a concern for the economically poor and marginalized populations, and both advocate a commitment of solidarity with these peoples in a process of conscientization, with the purpose of improving one's situation within the larger society. Both discourses assert that this commitment and process provides hope for the oppressed and marginalized as well as for those who work with and on behalf of the poor and the marginalized.

These elements of critical pedagogy and liberation theology, already a part of the Catholic fabric, now challenge the role of Catholic schools amid the contemporary reality of diversity and "new" immigrants: How does the Catholic Church, particularly, through the Catholic schools, serve these diverse and immigrant peoples? Domingo Rodriguez (1994) pointed out that all "immigrant groups though different, have certain common experiences which characterize and influence their behavior: (a) poverty, (b) margination and (c) uprootedness" (p. 2).

Charles Keely (1989) challenged the Catholic Church to address another "new" immigration, the refugee movement. "It is," he said, "important to determine whether Catholicism can play the historic role for the newer immigrant groups of today that it performed in the integration of the Germans, Irish, Slavs and Italians" (1989 , p. 30). He further observed that "Catholicism must admit it is still an immigrant church, just as America is still a nation with mass immigration" (p. 33). Thus, Catholic schools still face continual challenges in regards to how they serve new immigrant populations, and they need to answer this challenge while demonstrating respect for the dignity of each human person.

David Augsburger (1994) recently expressed a similar concern for the response of the Catholic Church to the changing diversity of the country. He pointed out that "the largest ethnic groups in America are German, Black and Latinos in that order" (p. 1), and he explained how this diversity affects the ministerial concerns of the church: "A theology and practice of ministry which prizes and celebrates diversity (affectively and experientially) energizes the slow, difficult work of changing our cognitive structures, our perceptual fields, our long-term habits, practices and communal behaviors. . . . It accelerates movement towards both—and establishes processes that allow us to crossover into another form of reference and return with new insight and renewed spirit" (p. 5). These concerns and movements also require a language of critique and possibility in responding to diverse populations. This new concern of church ministries must also generate hope among the poor and the oppressed, as well as in the lives of the ministers.

Peter Phan (1994) described the urgency he feels for the Catholic Church to address the current situation of diversity and multi-culturalism:

> Sociological studies have suggested the following changes in the shape of the American Catholic Church in the next generation: First, the Church in the U.S. will be highly diverse in ethnicity and culture. Second, the new ethnics—i.e., Hispanics, Asians and African Americans—will become the majority in the Church. Third, despite being the minority, the old ethnics (e.g. Irish, Italian, German, Polish) will still maintain at their disposal the bulk of social, economic, and educational resources and will continue to hold a greater number of ecclesiastical offices. . . . Unless some long-term planning is made to meet the challenge of the presence of these new ethnic Catholics, the American Church runs the risk of bifurcating into two groups deeply alien to one another culturally, socially, economically and spiritually (pp. 6-7).

Phan's disturbing prognosis challenges the Catholic Church and Catholic schools to respond to this contemporary situation. Earlier, however, Beutow (1988) developed an even more specific challenge to Catholic schools facing the new diversity:

> Catholic schools, with a long tradition of welcoming newcomers, continue to provide multicultural education to the new arrivals: the Hispanics, Blacks, Vietnamese, Koreans, Haitians, and others who have replaced the Irish, Germans, Italians, and Poles of yore. Catholic schools, wary of attempting a "melting pot" that might rob minority students of their identity, try instead for a sensitive course between isolationism and assimilation (p. 283).

The challenge Phan and Beutow and others (Chrobot, 1994; Dolan, 1994) issue to Catholic educators is the need to undergo the process of critique en route to accommodating the demographic changes within the Catholic community and in the country. Catholic schools must demonstrate an unmistakable commitment to these new ethnics—namely, Hispanics, African Americans, and Asian Americans.

Critical pedagogy during the last several years has, indeed focused on the concept of difference and the issues surrounding diversity. Giroux (1991, 1992, 1993) continually emphasizes that critical pedagogy is an experience of crossing one's borders and that teachers are increasingly understood as cultural workers and transformative intellectuals. Sleeter and McLaren (1995) integrate critical pedagogy with multicultural education and use them as a compound subject throughout their recent edition. They understand this integration as building "a coalition to enable dialog, to identify terrains for mutual support, and to articulate common concerns and agendas" (p. 8). They state that "both refer to a particular ethico-political attitude or ideological stance that one constructs in order to confront and engage the world critically and challenge power relations" (p. 7).

The development of a sense of community inheres in the discourses of liberation theology and critical pedagogy as well as in the practices and culture of Catholic schools. Church documents since Vatican II and resultant practices emphasize this sense of community, both as a characteristic of Catholic schools and as a characteristic of the Church itself understood as a community of believers (Castelli, 1995).

The Catholic Church has always understood itself, at least theologically if not in practice, as the "People of God" rooted in the beliefs of individuals in Jesus Christ and the Kingdom of God. The Catholic Church now acknowledges that its community is not per se the Kingdom of God, but is rather a means to the Kingdom. The documents of Vatican II provide the theological basis for this paradigm shift in the Catholic Church's own sense of identity. The Catholic Church now finds the Kingdom of God wherever there is peace, justice, freedom and love. These same qualities must become part of the climate and identity of Catholic schools. Beutow (1988) specified justice as a goal of Catholic schools to be achieved as a result of the community, which "is to be lived in the Catholic school," and he observed that "Catholic schools face a risk in presenting justice as a goal. If they accept a role as a carrier of messages for justice, an agent of change in society, they risk offending the rich and powerful, some of whom support Catholic institutions. But the risk must be taken, because the result of justice and love will be the peace on earth which all people seek" (p. 84).

The discourses of liberation theology and critical pedagogy also emphasize the community experience as part of the process of changing one's world. Both liberation theologians and advocates of critical pedagogy hope to develop a community of people characterized by peace, freedom, justice and love, the ethical basis central to both discourses, as well as for Catholic schools. Both discourses project the goals of peace, freedom, justice and love as individuals construct their own identities as a process of conscientization and as they become political agents of change.

Elements of Freire's works that influence liberation theology and critical pedagogy can easily become part of the language of a Catholic school identification. Catholic schools understand themselves as providing students with a language of possibility for themselves and the world. They understand, as well, that being agents of transformation is part of what it means to practice one's faith. A close reading of Scripture and the Catholic Church documents compels the conclusion that the day-to-day Catholic faith practices must include a concern for and solidarity with the poor and oppressed.

Moreover, many modern Catholic theologians suggest that this concern for the poor must exist as more than just a preferential option but as an acceptance of the call to live out one's faith commitment in response to the Gospels. The tendency to view schools as political sites instilling concern for the poor and marginalized, they say, should become part of the conversation of the identity of Catholic schools, and even more so, of Catholic school practices and curriculum. Beutow (1988) exemplified these sentiments: "Liberation as a Catholic goal of education will adopt the established forms of knowledge, and then add a deep faith in human creativity, a hope without much limit, and a profound love of the world and of men. Education should not end in stagnant inaction, but the action in which it results should be prudent and meaningful" (p. 92).

The emphasis on the voice of the learner, which characterizes both liberation theology and critical pedagogy, also needs to characterize the identity of Catholic schools. Recall that Freire understands this dialogue as an act of love, and of solidarity with the poor and oppressed and of commitment to others. In fact, Freire insists that one consider education itself as an act of love.

Concerning this dialogue in schools, critical pedagogy continually emphasizes the primacy of student experiences and voices. Giroux (1988a) stated that "at the heart of any critical pedagogy is the necessity for teachers to work with the knowledges that students actually have" (p. 197). McLaren (1994) echoed these sentiments. "[A] critical and affirming pedagogy," he said, "has to be constructed around the stories that people tell, the ways in which students and teachers author meaning, and the possibilities that underlie the experiences that shape their voices. It is around the concept of voice that a theory of both teaching and learning can take place, one that points to new forms of social relations and to new and challenging ways of confronting everyday life" (p. 226).

As he described the critical pedagogy of Freire, Shor (1993) too recognized that critical pedagogy must "challenge teachers and students to empower themselves for social change, to advance democracy and equality as they advance their literacy and knowledge" (p. 25).

These two elements—the role of the student's voice and dialogue—must become part of the climate and curriculum of Catholic schools as they undertake to articulate their own identity. Catholic schools already assume an important role in helping students effect social change as they articulate the meaning of their lives. The believing community acknowledges that in one's own experiences one comes to know God and meet grace. Spirituality in one sense involves reflecting upon one's experiences to find God's presence there.

As we have seen, the discourses of liberation theology and critical pedagogy include both a language of critique and a language of possibility. Paulo Freire identified in these two languages a process of denunciation and annunciation. The development of a critical awareness and one's conscientization leads to political and social actions that help to transform the world. Critical pedagogy insists that teachers treat education as both a font of possibility and a source of liberation. Giroux (1988a) insisted that "school and classroom practices should in some manner be organized around forms of learning that serve to prepare students for responsible roles as transformative intellectuals, as community members, and as critically active citizens outside schools" (p. 201). Again, these elements characterize the aspirations of Catholic educators, and the curricula and practices of Catholic schools must incorporate these qualities in learning objectives and student experiences.

The integrative model of the common elements of liberation theology and critical pedagogy that concluded the last chapter provides a format of evaluating how "Catholic" Catholic schools are. The Catholic church and Catholic educators certainly value these elements. One of the aims of Catholic education is to teach and help students become critical of the world and their own current experiences with the hope of making the world and their lives more caring, humane and just.

Catholic educators also work to provide students with a way to change their worlds as well as the larger society through conscientization, dialogue and action. Teaching and learning and the climate in Catholic schools have for many years included the traditional three points of the Catholic action movement of the early 1900s: see, reflect and act.

The other elements shared by the discourses of liberation theology and critical pedagogy also make up the identity of a Catholic school as ordinarily understood. Catholic schools have shown a traditional concern for the poor and oppressed, and the tradition should, ideally, extend to the new ethnics of the Catholic community. This commitment to the poor and oppressed must now result in a solidarity with these individuals in developing a more humane and just community. Liberation theology, critical pedagogy and a Catholic education must all provide a sense of hope in a world that to many facing injustice may appear hopeless. Traditional Catholic theology has, of course, always emphasized hope as a key virtue along with faith and charity.

A change in how one perceives oneself and one's world characterizes what happens as a result of a Catholic education as well as a result of liberation theology and critical pedagogy. From the perspective of theology and spirituality, one can understand this change as "a conversion experience." The practice of one's Catholic faith or the experience of a Catholic education, like the discourses of liberation theology and critical pedagogy, constitutes an ongoing recursive process of reflection, critique, possibility and action—a process of praxis, or the integration of reflection and practice. (As we have seen, both liberation theology and critical pedagogy are recursive, since one's process of conscientization encourages personal development and serves as a transformative agent of social change.) One's practice informed by religious conviction or spirituality is, indeed a recursive process: a continual journey of conversion.

All of these common elements and themes in the discourses of liberation theology and critical pedagogy are part of both the Catholic tradition and the contemporary conversation about the qualities and elements of the Catholic school, elements with a base in Scripture and Catholic Church documents.

East St. Louis, Illinois

My interest in studying the practices of schooling from the perspective of liberation theology and critical pedagogy led me to consider a school in East St. Louis, Illinois. I knew of East St. Louis from the first chapter of Jonathan Kozol's (1991) book, *Savage Inequalities: Children in America's Schools*. My familiarity with Catholic schools, mainly through my religious community, helped me to identify an alternative Catholic high school there, specifically Vincent Gray Alternative High

School (VGAHS).

My research at VGAHS and my subsequent descriptions of VGAHS have made the school an integral part of my own educational journey, a journey Quantz and O'Connor (1988) presaged: "[I]n researching and writing ethnography, one must describe the dynamic and conflictual nature of marginalized cultures, record the dialogues that bind the individual into a private world and a social community, and reveal the many voices struggling for expression" (p. 104).

My work at VGAHS parallels, in some ways, that of Jesse Goodman (1992) with his concern for how elementary education can promote critical democracy. His work with Harmony School drew heavily upon the writings of John Dewey and critical pedagogy. As I approached my own ethnographic work, I asked myself some of the questions Goodman posed on his very first page in regards to Harmony school:

> How might a school for critical democracy be structured, and what type of power dynamics might exist within it? What content might be taught, and what values might be embedded within the formal and implicit curriculum? What type of learning activities would dominate the instruction found in such a school? What dilemmas or struggles might teachers face as they try to manifest the goals of such a school? What factors might hinder the democratic empowerment of students and teachers within such a school? What aspects of this type of schooling could be transferred to other contexts, such as mainstream public or private schools?

Goodman intended "to explore as a 'lived experience,' the possibilities and constraints for developing what some have called a critical or liberatory pedagogy" (pp. 1 -2). Similarly, I present my experiences at VGAHS—particularly through the voices of the students, administrators, and teachers—as a lived experience of a school, an alternative Catholic high school where I could use the discourses of liberation theology and critical pedagogy to describe what transpires there while joining the discussion of the identity of a Catholic school. From this point on, I proceed from a theoretical discussion of the identity of Catholic schools, the discourses of liberation theology and critical pedagogy, and the relationship of these discourses with Catholic education to an account of these concerns in the context of my research and experiences.

East St. Louis certainly qualifies as a marginalized culture. African Americans form 98 percent of the population of 40,944, reflecting industrial abandonment and white flight. Its history is complicated but similar to that of many other industrial cities. At one time, East St. Louis was predominantly white, its population representing various European countries. Its people included mainly Poles, Germans, French, Irish, Lithuanians, Hungarians, Italians and Russians. These people brought their languages, customs and religion to East. St. Louis, and one can trace the neighborhoods where they used to live by the names of churches: St. Adalbert, St. Henry, St. Patrick, Sts. Cyril and Methodius. Many of these Catholic churches are no longer standing or are used for other purposes now. Some of these churches once had their own schools, but the schools no longer exist.

Many educators learned, as I did, about East St. Louis from Jonathan Kozol's descriptions. Kozol (1991) brought East St. Louis to the attention of educators and, in a sense, put it "back on the map" and "gave it a new focus." Kozol's *Savage Inequalities; Children in America's Schools* remains an outstanding example of socially committed literature. One can hardly read Kozol's accounts of the injustices in our public schools without wanting to address these "savage inequalities," though, a few may remain indifferent to these injustices or respond, like Chester Finn (1993), by claiming that *Savage Inequalities* is an "educational dinosaur" trading on an "endangered belief . . . that the only serious short-coming of U.S. education is that it spends more in some communities than in others."

Kozol described how political, economical and social injustices and corruption over the last few decades devastated East St. Louis economically. Now "the city, which is 98 percent black, has no obstetric services, no regular trash collection, and few jobs. Nearly a third of its families live on less than $7,500 a year; 75 percent of its population lives on welfare of some form. The U.S. Department of Housing and Urban Development describes it as 'the most distressed small city in America'" (p. 7).

One of the first persons Kozol introduced is Sister Julia, one of his key informants, who was also featured on a *60 Minutes* segment depicting East St. Louis. I met Sister Julia and our paths crossed often at various meetings and at worship services. She told me that Kozol visited East St. Louis for about a week during March of 1990 and used her office at the Villa Griffin Housing Projects for most of his interviews and as his own office. Many people had come to meet him and to be interviewed. Sister Julia had accompanied him on his many visits throughout East St. Louis.

She went on to say that what Kozol concluded about East St. Louis is true and should be taken seriously. She sees little possibility of change in her city, but valuing the people there continues to motivate her. She expressed a commitment to living the Lord's preferential love for the poor of East St. Louis and "giving a small gleam of hope to these people who are worth so much in an environment and life situations which are so unfair, unjust and unequal" (conversation of November 17,1992).

Kozol had walked through Villa Griffin gathering impressions of this dismal housing project and the neighborhood school. During my stay there, the people of several project dwellings were relocated so that a new sewage draining system could be installed and several of the projects could be remodeled inside and out. Nevertheless, I saw many dwellings with boarded windows–individual dwellings, Sister Julia said, where the lead poison count is so high that no one can live in them.

Kozol described the old neighborhood elementary school, Jefferson School, and right next to it, a poorly constructed new school, which is unusable. By the time I arrived, Jefferson School had been torn down, grass grew over its site and the children of Villa Griffin used the area as a playground. The new school, now known as Mandella School, had been properly rebuilt and is now the elementary school.

I spent three days with Sisters Julia and Diane at the Griffin Center and at DeShields Center. My observations there conformed with Kozol's descriptions of these housing projects and his admiration for the efforts of the two sisters among the people who live there. Along with Sister Diane, who serves as a liaison between the schools and the families of the projects, I visited East St. Louis High and Landsdowne Junior High School, and met their principals.

Seeing the places and meeting the people Jonathan Kozol described provided me with more hope than I had expected. Kozol's descriptions of East St. Louis are unsparing and real enough, but he conveys few hints of hope about the situation there. Nevertheless, people like Sisters Julia and Diane exemplify abundant hope amid the harsh realities of East St. Louis, and many others like them work and live there.

Some interesting developments between the time of Kozol's visit and mine took place besides the sewage cleanup and the opening of Mandella School. East St. Louis High School now boasts a new multi-million-dollar football stadium and locker rooms and regular garbage pickups resumed in July of 1992, through grassroots instigation and the efforts of the Metropolitan East St. Louis Churches Association. In fact, Operation Clean-Up extends beyond garbage pickup; its efforts include cleaning abandoned lots, tearing down abandoned homes and other buildings and planting flower bulbs throughout the city.

Under such depressing conditions, people try to make their lives purposeful and meaningful, and it is no easy task. Rube Yelvington (1990) conveyed a sense of this conflict between despair and hope in the foreword (p. v) to his book, *East St. Louis the Way It Is 1990*:

> The ghosts of the past are evident in abandoned cars, trashed vacant lots, burned out buildings, so many garbage bags, so many piles of trash, of broken glass and old carpet and even old sofas and chairs. The ghosts are so common that after awhile you no longer see them. . . . The derelict business buildings and houses that still stand tell of a city that cannot make it; the boarded up "government property" buildings tell of families with government loans who could not make it, of housing projects that failed because the people who ran them were selfish opportunists. These are stories of defeat, sad stories, depressing stories, frightening stories . . . buildings vacant, buildings gutted, crumbling; threatening, dangerous buildings potentially housing threatening, dangerous people. And in the streets the children, the hope of the city, play. . . .
>
> Every few blocks you will find a liquor store or tavern, and just as frequently, a church. And on Sunday morning, in every part of town you will see people in their Sunday best on street corners waiting for a neighbor to give them a ride, or cruising down the street in clean, shiny cars, going to church; and at the same hour, here and there, a man with a bottle in a paper sack, swigging as he walks. Are they both symbols of a search for hope?

These portraits of East St. Louis suggest the devastation in this city as well as the incipient efforts to improve it along with the lives of the people there. In this city of pervasive gloom, I found hope. Hope was present, for example, at the neighborhood meetings as part of

Operation New Spirit, which has been instrumental in reestablishing garbage collection after several years and leading a massive clean-up campaign throughout the city. Hope was present at the parenting classes, the meetings of the youth groups, and the activities for adults and young people at the DeShields Housing Center and at Griffin Center. I could see hope in the faces of the children at the Catholic Day Care Center. It was present in the various projects of the Catholic Urban Development Center, whose workers I got to know. I found hope when I gathered daily with those people who work in East St. Louis and the local Catholic parish (St. Patrick's) for prayer and worship. Hope also appeared at Vincent Gray Alternative High School where I spent most of my time in East St. Louis.

The Vincent Gray Alternative High School

Vincent Gray Alternative High School (VGAHS) opened in September, 1980, through the efforts of two Marianist Brothers and a School Sister of Notre Dame and with the financial assistance of the Marianists. The school initially enrolled twelve students under these three teachers and graduated its first student in May 1981. The students pay no tuition, but they help clean the school each day in exchange for their education. Meanwhile, the school is financed by grants and contributions from individuals, foundations, corporations and religious communities, with some supplementary assistance from state and federal programs.

Vincent Gray, a Marianist Brother, had achieved deep respect in his religious order, even though he died of a stroke at the age of thirty-seven in 1967. A native of Detroit, Brother Vincent Gray joined the Marianists at the age of nineteen in 1949, the first African American to profess religious vows as a member of the Marianists. He was also one of the first African Americans to graduate from St. Mary's University, San Antonio, Texas. Brother Vincent Gray served as a teacher and principal and was active in civic initiatives protesting racial injustices and social inequities and promoting urban renewal.

His namesake school perpetuates both his memory and his vision for improvement in education and social justice. His life touched the lives of the school's two Marianist founders, and the first Student Handbook (1980) stated that "while he was alive, Vincent Gray was an outstanding educator, person, and friend to all with whom he came into contact. It is hoped that his spirit lives on at Vincent Gray Alternative High School." In the Student Handbook for 1992 I read that "the school bears the name of an outstanding African American high school teacher who inspired a large number of students during his career in St. Louis some years ago" (p. 2).

During many of my conversations with the Marianist Brothers, who live in East St. Louis and teach at VGAHS, I asked them for their recollections of Brother Vincent Gray. For example, I asked Brother Luke to tell me about Vincent Gray, and his response suggests the type of person Vincent Gray was:

> Tom: What can you tell me about Brother Vincent Gray?
>
> Brother Luke: I knew him indirectly by reputation for awhile, since I became a brother, that he was a very special, kind and gentle Black brother. We didn't have many Blacks in the order at that time. And the area of ESL where I grew up was a very prejudiced area. I didn't get to know Brother Vincent until I started my master's program up in Chicago. And we lived together for several summers at St. Mike's. He had started his master's program a year or two before I did, so I'd say maybe three or four summers we lived together. All the things you heard about him, about him being a very quiet, gentle, fatherly kind of person became true. He was a type of person that, even some of the studies that I was doing, I had no hesitation whatsoever to knock on his door and say, "I'm running into trouble with this. Can you help me do this?" And he'd slide his chair back and put his hands behind his head and take all the time in the world: "Right now you are the most important thing on my mind." It just struck me at the time, you know, how he could stop and give you that sense of feeling that you were extremely important. Whether it took five minutes or three hours, he made you feel that it wasn't a waste of time, that he would do everything he could do to help you out, whatever your problem or question was.

Brother Vincent Gray's willingness to help others carries over in the practices of VGAHS, its staff assisting the students however necessary.

VGAHS began with the goal of helping students between sixteen and twenty-four who had left more traditional schools to earn high school diplomas conferred, until 1988, by the local Catholic high school. Since 1988, VGAHS has granted its own diplomas. From its origin, VGAHS has been recognized by the Bishop as one of the Catholic high schools of the Belleville Diocese.

VGAHS struggled with its own sense of Catholic school identity, however, and the Executive Director moved in 1992 to have its status as an official Catholic diocesan high school withdrawn, even though it continues to be considered part of the Catholic ministries to the people of East St. Louis under the "umbrella of the Diocese." VGAHS is also incorporated with the State of Illinois as a "general not for profit" corporation and with the Illinois State Board of Education as a non-public secondary school.

From its very beginnings, VGAHS saw itself as an alternative school, this report from the *East St. Louis News* of June 10, 1981, shows:

> The inclusion of "alternative" in the title suggests that Vincent Gray is not a traditional high school. "Alternative" means choice, and going to school at Vincent Gray is a choice students make. No one is forced to enroll at Vincent Gray . But by choosing to enroll, high school drop outs, age 16 to 24, can open up many opportunities for finishing their high school education. The reasons for attending Vincent Gray are varied. Some students feel they are too old to return to public high schools. Other students, dissatisfied with the impersonal air of traditional schools, are attracted to the individual attention offered at Vincent Gray. For most students, Vincent Gray is a better alternative than staying out of school (Scott, 1981, p. 1).

In an article in the *St. Louis Post-Dispatch* of January 29, 1984, one of the founders described the purposes of VGAHS as having three goals: "First, to get the students jobs; that starts while they are here. Then to give them the self-confidence to go out and to try to master things, be independent. And finally, to get them that high school diploma" (Grimes, 1984, p. 1, 7).

VGAHS began in the rectory and convent of the former St. Adalbert parish, an arrangement explicit in a lease between the Diocese of Belleville and the Marianists. In 1989, a second campus opened in the former elementary school building of St. Patrick's parish. The St. Adalbert campus became known as the VG Downtown Campus because of its location, and the second campus became known as the VG St. Patrick's Campus. While in East St. Louis, I divided my time between the two campuses. In March of 1993, stringent financial conditions dictated that the campuses merge into one, and the St. Patrick Campus became the site of VGAHS beginning with the new school year in September 1993. In 1988, VGAHS also expanded its programs with an Adult Literacy Program that has expanded each year since and usually serves 150 students of various ages at any one time.

In one sense, VGAHS provides a last-chance opportunity to earn a high school diploma. Many of the students who attend this alternative high school have been deemed incorrigible by the courts, unteachable by the schools, or lost causes by their families. They have fallen through the cracks of schools and society. VGAHS knows that not all its students will succeed. The Executive Director (1992) reported one teacher remarking that "in the last three years, six young men I taught dropped out of school before graduating, and they subsequently were found murdered on the streets of East St. Louis." About 120 students now attend VGAHS during each school year and in May of 1993, the 100th graduate since 1982 was honored at the commencement exercise at the end of the school year.

During my visit, VGAHS employed three administrators: the Executive Director, the principal at the Downtown Campus (a Marianist Brother and one of the founders) and the principal at the St. Patrick's Campus (a Daughters of Charity sister). The faculty included a Dominican Sister, a School Sister of Notre Dame, four laywomen, a Vincentian priest, four Marianist Brothers, a young Jesuit lay volunteer, and a young man who is an Oblate of Mary Immaculate aspirant. All of the staff members were white except for two African American laywomen. All of the staff members belonged to religious congregations except for the Executive Director, the Jesuit lay volunteer, and the four laywomen. Thus the administrators and teachers are mostly religious and priests, proportionately more religious than that at most regular Catholic high schools.

Despite a student body of "at-risk" young people, VGAHS confronts no discipline problems, no graffiti, no weapons, no beepers, and no drugs or alcohol on campus. With a student-teacher ratio of four to one, a family atmosphere promotes mutual respect, self-discipline and an appreciation for strong family ties and community involvement. In providing a safe and secure environment and an atmosphere that promotes academic success, the school encourages these young men and women—often for the first time in their lives—to learn, to taste success, to believe in themselves and to develop a hopeful outlook on their own futures.

Colman McCarthy (1992), Director and founder of the Center for Teaching Peace, Washington, DC, described VGAHS in a syndicated column that appeared throughout the country. He wrote that "Gray thrives because it is a school of alternatives, the main one being the love offered by the teachers and appreciated by the students. The kids know this is their final comeback." In an article for the *St. Louis Post-Dispatch*, Patricia Rice (1992) described VGAHS as specializing

> in the second chance, and sometimes the third and fourth chance. All students have dropped out or been kicked out of other schools. All are 16 to 24 years old. At Vincent Gray, all classes are round-table discussions with no more than seven students and one teacher. There are no grade levels. . . . The two campuses offer an identical liberal-arts education. Setting the students on fire with the desire to learn is the big challenge; once that happens, the rest falls into place. . . . The work is sometimes basic, sometimes advanced. Often remedial work must be done before new students enter academic classes. Those who read below the sixth-grade level must be tutored. Besides academic courses, there are computer, parenting, woodworking, sewing and cooking classes (p.1,6).

Like most other schools, VGAHS prints a faculty handbook and a student handbook. VGAHS also has school colors, black and gray, and a school symbol, a viking. The school newspaper, *Shades of Gray*, circulates well beyond the students and East St. Louis, as it is also used as promotional and fund-raising literature.

The school day consists of six teaching periods of fifty minutes each. The curriculum is similar to those in other high schools but also includes such courses as African American Literature, Criminal Law, Civil Law, Sewing, Crafts, The Human Body, Fine Arts, Practical Arts, Woodworking, Consumer Education, Parenting and Practical Employment Skills. On Wednesdays, the fourth, fifth and sixth periods meet in the morning with the afternoon given over to such physical activities as volleyball and basketball, and to such passive activities as card playing and board games. These Wednesday afternoon activities constitute the Physical Education class and also help develop a community spirit among the teachers and students.

On Friday mornings, only the first, second and third periods meet, followed by the weekly all-school meeting with the administrators, teachers and students. These sessions, usually organized and run by the students, include guest speakers, and they often address personal goals, career interests and educational opportunities. Once a month, this time also includes birthday or holiday celebrations and other special occasions and events. Students are dismissed for the day at 12:30. After lunch, the teachers and administrators gather to discuss an array of topics, which always includes each student's progress and development and how the teachers and administrators might help their students more.

At its very beginning, VGAHS established its ideals as the school's driving force and as the reason for its being, and I found this philosophy alive and influential. A newspaper article (Middeke, 1981) marking the first year of VGAHS as "almost a prayer of thanksgiving —not only for an opportunity which didn't seem possible a year ago— but for the interest and time which was never given before."

The current VGAHS philosophy differs little from the original philosophy statement expressing many of the elements of our two critical discourses as well as those qualities that traditionally characterize Catholic schools. Here it is as stated on the first page of the 1992 Student Handbook:

> VGAHS is a community of staff and students in East St. Louis, Illinois, which provides an opportunity for those students to acquire academic skills, vocational experiences, and spiritual and social traits necessary for self-esteem and the power to contribute to a better society. It is an aim of both staff and students of VGAHS not to discriminate in any way because of sex, race, or creed. Together, both staff and students maintain a Christian atmosphere in the school. The staff seeks to extend its role as teachers by spending time with the students beyond the normal school hours. It is hoped that each year VG is "re-created" by both staff and students and that the school continually reflects the needs, values, and aspirations of the current student body and staff. Policies and procedures at VG reflect the concern of all that the spirit of VG be one of honest searching, mutual respect, and growth of each person to his or her fullest potential.

In addition to the spirit and welcoming climate of VGAHS, one can find religious symbols throughout the building and classrooms. Crucifixes, statues of the Virgin Mary and saints, and banners and posters with motivational and inspirational sayings adorn the classrooms and hallways. Some teachers begin their classes with a prayer or a moment of quiet reflection. The school year includes times for such communal religious celebrations as a prayer service to mark Thanksgiving Day and Martin Luther King Day. The graduation ceremonies take place in St. Patrick's Church, and, besides prayer, they include testimonies by graduates to their own experiences at VGAHS. Such symbols and practices typify most Catholic schools and are considered traditional aspects of the Catholic school identity.

These, then, are some of the realities of both East St. Louis and VGAHS I came to know during the time I spent there. Of course, buildings and cities take on meaning only because of the people one meets there. The people of East St. Louis and of VGAHS became both a part of my life and a part of my learning, especially about critical discourses and the challenges they pose for schooling practices.

My experience at VGAHS demonstrated for me that the discourses of liberation theology and critical pedagogy can indeed become part of a school's day-to-day practices. The students, teachers and administrators articulated several of the common elements of these two critical discourses, as I show in the next three chapters. Similarly, my experiences confirmed my premise that a Catholic school can proceed from the perspective of the discourses of liberation theology and critical pedagogy. VGAHS provides one example of this possibility, and I believe that its history can inspire other Catholic schools to understand their own identity from this perspective.

Chapter Six

Student Voices

> A student's voice is not a reflection of the world as much as it is a constitutive force that both mediates and shapes reality within historically constructed practices and relationships of power. Each individual voice is shaped by its owner's particular cultural history and prior experience. Voice, then, suggests the means that students have at their disposal to make themselves "heard" and to define themselves as active participants in the world.
>
> - Peter McLaren, in *Life in Schools* (1994, p. 227)

In a public speaking class in September of 1992 at Vincent Gray Alternative High School, the teacher had asked three students in the class to choose a poem by Langston Hughes to read before each other formally, focusing on their delivery in voice and posture. A young single father, expelled from public school in his sophomore year for hitting a teacher, has returned to school in hopes of earning his high school diploma. After reading "As I Grew Older" (Hughes, 1932), he said he liked this poem because "it expressed some of my own feelings about my own life." The young woman in the class, a single mother who had left junior high school pregnant and bored, read Hughes' poem, "Mother to Son." Her own experiences animate the lines "For I'se still goin', honey, I'se still climbin', And life for me ain't been no crystal stair" (1932, p. 73). The other young man in this class had also quit high school out of boredom. He read "Judgment Day," lending dignity and hope to "Lord in heaben, Crown on His head, Says don't be 'fraid, Cause you ain't dead" (Hughes, 1932, p. 54). These three people, I realized, have aspirations, hopes and dreams which were expressed not only in the poetic words of Langston Hughes, but in their own voices.

Thus, these three students brought their unique histories as African Americans today and as students at an alternative high school in the city of East St. Louis to the words of Langston Hughes. Hughes emerged as a celebrated African American poet during the Harlem Renaissance of the 1920s and '30s. In 1926, Alain Locke, reviewing Hughes' "The Weary Blues," proclaimed that the Negro masses had found a voice in Hughes (Wagner, 1973, p. 394). Through his poetry and essays, Hughes expressed the African American experiences of his time, picturing people caught up in a repressive society, emphasizing "the common Black man's vigor and contempt for restraint" (Perry, 1976, p.54). Hughes knew that "the major aim of his writing was to interpret and comment upon Negro life, and its relation to the problems of democracy" (Perry, 1976, p. 49).

A lot has happened in the lives of African Americans since Hughes composed his poetry. But these three students, like the others at VGAHS, at once give voice to the poems and to their own experiences as African Americans, still bereft of schooling in the community of East St. Louis. They speak of their own lives in terms of knowing what it means to have fallen through the cracks of education, and yet still hoping to change their lives.

The voices of the VGAHS students also express the common elements and themes of the discourses of liberation theology and critical pedagogy, and they demonstrate how critical discourses can indeed help one understand what transpires in their own lives and at school. Besides observing classes at Vincent Gray Alternative High School, I interviewed several students and graduates, as well as teachers and administrators. These interviews with the students and graduates followed an unstructured format. Usually, my questions came in response to the interviewee's remarks. I usually began these interviews with questions about how the student had come to VGAHS and their previous school experiences.

These interviews presented an experience of dialogue in the Freirian sense of my coming to understand reflection, action and transformation from the perspective of the students. Freire described the experience this way:

> We attempt to analyze dialogue as a human phenomenon, we discover something which is the essence of dialogue itself: *the word*. But the word is more than just an instrument which makes dialogue possible; accordingly, we must seek its constitutive elements. Within the word we find two dimensions, reflection and action, in such radical interaction that if one is sacrificed–even in

> part–the other immediately suffers. There is no true word that is not at the same time a praxis. Thus to speak a true word is to transform the world (1989, p. 75).

The integrative model of liberation theology and critical pedagogy presented in chapter four, described these two discourses in dialogue—interacting—with each other. The model became more concrete as I explained these two discourses to others. But, this integrative model of liberation theology and critical pedagogy came most to life as I contemplated what the students and alumni had said in East St. Louis, and even more so, as I reread and coded the transcripts of my interviews.

In fact, I first constructed the model after coding my first five student interviews. This integrative model of liberation theology and critical pedagogy represents both an etic and emic experience of a researcher on site and then the analysis of the voices of the participants. Yvonna Lincoln (1995) partly describes my own experience as a researcher when she states that "the major contribution of critical theory to this search for student voices is the focus on helping students examine the patterns in their lives in such a way as to discern the nearly-hidden structures that shape their own and others lives" (p. 92).

As much as possible in the early phase of analyzing the transcripts of the first five student interviews, I tried to maintain an inductive stance, allowing the experiences of the students and how they expressed themselves to serve as the source of the elements that then became the integrative model. Nevertheless, I continually read and coded the transcripts, alert to any expression of the two discourses in the students' words. Before my VGAHS interviews, I recognized common elements in the discourses of liberation theology and critical pedagogy, but by reflecting on the lists of the codes, I felt assured that I could use these key codes or signifiers to construct a theory of commonality between these two critical discourses.

This chapter shows how the students, and alumni, voice the common elements and themes of the two critical discourses as shown in the integrative model. Thus, I present the voices of the students in relationship to the three major parts of this integrative model: (1) a critical discourse, (2) a method of change (a discourse of possibility), and (3) other common elements the discourses of both liberation theology and critical pedagogy include. As I read the transcripts, I recognized that these students had an intuitive sense of some aspects of liberation theology and critical pedagogy, even though they rarely used the specific language of either discourse. The content and length of any one voice or section reflect my own decision guided by the principle of saturation. My goal in this chapter is to demonstrate that the voices of the VGAHS students do present elements of the integrative model of liberation theology and critical pedagogy, thereby demonstrating that the two critical discourses could become part of the discourse of Catholic school identity.

I chose the voices of nine students, past and present, out of the many I interviewed, as the most representative. The current students I interviewed were chosen by one or the other of the two principals. The interviews in this chapter represent a balance between young men and women, in the length of their VGAHS experience, and between students from both campuses. My interviews took place either in the students' lounge at St. Patrick's campus or the living room lounge at the Downtown Campus. My interviews with the alumni, arranged by Brother Steven (the principal of the Vincent Gray Downtown Campus), took place wherever I could conveniently meet them. Finally I should point out that these nine voices were the clearest and most audible and articulate. Some of the other interviews include simple, often monosyllabic responses and were brief and lacking in description.

The Language of Liberation Theology and Critical Pedagogy As Descriptive of "My World"

Liberation theology and critical pedagogy are critical discourses. By this I mean that each provides a language for describing one's current world and its problems. But, besides being discourses of critique, they are discourses of possibility. While including the observation that something is wrong with "my world," an individual may also acknowledge the possibility of making "my world" more caring and just by eliminating some of the oppressive, "wrong" aspects. Over and over again, the VGAHS students expressed the idea that "something is wrong with my world" as they discussed that world, their experiences and their hopes for changing either themselves or their current situations. Some of the students talked in a critical way about East St. Louis, and others focused more upon their own lives and experiences. Not all of the students expressed hope or possibility for changing conditions as they discussed East St. Louis, but some raised the possibilities of changing their own lives.

In this first section explaining how the voices of the students speak a critical discourse, describing "my present world" and its problems, I chose to present the voices of each of the six students currently enrolled at VGAHS and two of the three graduates. I expect to add some body to the eight voices by presenting some personal information about each one. Each voice tells its own story and describes its own situation in life, but these voices also represent personal histories similar to those of many other VGAHS students.

Finally, I present the voices as emergent, proceeding from struggling adolescents, the single parents, the former addicts, to the alumni who are now parents trying to keep their families wholesome and intact. The link through all these voices is that they express a critical discourse as they view their worlds.

Felicia: Being Pregnant for the First Time

Felicia, a young woman, pregnant with her first child, had been at VGAHS for eighteen months and graduated in January 1993. Felicia assisted in Sister Anne's office (the principal's office at the St. Patrick's campus) each morning checking attendance, answering phone calls and entering mailing labels and other data into the computer. There I engaged her in many informal conversations, especially during the week I shadowed Sister Anne. During our formal interview in the students' lounge, she revealed that she had quit public school because of the violence there. Leaving, she felt, was the only way she could begin to address that violent world. Felicia described the violence she had experienced as a sophomore at East Side Senior High:

> At the time I was there, I'm standing out on the parking lot and this one guy got stabbed by his girlfriend with a pair of scissors. I said I stopped going because I didn't feel that I should have to any time see anybody get hurt. I should not have to look around and see, you know, wondering if I am going to be next. So I just stopped going to the public school.

I was interested in what she was experiencing in her East Side classes and if she had seen any violence inside the school:

> They were O.K., I was passing all my classes. I was making As and Bs. But it was just the violence in there that stopped me from going.

I pressed on, asking if she had experienced any violence other than the one event she had already described:

> Tom: Have you experienced other violence, other than the kid being stabbed with scissors?
>
> Felicia: When I was going there, people would be going down the hall pushing and just for no reason walk up and push you or pick a fight with you, just for no reason. I can't take that.

Felicia also described her experiences of violence as a student during her earlier years at Clark Junior High:

> It was fun at junior high. I miss it. Going to school there was O.K. The violence there was like with gangs and they were like shooting in the morning or shooting in the evening. I made it home, though, before they start shooting like that.
>
> Tom: You would hear the gunshots?
>
> Felicia: Yes. We were standing on the corner from the school park and they were always shooting like that. They were always shooting. It didn't matter where I was at or what time. You always had a shooting.

Thus, Felicia described the violence she had experienced as a public school student. She wanted to avoid this violence so she opted out of school. Now, however, she wanted to change her life as a young dropout by earning her high school diploma. Even though Felicia was in the early months of pregnancy, she overlooked her pregnancy to focus on the violence in her life and how she hoped that her world would one day be less violent; at least as a VGAHS student, her world of school knows little, if any, violence.

Ray: A Young Man with Energy Amidst Violence

Ray turned twenty the day after our interview; thus I took part in his birthday celebration at VGAHS. He hoped to graduate in May 1993, which he did accomplish. Ray was one of the elected student representatives and, thus, a student leader who conducted some of the weekly meetings. He expressed his interest in becoming a carpenter.

Ray described his neighborhood and East St. Louis experiences during the interview. He saw the good and the bad, and he considered himself capable of handling both. He acknowledged the East St. Louis violence as part of his life; however, during our interview Ray offered no solutions and expressed no possibilities of changing his neighborhood violence:

> There's not much to say about East St. Louis. Some areas are bad, you know, some areas are evil, and others are all right. You don't have to worry about nobody messing with you as long as you, you know, carry your own, hold your own, keep to yourself, unless you know the person. Some places you can't dress a certain way.

I went on to ask Ray to describe "some of the stuff that happens" in his own neighborhood more specifically:

> Fights, shooting, dope you know (pause). I know just about everybody over there, as long as they know your face, you know, ain't nothin' to worry about.
>
> Tom: Are there gangs there?
>
> Ray: There's gangs all over. I guess they call it a business, you know, making money. It was like that, see each other, have a fight or whatever. I guess they're makin' money now though.

As Ray described this violence as a gang experience, I wondered if violence had been part of his own experiences. Ray answered my direct question, "What is the most violent thing that's ever happened to you?"

> I got into a misunderstanding once; I got stabbed! See, it was over a guy, you know, and my girl friend. This began at school. This guy wanted to jump on her sister and my friend. So we got into it, and we got into it really good one night. You know it was like me and my other friend, we ran into each other over my girl's house. It was while she was at work and this guy came to the house and we got into a fight really good. But when I got to my home, I felt my back was all wet. That's why I called my uncle and told him to look at it and I had six holes from an ice pick. That's about the worst thing that's happened to me.

Ray, like Felicia, understood that violence characterizes his neighborhood or public school life in East St. Louis. Ray also wanted to reduce the violence, earn his high school diploma and find a job as a carpenter.

Lisa: A Single Mom

One of the first students I met at VGAHS, Lisa was enthusiastic about completing high school and looked forward to graduating in January 1993. She had attended VGAHS for two years, and hoped to enter the local community college to pursue a career as an accountant or teacher, and I observed her performing credibly in her calculus class. Lisa is a single mother with a young son, for whom she expressed a lot of love and concern. During the school day, she left her son across the street at the Catholic Day Care Center.

Our interview began with Lisa discussing East St. Louis, which she believed to be no different from other cities:

> Well, it's not the best place in the world and it's also, it's no worse for me, my own personal opinion, it's no worse than the places like Chicago, New York and you know how they have it on *60 Minutes* and all that stuff. I mean to me, it's no worse than other cities.

Nevertheless, Lisa had a feeling that other people view East St. Louis negatively because the majority of the people living there are African Americans:

> And I don't know, I guess maybe people are down on it so much because basically it's an all Black community. And in Chicago and New York, California and all that stuff you got like a lot of different races and stuff, and here, it's just all Black.

Clearly, Lisa perceived East St. Louis, her world, as somehow wrong. Frank about being a single parent and giving birth when she was sixteen, she still hoped to make her world better and more caring. In other words, she envisioned a more humane world for herself and her son out of a world that was far from being perfect. Lisa believed that praying, studying for a high school diploma and possibly obtaining a college degree would be the appropriate steps toward improving her own situation and that of her son:

> In these days and times you gotta stay praying, all the stuff going on. I know I like nice things, I want to get my son nice things. In order to get nice things, in order to have more money, I know I got to have more knowledge, go to college, do all that, you know. But I don't want to go to college because people are like, you should go, you should go, I want to go on my own, because, it's something I want to do, because I want more money (chuckle) it's just, you know, just gotta do something.

She went on to point out that she often felt captured by the system of social welfare as a single mother. But she saw earning a paycheck as a way of changing her world by implementing the motivation to do something different than the system currently allows her to do:

> Because, being in the system, when I say in the system, like, being in low income and low housing and public aid and stuff like that. It helps you out, but it also holds you down, because it limits you too, like there's only so much that you can do. It's like—how can I put it? Like you get a check once a month and then say if you was to get a job, and you might not even be making more than what aid was given you but they would still take the aid away from you. I think that's why a lot of people probably just don't have any desire to do anything, or else they are probably like, "Sure I can just sit home and get this free check and I don't have to work." And then they'll probably feel like, "And then if I start to work I won't get that money anymore, so why work when I can get this free?" So that's why a lot of people get stuck at home. At least I always like to have some kind of job, something to keep me motivated so I won't be stuck at home. Even if I were mopping floors or cleaning toilets, gotta do what you gotta do.

Though critical of both East St. Louis and the welfare system, Lisa wanted to change the realities of her life and that of her son. She accepted her world as far from being perfect, but it was her world, and she wanted to do something about making it a little better.

David: A Single Dad

David is a single father in his third year at VGAHS, with hopes of graduating in May of 1993. David had been expelled from the public high school in sophomore year for hitting a teacher. He talked not only about life in East St. Louis but also about his own life as a young Black man. David's comments echoed some of Ray's feelings in regards to the violence in their lives and in the city. David described the violence he had seen in East St. Louis and how Black men are victims of this violence, police harassment, and unemployment, simply as a result of being Black.

> Okay, life in East St. Louis is like this. It's hard in a sense if you make it hard it's hard. It's kinda hard to stay out of trouble in East St. Louis. You got a whole lot of drugs and that be harder to deal with you know. Sometimes you get a whole lot of harassment here, too. State police comes out here and gets a Black man, but they don't do much to harass people like you. . . To be a Black man, you know, yes, it's like a stroll. You have to survive. If you let yourself down, if you just give up man, you ain't going nowhere. You just like, ain't that many jobs for Blacks here in ESL. You go somewhere else, you, as a Black man, compete against a white man. And the white man eight times out of ten, will get the job. It's reality, because like in ESL you can get on the street. Man, you get shot up. Just the wrong time. I say so what if I was to get shot.

As I was with Ray, I was interested in David's own experiences of violence. He told me that some of his friends had been shot, and I wanted to know what effect this experience had had on David. David continued to describe this experience from the perspective of how white society constructs Black males as the criminals, even though crime cuts across racial boundaries.

> Tom: Some of your friends have been shot?
>
> David: Yeah.
>
> Tom: What does that do to you?
>
> David: That could have been me. I was right there. That goes through your head. It just wasn't me. Probably wasn't my time. That's the way I look at it. It's, man, like out here people sticking other people up, jacking people for their car and for their jewelry. I was loaded down with jewelry last year. It was sticking people up

> for the jewelry and stuff people have, but they don't. I feel like man if you wear some, then somebody else will go out there and try to get it. Nine times out of ten, it's a Black man, it's a Black person shown [on TV?] doing that. That's what they show. They hardly show a Black man. They might show like I'll show three times out of ten a white man out there shooting somebody. It's mostly drugs, mostly a Black man doing this. A Black man doing that. The Black man, that the reason our crime is so high, because the Black man is doing it. The Black husband is doing this and doing that. They hardly show that for the white, and you know everybody ain't perfect. Yes, it's true that Blacks do this or do that, but whites in our society, they really do the same thing. They might do it a different way, but it's the same thing, doing wrong, repeating itself. Like in St. Louis, man. They try to say East St. Louis is bad. It's bad to a sense, but if you'll really take a closer look at a white man, you'll probably see the same thing.

David's world as a young Black man may be marked by violence, but the violence helped him appreciate his own life and find a hope that his life and life for other young Black men might be improved. Having been expelled from school for his violence, he had found the hope to complete high school.

Jody: A Former Drug Addict and Mother of Two

Jody, a twenty-five-year-old woman with two children, had been a drug addict. She expressed her desire and need to create a more caring world for herself and her neighbors. Jody began by observing how the people of East St. Louis hinder and help the community through the choices they make:

> You know what? At first, I was like I wanted to get away from East St. Louis, ain't nothing here. But it's all in what you make it, you know, in what you try and achieve in East St. Louis. If you want to hang around with the bad bunch, then that's where you're going to be, with the bad bunch. There are positive people in East St. Louis, and there's a lot of things you can do to help the community. I mean a lot of people want to just dump trash everywhere, you know. But some days on the weekend when you're not doing anything, pick up trash.

She was trying to make some good choices by going to school, yet she acknowledged that one of the weakness of the Black community is a reluctance to affirm and support each other and the tendency to put one another down, usually out of jealousy:

> One thing about the Black society is that they don't help each other. We tend to be jealous of each other and try to hurt each other. And I know it's hard, it's hard out here, but it's all about trying to just make it to me. That's why I'm going to school, trying to do something with my life so I won't have to live, you know, so I can live the way I want to live. It's up to you. You got a choice. Go to school, get some kind of trade, get a degree, whatever. That's how I feel about it.

Jody's world had recently changed a whole lot, but she realized that her new world could continue to improve only if she remained reflective about her life. Her life had entered a new focus without drugs, with a husband, with children and with her studies. Jody exuded joy and peace as she answered my questions and, in fact, whenever I saw her.

Washington: A Former Drug Addict and Alcoholic
Washington always came to school looking clean and neat. His life history, I knew, included off and on attendance at a local public school, and a three-year residence at a drug and alcohol treatment center. Washington freely admitted his addictions but was trying to stay clean. His comments about East St. Louis echoed the same frustrations the other students had expressed. He saw a lot of violence in the city and associated it, in part, with an all-Black racial make-up. Still, his closing remarks revealed a scintilla of hope for the city:

> Tom: How would you characterize ESL? What could you tell me about ESL?
>
> Washington: It's pretty all right. It ain't like that all over. It's bad like an all-Black community. People say how bad it is, you know. Lot of gun fights every day. But it ain't really like that. There's a lot of robberies and car thefts, but not too many. It's like Harlem, half of it, just split in half, half of that crime rate. Just be yourself. Don't be scared. Speak up for yourself. There's a lot of drinking. Everywhere you see on the corner is a liquor store. That's what

> makes crime, too. When you get high, you want to do things. You think you're God. When you wake yourself up, you're like a whole different person. It's like, "I did that. Ah, I did all that." Or you might wake up in jail, some of the things you do. I guess East St. Louis is an all-Black community trying to get somewhere, but ain't nobody just helping.

Washington had been involved in some of the violence as a drug and alcohol addict committing crimes. During the early part of the school year, Washington expressed a hope to make a change in his life by abstaining from drugs and alcohol and by returning to school, but after several weeks at VGAHS, he resumed his drug habit and stopped coming to school.

The Alumni: Two Mothers with Families

Marcia graduated from VGAHS in 1984; thus she was among the early graduates. By 1992, Marcia had four children and her husband, the father of her children, lived with her. During her days at VGAHS, Marcia had worked at the Catholic Day Care Center, a job she kept after her graduation. She took a break from her job, however, to take several classes in child care at the local community college. I interviewed Marcia at the Day Care Center during one of her normal work days, and she spoke of East St. Louis much more positively than some of the current students had. Yet, while describing her hometown with a sense of pride, Marcia's comments also reflected the tensions in East St. Louis.

> Tom: How do you feel about ESL being your home?
>
> Marcia: I'm proud of it. I like it because it's where I was born. It ain't the town, it's just the people in the town. That's what makes the town. Ain't nothing wrong with the town. It needs lots of cleaning up or whatever, but ain't nothing wrong with the town I was born in. I don't want to leave the town. This is my home and I really don't want to leave it. I'm proud of ESL, and I will tell anybody that I am from ESL.

Another VGAHS graduate, Cynthia, described East St. Louis similarly. Her comments described the contradictions in the city but included the wish for her city to improve. The realization that East St.

Louis is a home for themselves and their families probably encourages Marcia and Cynthia to hope for a more humane East St. Louis. Their evaluations seemed more positive and hopeful than those of the current students.

> East St. Louis, [Cynthia observed], our poor little town has such a bad reputation. The past mayors, stealing and what not, but I am still proud of my little town. We've lost thousands of jobs here. But still you have people who have gone on to better themselves in college and get great jobs or what not. Still, they won't leave. They're determined to stick it out here. I thought about leaving for awhile when it was really bad in my neighborhood, shooting and drugs. Who wants to raise their child around something like that? I thought about leaving. I don't know. I still may leave. I always say if I leave, I'll leave for awhile. But I know I'll be back. Because this is home. Regardless, it's home. So you can't say all of ESL is bad.

Cynthia also described the projects where she lived and how some people think about them. She noted that she changed in how she felt about these projects after she had lived there herself:

> And being in ESL, everyone knows, the projects I live in. These projects had a very bad reputation, long before I moved into them. I didn't even want to move in but after I've been there for a while, it's not as bad as they say. When people are, you know, well think people goes when I tell them I'm from ESL, they go, "Ohhh!" . . . It may not be the best, but you have to work with what you get. That's how our whole district is. You work with what you can get.

Cynthia went on to point out that East St. Louis offers few employment opportunities, but some low-paying jobs remain available. Meanwhile, she hopes for the arrival of some industry to provide more work:

> Well, a lot of people are losing, have lost jobs, but there are other menial type jobs, minimum wage. I was unwilling to take a minimum wage job, and it just so happens that this job happened to come in that I have lined up now. But still I plan on staying around in the city. We've accomplished some things, getting our

> streets fixed. And I do hope we can get some type of factory jobs or something like that lined up.

Cynthia continued to talk speculatively about developments on the East St. Louis horizon, like the Riverboat Casino that now docks in the city, and the fountain along the Mississippi River. As she spoke about these developments, Cynthia's words betrayed concern about the problems these developments might add:

> I know they've been talking about the Riverboat Casino thing, that's supposed to come through. Okay. Yes, that's going to provide jobs. But you have to look at both sides of the coin. It will provide jobs and Lord knows that we need jobs in this city because there's so many unemployed people. Yet it still makes you wonder, what about the knucklehead people who may come and try to mess it up. You have your alcoholics and drug addicts and what not and I can understand the people saying you don't want them hanging all around making business bad. Some ways it's kind of a no-win situation. You need it. But again, you don't like to cause any more problems than what we already have.

For Cynthia, these developments would hardly respond to the needs of the young people. She pointed out the irony of increasing the number of taverns in the city but failing to find a place for teenagers to meet socially:

> We're getting more taverns than anything else. We just getting ready to open a new one downtown called the "Royal Flush." Do we really need another joint? Please, no way. We really don't need that. Make something else constructive. We need a place where these teenagers can hang out at. Open up another video arcade room. We did have one downtown but it burned down some years ago. The kids don't have a place to hang out at. There's the Boys' Club, but everyone doesn't want to go to the Boys' Club. I wish you all would think about children.

Marcia and Cynthia recognized the many shortcomings to their East St. Louis world. But it is their home and the home of their own families and they both expressed hope that life in East St. Louis might improve. Still, in spite of what East St. Louis is or isn't, they both work to improve their world.

The Students Speak a Critical Discourse

At the same time these students spoke critically about their own world and experiences, they conveyed their hopes for change. They all realized that the media projects East St. Louis as pathological, violent and sinful—mostly, they suppose, because of the high percentage of African American residents. They have deconstructed this media representation as an incipient step toward improving their lives. For example, they criticize and withdraw from the violence, the unemployment, and resent the influence of drugs and alcohol. Their voices expressed the strong conviction that something is wrong in their world, and that it should become more caring than it is.

The students, in short, were willing to examine their world critically. Of course, many others—often those of the dominant culture—see much wrong with East St. Louis and despair of reconstructing or transforming it. To the dominant culture, terms like hope, justice, equity and care might seem out of place in East St. Louis. But the voices of the VGAHS students suggest a critical discourse, though perhaps in muffled tones, and at least, they can view their city and some of their own experiences critically.

Liberation Theology and Critical Pedagogy As Conducive to Change

The discourses of liberation theology and critical pedagogy propose a method for changing the reality of one's world, thus, these two discourses move from being simply critical toward being interventionist. Both discourses provide a method for change known as praxis—that is, an integration of theory and practice. This method moves through three steps: (1) developing an awareness of those conditions that spoil the world must therefore be changed; (2) proposing solutions that could transform the world; and (3) implementing those proposed solutions. The method moves the discourses of liberation theology and critical pedagogy from theory to action: discourses of "doing theology" or "doing pedagogy." This method also presumes the discourses of liberation theology and critical pedagogy as discourses of possibility, not merely criticism.

The students and the alumni often sensed this possibility as they discussed their lives. Their words mapped out the three steps of the method. They expressed an awareness of their world in need of transformation. Their voices also suggested solutions they hoped to implement or are already implementing. Hope leads to the effort to improve a world, and they have hope in terms of changing what they now experience as students, going beyond simply the hope of acquiring a high school diploma.

Ray

Ray told me he wanted to earn his high school diploma at VGAHS and use it to find work at a decent wage. Ray quit high school during his junior year and he and his friends began drinking beer and whiskey and gin out of boredom. But Ray found VGAHS far from boring and it provided him with the means for changing the current realities:

> I want to get more done, you understand. I was just, you know, like stuck on a burnt bridge, you know. I want my diploma and I want to find some work, and get pay for it, 'cause you know, I don't want to be stuck in dead end like I was. That's why I'm sticking with, you know, up here at school.

Returning to school, therefore, was Ray's affirmation of the need to transform his world of boredom and disgust.

Lisa

Lisa, too, saw school as a way to make a difference in her life and a route to a career. Lisa recalled the advice of her grandfather to value schooling as a means of improving one's situation as a Black person in a white society:

> My grandfather before he died used to always say, go to school. I could talk to him five times a day and no matter what I'd say, he'd be like, "Just make sure you go to school and get an education." That's all he'd say, cause he'd say, "I know, I only made it to the third grade" and "You ought to be blessed because in my days we had to pick cotton and have to do this or do that." Oh, what else did he used to say, uh, "Just keep your pants up and your chest flat" [laugh], and he would say, "Make sure you don't have no babies." Oh, and he'd be like, "Once you get an education that's the one thing the white man can't take away." And he used to say stuff like that, and he'd say, "Only the strong survive," or like, "The longest road gotta end," meaning if you're having rough times, it

won't last forever, it'll soon be over with.

Lisa's first step to changing her situation was to complete high school. Explaining how she came to VGAHS, she described the conditions in the public high schools of East St. Louis. One high school had a long waiting list for admission of new students, and the other she characterized as violent. At the time Lisa began VGAHS, she was living in an apartment across the street from the VGAHS Downtown campus:

> I was at the foster home that was right across the street and, um, at first I tried to get into Lincoln, but Lincoln was always saying they had a long waiting list. Lincoln is one of the other high schools in District 189 besides East Side, and I didn't want to go to East Side because people would say, "You don't want to go to East Side because at East Side they fight every day and this and that." So VG was just right across the street so I just came here.

Upon completing high school, Lisa had hopes of going on to college. "When I graduate from here, I plan to turn right around and go to the local junior college." She wanted to become an accountant or a teacher, and earn a good salary. Lisa also indicated her willingness to continue her education, even to the master's degree level:

> At first I thought about a school teacher, but I want to do something that I like and also make money [laughter]. I mean they make enough money, but I guess, East St. Louis has some of the highest-paid school teachers. I guess in order to make money in anything it takes time and experience to be in a job for a while, unless you go back and get your master's. So it will probably be something like teaching or accounting, something like that, 'cause my favorite subjects are math and science.

Lisa then, hoped to transform her world by continuing her education. She had come to value an education as her grandfather had urged her to do.

Jody

Jody struck the same theme: realizing something is wrong with her world, proposing solutions, and trying to put them into action by returning to school. At a certain point, Jody, as a drug addict, knew she had to change her world into something better. In fact, she quite literally wanted to reconstruct her world as a wife and mother. She began her remarks by acknowledging that her drug problem involved more than simply drugs, but also reflected her dissatisfaction with who she was and her frustration with her life:

> A lot of times the reason you get caught up into drugs and be addicted is because. . . the drug just be one percent of your problem. You have all these other problems that cause you to, if I felt so good about myself and I was so happy or whatever and was doing what I want to, man, I wouldn't have done it. I would have said I ain't going to take this, because I know it will kill me. But I was disgusted with myself, I just, I don't know, I was just looking for something. I couldn't deal with life on life's terms, and I'm learning how to do that today. Just because something doesn't go my way don't mean I have to go use, because the problem is still going to be there.

Jody first realized that a twelve-step treatment program would change her world for the better. Jody, in other words, changed her world by changing herself:

> I just thank God I got into treatment. I made it through treatment, and I didn't have to lose my life, or my kids or my marriage, you know. My husband, he's in treatment too, we're doing this together—one day at a time. As long as he stays on the right road, then we can be together. But it's all about me today. I ain't going to sit here and put my life on the line because of him. I have to think about my kids. One of us going to have to be strong. We both can't be weak, because our children need us and I don't want nobody else to have to raise them. I laid up and did what I had to do to have them and it is my responsibility to take care of them and teach them the way of life.

Jody now knows that her world can change only while she concentrates on eliminating those conditions that threaten to make her life less than she wants it to be. She has proposed solutions to her problems: being addicted and being uneducated. She is now acting on those proposals.

Washington

Washington, like Jody, felt pride in knowing that his life had changed for the better. He had abused drugs and alcohol, and had been a thief and a gang member. He clearly expressed the dynamics of the three aspects of the integrative model methodology: an awareness of his world, an inclination to change it, and a course of action based on the inclination. He also told me how his VGAHS experiences had helped him change "my world." Washington began this part of our conversation by reflecting on his current world in light of his past experiences, and on his desire to improve his world:

> I'm trying to change from bad to good. . . . It got worse. I end up down on probation because of skipping school and doing bad things. I used to fight a lot and stuff. I went with my friends. I had wanted to change then. Since my friend got killed, I wanted to change my life. I didn't want to go out like him. I want to be here and stuff. I gotta play straight. I never bothered since. I really don't like to think about it, but I have to face up to it. So now I can face up to it, straight. I know my way around now. I consider myself better now than when I had been in school last time. 'Cause when I see myself back, I was bad. I can see myself now, I'm better than then. I used to steal . . . steal cars and stuff, sell dope, live in the fast lane.

Washington attributed the changes he was undergoing both to his time in rehabilitation and to his current VGAHS experiences. At VGAHS, Washington found respect as a person and as a student learning academic subjects and earning his high school diploma.

> Tom: So you've done much better now and you feel that coming to VG has helped you?
>
> Washington: Yeah. They teach you how to be a decent person. You try to act cool and do all that. They kinda put you in the right place. You know the thing you ought to know, they'll teach you.
>
> Tom: How has VG helped you with yourself?
>
> Washington: VG, there's a lot of things. They helped me with all my math, English and addition all the things I had missed. I got

caught up. I know what kind of life I'm in. I like to do it here, staying together, because they listen to you. They ask you if you will speak up, express yourself. When you express yourself, they'll listen. That's why I chose this school, plus I know the teachers that are here. They helped me. So I came, new life. Since I'm here, I feel much better.

My conversation with Washington then focused upon his gang experiences. As Washington described these experiences, he mentioned the changes he had gone through realizing the consequences of his behavior as an active member.

Tom: Were you part of a gang?

Washington: Yeah.

Tom: What kind of gang was it?

Washington: It was Fireside. I used to be invited to everything that happened every night. I was to the point where I didn't care. I let them rule. It was like a front. Then when I got to begging, I start doing it. I said this ain't worth going to jail for, 'cause I been to jail about six times. Every time I quit a job, I thought "This is a mistake. You should have thought what could have happened." I never thought of that. I was just like, "Go with this, do it." Now I just sit back and like well, "I shouldn't have done it." Now, I'm accepting the fact and now I can change.

Tom: As part of a gang did you experience any shooting or being shot?

Washington: I got shot once in my right arm. I was drunk, high and being careless. I got shot here, too (pointing to the side of his left leg).

Washington had left the gang, even though some members still invited him to join their activities. Washington let them know that he feels differently about himself and is struggling to remain free of drugs and alcohol.

> Tom: You don't need that (belonging to a gang) any more?
>
> Washington: Nope. They still kinda come to me at night . . . cause some of my friends are in jail, some of them on the run. I'm just glad I'm here. At night I can, like you know, new people come and try to talk it over and all that. They want to see what's happening to them. I try to talk to them. I just tell them throw that stuff down, 'cause it ain't worth like going to jail, doing time. You got to do that time. You don't think about that, "Why, I shouldn't be here or I should have done this." What you should have done you should have walked away. You shouldn't care what people say about you. It don't matter. Respect yourself, don't try to show off. That will get you in deeper trouble. I try to talk to people, 'cause I know myself, I'm straight. All I try to do is help somebody here. If they don't want it, fine. They'll have to find out the hard way like me.

Trying to change his life as a member of a gang, a drug addict and an alcoholic, Washington demonstrated an awareness of (1) his former world and of himself, (2) solutions to these realities, and (3) his present attempts to change. In time, as I said, Washington returned to his addictions. But, during his brief time at VGAHS, he believed he was making a change in his life. One hopes that Washington occasionally reflects on his experiences at VGAHS and wishes still for a new beginning or a better life.

Marcia

Almost ten years after graduating from VGAHS, Marcia recalled how she had experienced a change in herself and in her attitude toward school. Marcia also recalled how her VGAHS experience had given her confidence in herself. She further felt certain that others who came to VGAHS would experience a similar change in themselves:

> VG is an encouraging school. The place makes you feel confident about yourself. The people there give you a lot of confidence. They gave that to me. They gave me a lot of confidence, made me feel like if we can do it, you can finish here. You can because we're going to stand right by you and help you until you finish getting your diploma. That's what means the most. You're gonna do it in the end. Some people like drop out . . . . Before you know it, I was

> like finished. . . . I would encourage any student or teenage dropout to go to VG.

Marcia remembered that even her attitude toward school changed once she entered VGAHS:

> I was happy to go to school. Previously it was Oh-h-h-h. Before I had my baby, before I got pregnant, I was going to regular school and that's how it was. You know, my mom would say, "Marcia, it's time to go to school. You're going to miss your bus." "O.K. Mom." After I had my baby and heard about VG and got in there, I'm like, "You got all these privileges."

Marcia attributed part of her enthusiasm for VGAHS to her treatment there as a young adult with a right to respect. The VGAHS experience was also like being at home:

> At the time I was at VG, I was smoking. They would say, "Well, you can smoke here." Like I was grown, because I think I was 17 or 18. It was like you're grown. We're not going to be on your back. We're not pressuring you. Either you learn or you don't." That's how it was at VG. I was like, "This is school!" You get to bring your own lunch and cook whatever you want to eat and you don't have to eat what they're serving you. It was like at home, so why not go to school. You felt just like you were just right at home. A couch is what you sit on to be comfortable. Why not get up and want to go to a place like this? This is school. You felt like you were at home. You got sick you could lay down or something like that. Every morning I woke up, "Hey, I'm going to school. If school's today, hey, I'm going." I was right there.

This completely different school experience helped change how Marcia felt about her own life and encouraged her to earn her high school diploma.

Ronnie: Hope for a College Degree

Ronnie graduated from VGAHS in January of 1992, after eighteen months there, and he was planning to study communications at St. Louis University in January of 1993. Our interview, in the kitchen of the Downtown campus, was interrupted by students coming in for snacks during a special Monday lunch day. After the interview, Ronnie and I joined the teachers and students in whatever remained on the table.

Ronnie, like Marcia, recalled his frustration in public schools and described how VGAHS had changed his attitude towards school and himself. Ronnie had accumulated lots of absences at public school partly because of his impoverished home:

> Tom: What was your experience before you came to VG?
>
> Ronnie: It was all right. When I was going to East Side, it was all right. What really messed me up, I was having problems with my family and like the location, it was difficult to get there, so many problems were stopping me. It was problems at the school.
>
> Tom: It was problems at the school, right?
>
> Ronnie: It was like with most of the teachers, and the classes were so large. It was like they couldn't pay you any attention, pay no attention to just you. They couldn't really give you any real attention.
>
> Tom: Were you asked to leave school or did you leave school on your own?
>
> Ronnie: I was asked to; really, I was asked. Mostly because of my absentees. It was hard getting back and forth. I had to walk at least two miles, two or three miles, about three miles even in the morning.

Ronnie had enjoyed junior high, but his family's problems began while he was going to high school. He also remembered being ignored by and lacking acceptance among the other students and teachers since his clothes reflected neither popular styles nor money.

> Tom: What was going to junior high like?
>
> Ronnie: It was nice. My junior high days were nice. It's just that when I got to high school, that's where all my problems mostly came. That's when mostly my problems came in high school. . . . I really didn't have that much money, like clothes or like mostly I

> wear the same clothes and stuff. I didn't really have the money or anything. I had to catch the bus always or walk to school and stuff.
>
> Tom: How did the students tend to treat you ?
>
> Ronnie: Not really treat me no way, but it was like, "They're poor. Here's that kid wearing the same clothes." Poor, kept me isolated.

VGAHS provided Ronnie with renewed confidence because he began to be noticed by others, including teachers. He also believed that VGAHS gave him a sense of possibility for himself as a student and a person.

> Tom: Do you feel being at VG made a big difference in your own life in terms of being motivated, wanting to go to a university and become a professional? Did it make a difference for you?
>
> Ronnie: I think it did. I think if it wasn't for VG, I [long pause] I wouldn't have my diploma now. It was like I really gave up until I found about VG. I started to give up, but I came here and got motivated for my future. I went around with mostly teachers, and they give you inspiration to try harder and stuff. They motivate you to try harder. VG showed me that there's more out there. Don't give up. Don't give up. Just got to try harder. Everyone has problems, but you can't let them stop you. You gotta keep going.

In brief, Ronnie at first resented school and felt oppressed by the students, his teachers, and his own family's economic situation. But, achieving his high school diploma at VGAHS made a difference in his life and helped him to create an altogether new world.

Cynthia

Cynthia graduated from VGAHS in 1986. She had started there in 1983 but took part of her second year off to give birth to her third daughter. She had quit regular public school because she was a teenage mother with two daughters. In 1992, she lived in one of the government housing projects with her husband and three daughters, aged 16, 13 and 8. Each one of them is going to the public school and succeeding in her school work and extracurricular activities. Five years ago, Cynthia had undergone surgery and subsequent treatments for cancer. The disease remains in remission.

Our interview took place in the cafeteria of St. Mary's Hospital just after her Certified Nursing Assistant classes. She was preparing to take her final exam in this three-month course at a local technical college and expecting to graduate the next week. She explained how VGAHS provides an atmosphere conducive to changing how students feel about their lives and themselves. Cynthia also described how her attitudes toward school had changed at VGAHS, mostly because she felt respected and was treated like a young adult:

> At VG I went to all my classes. I know in high school I couldn't stand them. I guess I felt the way the teacher went about doing it: "I'm a teacher, you're a student," instead of just saying, "You're a person, I'm a person. I'm going to help you learn." I understand teachers have their way, how they must teach a subject. But what I'm always trying to tell the teacher is "Everyone is not the same, so you can't always try to get everyone to grasp onto this one way. Sometimes you have to go out of your way and help someone else." Other people learn to do it slightly different way. At VG I did a lot of that.

As our conversation continued, Cynthia talked about how she encourages some of her younger friends to return to school at VGAHS. Cynthia concluded by acknowledging that she had gained hope being a student at VGAHS:

> VG gave me a lot of hope. Without them, I don't know. It made me want to go on with my life and get a career going. A lucky thing that VG knew that I was determined to do something anyway. With all the things I had to go through and the time I first started until the time I graduated and having a child.

Like Ronnie and Marcia, Cynthia reported that her experiences at VGAHS helped her create a new sense of self and a world for herself different from the one she had known. Through her VGAHS experiences, Cynthia put into practice a method of changing her life.

Students' Voices Describe a Methodology of Change

Various VGAHS student interviews revealed the methodology of constructing a new world. Some of the students drew upon struggles and situations,such as their addiction to drugs and alcohol, their negative attitudes toward schooling and their new desire to earn a high school diploma and gain meaningful employment. They also hope to see this methodology succeed in improving their lives and the lives of others in East St. Louis. Some of the students specifically credited the atmosphere and structures of VGAHS for providing the opportunities and incentives for them to create new worlds for themselves. VGAHS provided some students with more than a high school diploma, it gave them a new sense of confidence, respect and esteem their former schooling experiences had denied them.

These student voices demonstrate that the methodology of the integrative model of critical pedagogy and liberation theology provides a praxis in their lives, integrating action and reflection as a means for achieving change. The interviews demonstrate students moving from expressions of a critical discourse to expressions of a discourse of possibility. Thus, these students experienced themselves as agents of change in their own lives, moving from their "current" world to a "new" world.

The focus of this change, however, is themselves—namely, earning a high school diploma to enter a world in which the dominant culture still uses education to define success. The changes in their worlds remain on an individual level of change. It remains for them to confront how these positive changes might move out into the wider community, making the students more political and agents of change in the larger context of, for example, the collective struggle of the people of East St. Louis or other poor and marginalized people. But, as long as the dominant way of defining success includes test scores, credits, diplomas and credentials, these students can achieve little change in their own lives without their high school diplomas. Students learn, some more quickly than others, that a high school diploma opens the doors to opportunities and possibilities for employment and further education.

Meanwhile, these voices show how individuals can improve their own self-respect and confidence. This new acceptance and understanding of self can, in turn, help them affirm themselves and their lives as meaningful and successful. The dominant culture should, of course, prize successes like those over academic or monetary standing, and a need to prioritize success is one of the lessons VGAHS offers these young men and women. The realization that the lives of young men and women in communities like East St. Louis have value could be a lesson for a dominant culture partially responsible for the dire realities in this city and others like it (Kozol, 1991, 1995). These poor, young Black men and women can be critical of their world, propose solutions for changing their world, and implement these proposed solutions to help banish such impressions as the inevitability of "their" victimization. Likewise, the dominant culture should realize that others can address and transform the world. In these voices, one can hear the power in each person once he or she is encouraged to become an agent of change.

Elements of Liberation Theology and Critical Pedagogy

The voices of the students at VGAHS also express the other common elements of the integrative model of critical pedagogy and liberation theology. They represent oppressed or marginalized individuals in the marginalized community of East St. Louis. They have all tasted failure for one reason or another in the public school system. Their early schooling experiences have added to other experiences of being oppressed and marginalized. But, their VGAHS experiences introduced a feeling of community in which they came to know what it means to be accepted and affirmed. They experienced a solidarity with each other, both students and teachers, as part of the VGAHS community. Their voices also express the hope for a better world, for a change in their own worlds and for the recursive experience of ongoing change.

The voices presented in this section follow the familiar pattern of the integrative model of liberation theology and critical pedagogy. Each of the students and alumni described how they experienced a sense of community at VGAHS, how they gained hope, how they changed an understanding of themselves at VGAHS and how they learned the need to be continually reflective about their lives to keep improving their world. In order to avoid redundancy, the voices to follow are those that most clearly addressed the elements of liberation theology and critical pedagogy as presented in the integrative model.

Experience of Community

The students often described the sense of community they felt at VGAHS. This sense of community appears in references to being helped or helping others at school. For example, Felicia felt that VGAHS had changed her entire attitude toward school. She found there a nonviolent atmosphere and a place to learn, mainly because of the concern the teachers demonstrate:

> The teachers here are nice and VG is not violent. You learn. You learn more than what you learn in the public school, because there it's like they just really shove the work in your face and told you, "Do it or get an F." Here they'll tell you how to do and take their time with you. It's not like East Side. Here you can go to any one of the teachers and they show you how to do this and show you how to do that. If you don't know how, then they explain it to you. The teachers are nice.

Felicia also found that the students tend to get along and show concern for each other:

> I like it because everybody can get along here. We very seldom hear that somebody wants to fight somebody else. Other than that, everybody gets along.

Ray also expressed his sense of community at VGAHS as characterized by the friendly interactions between the teachers and the students:

> Teachers here are not real strict and you know, they talk to their students. Besides doing work for them and with them, we talk to them as a friend, just talk to them. That's what I say. If you can do that better, you'll find out more about them, you can find out how to teach them better. Talk to them and let them know about you.

Lisa explained to me what she considered the all "good things at VG" in response to my question about her sense of the VGAHS community. Lisa attributed the caring atmosphere among teachers and students, and students and students to the small student body:

> The best thing for me is that it's a smaller crowd. You feel like you can't fit in if you have a hard time being in a classroom with like 30 people or just being in a school with like 1500 students or something like that. If you have a hard time like fitting in like that, you can go to VG. Basically most of the time if you have a problem, you can talk to the teachers; like if you're trying to help yourself, then they're basically trying to help.

Other students noticed that the teachers were concerned about them and willing to pay them attention. The students also felt a sense of belonging with and being affirmed by the other students. Jody emphasized the difference she found between the cooperation at VGAHS and the competitive struggles between students at other schools. Jody needed only two credits to graduate and spent only two quarters at VGAHS. (She began school in September of 1992 and graduated in January of 1993.) Jody began her comments by observing how students try to understand and help each other, as opposed to competing against and isolating each other:

> We all trying to get an education. Instead of trying to be mad at the next person 'cause he got a higher score than you, you help each other. If I understand this and you don't, I'm going to try and help you to understand it, you know, to my best ability. If I don't know something, you help me understand it. I'm not saying that all the students are like that, because you have your class clowns and all that, but you know, some of them, we help each other, and stuff.

Jody had also noticed how her teachers help the students understand and interact with students in a concerned way:

> And if we do have a problem we can't solve with each other, we go to the teacher. The teachers aren't so bad where you be, like, "I don't want to talk to him because I don't like the way he be talking or nothin'." They all are concerned about what happens, what's going on with you, how you're feelin'.

Jody moved from the general to the specific in expressing how certain teachers at VGAHS had helped her make a difference for her own life and increase her enthusiasm for being back in school. She also felt a sense of being affirmed by and belonging to the VG community:

> Sister Elaine will help me a lot. If I have a problem, I'll go talk to her. Brother Steven helped me. They help me, and I feel like I'm somebody. I enjoy coming to school.

Marcia, too, expressed this sense of community in terms of her cordial relations with the staff, and one teacher in particular. She also described the concern other staff members felt for her and the other students. In fact, Marcia continues to feel herself a member of the VG community and participates in the annual alumni picnic:

> Tom: What are some of the things you remember about VG, the people?
>
> Marcia: The staff or what?
>
> Tom: Yes, the staff.
>
> Marcia: The staff member that I was so close to was Sister Marilyn. She's no longer with VG. We were so close. The day she announced that she was leaving, brought tears to my eyes. Everybody, "You can't leave. When I started at VG, you were here and you're supposed be here till I finish." She was at my graduation when I finished. The day she left it just hurt me. It just took a part of my heart away you know, when she left because we were so close. Everybody gets along with each other. Sometimes the teachers be playin' like volleyball with us, sometimes. Brother Steven was in the activities. Brother Harold liked me and when I was just working on stuff he spent most of the time in the office. I met him last year, not this year at the graduate picnic; he was over there. I was very glad to see him, because I hadn't seen him in so long. He was surprised to hear how many children I have and all of that, and that I'm still around. I was working here. He told me he was happy for me, "Keep it up and try to hang in there."

The community aspect of VGAHS had been part of Cynthia's experiences from her first days throughout her three years and she still maintains a connection with the VGAHS community even after ten years. As a student she felt right at home and received a lot of concern from the teachers:

> I was determined to at least finish high school. If nothing else, I was determined to do that. I decided to give the school a call and they set me up for an interview, and I started there. The first week, you know, it takes a little time adjusting. I guess after the first couple days, I felt right at home, right at ease, because you could sit and talk to the teachers about any problems you were having. It was one-on-one adult, not like "I'm the teacher, you're the student,

> so you just sit down and shut up." I loved the way the teachers teach, talk to you and help you. They would just keep helping you and helping you and helping you until you got it. Where a lot of them, it wasn't so easy, where for me, go over it a few times and then I would catch right on to it. They've helped me a lot.

Cynthia reported that this "feeling right at home" applied, as well, to the other students, as evidenced by how they related to each other:

> You also know all the students eventually. I knew everyone in the building right after I got there and before I left. You get to know everyone and you kinda get to know their ways, how they are. You get along. You go in the kitchen and you cook. I guess they still have the place where we used to fix lunch.

I noticed the efforts the VGAHS staff makes to value all the students as an important members of the community, and Cynthia remembered the students taking part in the decision making, helping to schedule classes and other school activities. This participation is most evident at the weekly meeting with the students and the staff:

> We determined some of the classes and how the teachers go. We had meetings every week. The students got up and did the talking. The teachers pretty much just sat there and listened, but if they had something that they wanted to put in they had their little input. We did the school together, run by the students more than the teachers.

Cynthia noted that the graduates have happy memories of their days at VG and their experiences continue to reassure them as they confront current situations:

> I run into some past graduates from VG, and they still talk about when we were there and how much fun it was, kinda wish they were back up there. Me too. God, I wish I was back up there, but we're older and we must move on.

"Community" does appear to be a major theme in the VGAHS student interviews. They expressed a sense of "belonging to the school," and the peaceful "getting along" atmosphere at VGAHS they associated with each other and the teachers.

The structures of VGAHS—for example, the size of the student body, the faculty and the classes—represent a deliberate effort to create a community atmosphere within the school. Other practices, such as the weekly student meeting, the personal advisor and the lunches prepared and served by various students also reflect the effort to develop a spirit of belonging. These efforts all help create solidarity among all those at VGAHS.

Having achieved an esprit de corps, the challenge for the students and teachers at VGAHS becomes the application of these micro-community experiences to the macro community. These positive experiences of community should help the students recognize an opportunity to share those experiences with others in their own families and neighborhoods. Ideally, the realization of a small successful community will awaken in the larger community the possibility of mutual concern where there has been violence and alienation. At least, the experience of community at VGAHS can help the students and teachers see that a sense of community might be possible for many more people in East St. Louis.

The Hope for a Better World

Hope for an improved world permeates the discourses of critical pedagogy and liberation theology. Hope leads directly to convictions about possibilities and thus to a willingness to attempt the transformation of the larger world.

Aware of her own impoverished situation in the projects, Lisa still maintained a sense of hope for herself and for her future. She pointed out the need for patience in achieving something more desirable than the current situation. Lisa identified this hope as part of having "soul":

> Lisa: I don't have that much, or all the things I want, but you gotta crawl before you walk. Take it step by step.
>
> Tom: Do you live with a lot of hope?
>
> Lisa: Do I?
>
> Tom: Yeah.
>
> Lisa: Yeah, I think basically because of my soul and what it means

> to me, just because you're like born in the slum, or something, doesn't mean the slum's gotta be inside of you. It ain't gotta be like that forever.

David echoed this theme of hope as he talked about achieving his high school diploma and the possibility of becoming a Marine or a law enforcement officer. His comments reflect the hope young Black men require as they look towards their futures:

> Tom: During your time here you've seen a lot of different students come and go. What makes you stay, some go?
>
> David: Some completely just leave. They might think they're coming just so it'd be easier. I just want to get my diploma. For other people it means that they don't want to do that. . . . I was thinking about taking law enforcement or joining the Marines.
>
> Tom: How'd you get interested in both of these?
>
> David: Since I was a kid, I was thinking about joining the services, but Marines, they got my attention. I want to do something that's a challenge. I don't want to just join. I want to make sure I join the law enforcement and keep myself focused, not just set down. . . . Being a Black man, it's like that if you want to survive you gotta keep strugglin'. If you give up, ain't going to survive. You're going to be a loser.

Jody expressed this hope as she discussed her life as a recovering addict. She imagined that life getting better with the assistance of others:

> One day, one day at time. Yep, there's more to life than drugs. But I didn't know that at first. But with the help of a lot of people and God, I'm on the right track, I'm on the right track.

Washington expressed his hope for a high school diploma as a way of changing his life. He also expressed gratitude that the teachers and the atmosphere of VGAHS helped him learn at his own rate and in his own way:

> I want to get my high school diploma here. I'm not going to sit and whine. Take my time and do the very best I can. At the other school you can't do that. You would be joking around, playing around, acting a fool. Like the teachers yell at you, and you yell at them. You ain't got time, not even at home, because you got duties when you go home, like I do. Here, I can just do my work and, of course, have fun. At the other school you can't do that. You can get a diploma here better than you can on the East Side.

Washington went on to acknowledge that he receives a lot of support from his family and teachers as he works to give up his addictions and former behaviors. This support provides him with some hope for a different way of life and developing a belief in himself:

> Tom: Do you find a lot of support also in terms of turning your life around?
>
> Washington: Lot of support here. I have one of the brother's support, my father's support, my whole family, plus I got support here—my teachers. They don't get lazy on you like the other ones do. There ain't nothing else I could change. Because it's already here, everything you need, support, meals, and teachers. Now I feel good about going to school. I can learn what I wanted to learn and keep going on.
>
> Tom: Do you feel a lot of strength inside you?
>
> Washington: Uh huh, I believe in myself that I can do it. I will make it.

Cynthia expressed hope and determination in various ways throughout our interview. In fact, her hope and determination appear to explain her intense enthusiasm for her life. She described herself as a person who doesn't give up. She also attempts to share this hopeful enthusiasm with her family and with others:

> People tickle me though, sometimes. They say certain things, you know, "I'm not going to do this or I wouldn't do that." I go, "Never say you will not." A person should never say that because you never know what the outcome may be. You may have to end up

> doing it anyway. I told my children yesterday that they [the people at the nursing home] wished they could take a cookie cutter and duplicate me from cookie dough. I said, "Really." One of the aides at the nursing home, she said, "Now you have three children?" I say, "Yes. I have a 16, 13 and 8 year old daughters." She said "Now, you go home you cook dinner." I said "Well that depends. If my husband is there, dinner's already cooked, my other uniform is already cleaned and ironed. So normally, I just go home and study or relax and spend the rest of the time with the children." She goes, "Okay, you have three kids. You are married. You have to work around the house. You go to school. You study for tests (because I had tests twice a week) and still you manage to work. Very cute and do all that." And I say, "Yes, I sure do." She said, "I just need to take a cookie cutter and duplicate you out of cookie dough."

Some of the students expressed hope in terms of earning their high school diploma and consequently gaining employment or a career. Other students voiced hope in a determination to change the realities of their own lives, as well as create a different situation for others in East St. Louis.

A Change in How I See Myself and My World

The experiences of hope and transformation that are part of both critical pedagogy and liberation theology as discourses of possibility lead to changes in how people view themselves. The recursive methodology of these two critical discourses keeps one continually aware of changes in self-perceptions and in one's understanding of one's own world.

Ray hesitated to acknowledge any change in how he perceives his world. But, he did express an awareness of some changes in himself. He confirmed a new and different attitude about school and that he now has more control over his temper. These two changes have brought more enjoyment to his life and world:

> Nothing's changed too much for me, except for [pause] I learned to be myself. Let me see, I learned a lot about school. I learned to control my temper though, you know, learning can be more fun than violence and fighting. I improved a little bit. Not much, but you know. . . . Yeah, I used to have a chip on my shoulder, you know. I had an attitude problem. Then I'd fight at the drop of a

> gun. I had a lot of nerve to fight and then laugh [chuckle]. Now it don't make no difference whether they fight or not. But you know I'm not going to trust nobody fighting with my hands, unless he puts his hand on me. Now I laugh and make fun in general.

Lisa observed that her grandfather's advice described earlier was just beginning to sink in. She indicated a change in a new awareness of her life and world.

> Tom: What's some of the stuff that's sinking in?
>
> Lisa: Like how important it is to go to school. Just being aware of the things that's going on around you, the people, the actions, be alert.

Likewise, David realized there had been a change in how he perceives and understands himself as one result of attending VGAHS. More specifically, David acknowledged a change in some of his behavior, particularly as it involved violence and drugs. He had begun to perceive himself as "good":

> Tom: Do you see a change in yourself, being here?
>
> David: Yes, 'cause I used be like, man, you know, the more I am good, the more I am calmed down. Cause I used to be kinda, what you say, well, "used to."
>
> Tom: Used to what?
>
> David: I used to like, I guess it was like, I run about with drugs and gangs. I guess you could say I was street smart, but I was educated, too. In a way, I was more street smart. Now, you learn something new every day whether you realize it or not. You learn something new every day. I realized I was learning new stuff.

Jody considered herself a better person as the result of her struggles with life. She had gained a sense of pride, as a determined individual with a different sense of her own world. She acknowledged her former perceptions of her self and her world, and seemed thankful that both had changed:

> I'm not ashamed of what I am, you know. A lot of times I'm thankful for the things I had to go through in order to get here to where I'm at today. I'm glad that the Lord put me through some things that He put me through because that made me a better person—to me, and that's all that matters. . . . See, I am determined. I am determined to do something. I've been through a storm, you know, and now it's settling down, and things are getting right. I just feel good, and I'm going to enjoy it while it lasts. It's not going to last all day, every day, but while it's lasting, I'm going to enjoy it. And I'm going to be ready to deal with any problem that comes my way too.

Enthusiastically, Marcia described how her years at VGAHS changed her self-perceptions and attitude toward school and learning:

> Tom: How did you hear about VG?
>
> Marcia: From a friend, she told me about it.
>
> Tom: How did you feel once you got here, compared to other schools?
>
> Marcia: I felt good about myself. I felt like I was really doing something once I got into VG. When I was in regular school, it just felt like I was barely taught. When I was at VG, I just felt good about myself.

I continued our conversation by asking how Marcia felt when she graduated. Her responses emphasized this new sense of confidence:

> Tom: How did you feel when you graduated?
>
> Marcia: Like a million dollars when I graduated from VG. I really felt good, like, "Boy, you finally did something yourself!"
>
> Tom: So it gave you a lot of confidence?
>
> Marcia: It did. It gave me a lot of confidence.
>
> Tom: And being there, during the three years, you felt also like

there was a change in yourself?

Marcia: I did. I really did. I felt like there was a change in myself. Just felt like a new person. It just changed my life. I feel that they should stay open always and give other students, other people, an opportunity once they drop out of regular school.

Tom: You feel the confidence you have today, a lot of it came from VG?

Marcia: Yeah, it came from VG.

Like Marcia, Cynthia described how her experiences at VGAHS continue to influence her and how she now interacts with her own children, almost ten years later:

Tom: Do you think that some of the things that you were taught at VG affect the way you have raised your own children?

Cynthia: I think a little bit of everything I learned at VG has been enforced like a great deal. When I do certain things or say certain things, I think of one of the teachers. It may be Brother Harold, though he's not here in the city. A lot of things I do or say has a lot to do with VG.

As the voices of the VGAHS students illustrate, many of them experience a change in how they perceive themselves and their worlds as the result of trying to make their world more humane. The students saw a future for themselves, a different future from the one they had seen before VGAHS. Many students confirmed that attending VGAHS had effected the changes they felt in their identities and in how they had come to understand their world.

The Recursive Model

The VGAHS students appeared to realize that a change in their world is part of an ongoing process and not simply a static condition reached by gaining a high school diploma. Both critical pedagogy and liberation theology continually integrate theory and praxis with reflection upon what one's world "is now" and "what it could be." It is a recursive process of reflection and action with the hope of transforming the current world into a more just and equitable one.

While observing classes, I noticed Felicia reading a copy of Toni Morrison's *Song of Solomon,* and during our interview I learned that reading is one of her hobbies. She had already read *Beloved.*

> Tom: What part of the day do you really like the best?
>
> Felicia: I like the evening better, because it seems like the day goes by quicker. I like the evening.
>
> Tom: You spend that time relaxing or what?
>
> Felicia: Yes, or most of the time I read.
>
> Tom: Reading school books or what?
>
> Felicia: Yeah, most of the time, like *Beloved.* Most of the time I take the book home and read it. But other times I am at home reading like magazines or other books. . . . The magazines are *Black Fashions*, *Ebony*, *Queens*, comic books.

I asked Felicia what she thought about the Black women in Morrison's novels, and she said that as she read Morrison's novels, she thought about the recurring need for Black women to reflect on how to keep changing their present situations. In other words, Felicia was able to integrate her reading into her current situation as a Black woman:

> Tom: Do you like the way Toni Morrison talks about the Black women characters in her book?
>
> Felicia: Yes. I thought her book was going to be boring, but as I was reading I thought they were very interesting. I think, stuff like, you know the Black woman, most of, you know and how they were treated back in the 18 or 19 hundreds. They talked about how they were treated and stuff. It was really interesting, her books. 'Cause she was saying, like in her book *Beloved*, that some men had raped her. Today Black men are still raping Black women. So I feel that it is still going on today. What she was saying. As you know, time hasn't changed.

She continued by focusing upon the role of Black women today:

> You know, in most of our families, there is no man. Just mostly a woman. That's probably why most women are leaders in meetings and stuff like that: because there is no man in the family. I feel personally that a woman would probably, well, do a better job than a man does.
>
> Tom: Even among young people ?
>
> Felicia: Yeah. I feel I do a better job than they do at everything. Because they are not really stupid when they act silly. There's a time to play and time to be serious, but they play all the time. It takes a woman to show them there's a time to play and a time to be serious.

Jody described the ongoing process of recovering from drug addiction and staying clean. Meanwhile, her interest in being a nurse helps motivate her academically:

> I know it's going to be difficult, but uh, I won't know unless I try. As long as I know that I tried, you know, that's all that counts. Even if I don't succeed, I can keep trying, keep trying, whatever. You never know. I might get to college and then decide I'm more interested in another field. But right now, you know, I feel like I want to study RN, be an RN.

Jody told me that attending VGAHS had helped her begin to organize her life in new, positive ways. A reader may recall that she said she lives her life "one day at a time" as she recovers from drugs:

> Tom: And you feel that coming to VG helps you with this, day by day?
>
> Jody: Yes I do. Because I'm doing something positive with myself. And you know, if I sit around the house and not do nothing, my mind will go to wandering the wrong way. As long as I keep myself busy and doing things that I enjoy in lieu of doing drugs. And I enjoy going to school. I get up at 5:30 in the morning, because I have to get my kids ready. And people be like,

> "How do you get up at 5:30?" I got a commitment, and that's coming to school, and getting my education and going on from there. I am a recovering drug addict. I've been clean for about seven months, so I'm really trying to get myself together, you know, because I have two kids to raise and I want to be a good mother to them, not somebody hanging out on the streets and stuff, you know. I want some other life, and I know the way I was going wasn't right, so, I went into recovery and I'm still in recovery. There's more to life than drugs. But I didn't know that at first. But with the help of a lot of people and God, I'm on the right track [a long sigh]. I'm on the right track.

Keeping himself motivated appeared to be Ronnie's constant struggle, even after earning his diploma and starting to focus on a college degree. Ronnie looked beyond himself, however, to include other young Black men:

> I think, it's like, to me being a Black male seem like you gotta try for it more than most of the other minorities. You gotta try for it, push harder to get ahead, to become somebody. You got trouble. Instead of 100 percent, you gotta give about 200 percent or more. You've got to try harder.

Cynthia described the continual process of reflecting on her life and world, with the hope for making life different and better. She tries to use her VGAHS experiences to impel new experience:

> I think a lot about it and without VG, I really don't know if I would have taken this step that I've taken. If we go there and we learn, we teach and graduate, they expect for us to move on with our lives. I did. I hated for myself to go through those two and a half, three years of trying to get a high school diploma and then just letting that be that. I was too young to just sit and do nothing. We got to go for something else.

Cynthia offered the example of her current involvement in a Certified Nursing Assistant program at a local technical college. Apparently, this is work Cynthia always wanted to do but is only now learning:

> When I was there [VGAHS] for the annual summer get together, I told them, "I plan on registering for CNA [Certified Nursing Assistant] class." I told them I was going to do that, but it was just taking me a little while since I left to do it. Everybody was so happy. I was determined to do this. It's only a three-month course.

Cynthia explained how her plans for further study had been delayed because of her cancer treatment, she now expresses a satisfaction and joy in overcoming the cancer and continuing her education:

> I was determined to get through it because I had some illness along the way. The one thing that stopped me from already being a CNA was the fact that I had to go through a bout with cancer back in, well, I found out back in '86 that I had cancer. That meant putting that behind maybe another three years or so until I finished the chemo and regained my strength and some of my memory. I got over that and as a matter of fact I'm going into my fifth-year remission. In March, it will be five years ago. I thank God every day that I have made it this far. My family is very proud of me that I didn't let anything stop me. Three children—sending them to school everyday and taking care of the house. Where I work, it's hard work, but I am determined. I'm very proud of myself.

Cynthia has expressed similar sentiments in conversations with her daughters about the need to aspire to something better and to change the current realities. One of her daughters considers her an inspiration in this regard:

> My sixteen-year-old always says I'm her inspiration. She says, "Well Mom, you're raising three kids. You've gone through cancer treatments and everything. Here, you've popped back up. You've gone back to school. You're going to work with little children. Most people just can't stand little children. Still going back to school once you finish working." I have to keep going. I can't just sit. You don't accomplish anything by just sitting there. It's not going to work until you go, "Hey, here I am." I said, "You have to go out and get it."

The realization of the praxis, and namely, the integration of reflection and practice, appears repeatedly in my VGAHS interviews.

They convey a sense that a high school diploma is just the start of a struggle to address the problems of the world. The students realize that they must keep alive the hope of changing their "present" world into a "new" world. They have a sense of dealing with their own realities as an ongoing process. Some speak of this process in terms of recovering from addictions or their roles as spouses and parents. Others express this process in terms of the realities of being African Americans. But they understand the continuity needed to achieve a "better" world now, then renewing the effort.

Summary

Properly inferred, the voices of the VGAHS students describe the integrative model of liberation theology and critical pedagogy. These two critical discourses exist beyond just a reified state. The students speak to the various elements of the integrative model of liberation theology and critical pedagogy as criticism of and possibility in their current worlds. Their reflections on who they are, what they have experienced and what they can be represent both critique and possibility in action. Praxis is for them more than a theoretical construct; it is a way of life. Thus these students demonstrate an intuitive awareness of the need to be critical and to apply a methodology of praxis to change their worlds. They can do so, they sense, through the community they helped build at VGAHS, so as to acquire hope and anticipation, experience a change in understanding themselves and continually to reflect on their lives. While their voices do not speak the literal language of the discourses of liberation theology or critical pedagogy, their expressions contain the elements of these two critical discourses as presented in the integrative model.

Furthermore, the voices show the applicability of liberation theology and critical pedagogy to schooling. Even though the interviews focused on the struggles of individuals, they suggest how these two critical discourses can promote an understanding of what happens in the lives of high school students. The voices of these students also suggest how critical discourses can inform the dialogue on the identity of Catholic schools. Finally, the voices of the VGAHS students demonstrate how the common elements of the critical discourses of liberation theology and critical pedagogy can become part of the Catholic school evaluation process.

Chapter Seven

Voices of Administrators

> Transformative intellectuals need to develop a discourse that unites the language of critique with the language of possibility, so that social educators recognize that they can make changes. In doing so, they must speak out against economic, political and social injustices both within and outside of schools. At the same time, they must work to create the conditions that give students the opportunity to become citizens who have the knowledge and courage to struggle in order to make despair unconvincing and hope practical. As difficult as this task may seem to social educators, it is a struggle worth waging. To do otherwise is to deny social educators the opportunity to assume the role of transformative intellectuals.
>
> \- Henry Giroux in *Teachers As Intellectuals: Toward a Critical Pedagogy of Learning* (1988, p. 128)

The voices of the teachers and three administrators of Vincent Gray Alternative High School expressed their experiences in ways consistent with the elements of the integrative model of liberation theology and critical pedagogy, presented in Chapter Four. This chapter focuses on how these voices and experiences follow this integrative model of liberation theology and critical pedagogy, much as the voices of their students did. These voices, too, suggest a role for critical discourses in the dialogue over the identity of Catholic schools. The voices in this chapter, like those in the preceding chapter, come from unstructured interviews during the weeks I visited VGAHS in 1992. This chapter centers on the three administrators, including the chief administrator or Executive Director of VGAHS (sometimes referred to as the CEO), the principal of the St. Patrick's Campus of VGAHS, and the principal of the Downtown Campus of VGAHS. The next chapter concentrates on the voices of the teachers.

The administrators and teachers I interviewed embody a variety of education experiences at VGAHS and elsewhere. Some have remained at VGAHS since it opened; others began teaching there in 1992. They also represent both of the VGAHS campuses existing at the time. They represent from one year to thirty years of teaching. They also represent such different teaching locations as only VGAHS, only Catholic schools, only public schools, only at the elementary level, only at the secondary level, and various combinations of all these. The teachers also teach or have taught in such subject areas as reading, sewing, cooking, science, English, social studies and art.

The three administrators also are teachers. Mr. George Reynolds came to VGAHS as a teacher, leaving his first career as a chemist. After several years of teaching at VGAHS, he became the chief administrator when VGAHS acquired a second campus in 1989. Reynolds continued to be the chief administrator until the end of the 1994 -95 school year, and during that academic year he also assumed the responsibilities of being the principal.

Sister Anne has spent her whole life as a teacher, counselor and principal at various Catholic high schools. She served one year as the principal of the Downtown Campus until VGAHS spread onto it's St. Patrick's Campus where she became the principal. She continued in that position, then became the principal of the "new" VGAHS, as the result of the merger into one campus at the site of the St. Patrick's Campus in the summer of 1993. She was the principal until the chief administrator also took over this position. Throughout all of her time at VGAHS, however, she has taught English and computer skills.

Brother Steven is one of the VGAHS founders. Earlier, he taught and was the Assistant Principal at other Catholic high schools. He remained involved with VGAHS until the summer of 1993, when he initiated an innovative family care and counseling project at the site of the former Downtown Campus of VGAHS. He also taught a variety of courses at VGAHS, including math, typing, economics, woodworking and electricity.

The VGAHS teachers and administrators come from different worlds than their students, and they often view the students and events at VGAHS from different perspectives. All of the administrators are white and have lived in places besides East St. Louis, although all of them have also lived in East St. Louis. Brother Steven and Sister Anne continue to live in East St. Louis and George Reynolds lived in East St. Louis for about ten years but now lives across the river in St. Louis. All but two of the teachers are white. They live either in St. Louis or the neighboring towns around East St. Louis, except for Brother Luke, who, like the other Brothers teaching at VGAHS, lives in the Marianist community of East St. Louis. All of the teachers have furthered their educations and almost all have a master's degree and additional schooling.

Thus, the administrators and teachers often speak past the world of the students at VGAHS about their own worlds. Nevertheless, they appear to realize that through their own experiences at VGAHS, they have discovered changes in themselves and a sense of solidarity with the oppressed and the marginalized African American East St. Louis community. Interestingly, as I said, the administrators and teachers tend to talk from their own perspectives about the world of the students. Still, they realize that their worlds differ from students' worlds. Thus the voices of the teachers and administrators present the common elements of liberation theology and critical pedagogy from two perspectives: (1) the perspective of what happens to the students at VGAHS and (2) a perspective on what happens to them as administrators or teachers.

The Voices of Administrators

Transcribing my interviews with the three administrators, George Reynolds, Sister Anne and Brother Steven, I made notes in the wide margins to identify common elements of liberation theology and critical pedagogy. I had initially induced these codes from my student interviews. I sought to let the words of the administrators describe elements of the integrative model of liberation theology and critical pedagogy, and I worked to apply that model objectively between emic and etic categories as I identified emerging patterns and themes in my transcripts.

I found it easy to outline the unstructured interviews for each of the administrators since the flow generally seemed more structured than that of the students. These outlines led me to focus on some of the concerns the administrators expressed for themselves and for VGAHS. These outlines also illustrated how the worlds of the administrators differ from the worlds of the students. One of the main concerns during the 1992-1993 school year was the possibility of merging two campuses into one. My conversations with the three administrators also included their personal histories at VGAHS, the history of VGAHS itself, and the issue of the school's Catholic identity.

The interviews with the administrators differed greatly both in tone and in content from the student interviews. The administrators tended to focus more on the institution and the history of its current problems. In response to my first question, each interviewee spoke about becoming involved with VGAHS and coming to East St. Louis.

Despite their great differences in tone and content, I gradually realized the transcripts of the administrators' interviews revealed similarities between the voices of the students and their own. The administrators express strong commitment to working with the students at VGAHS and about developing a sense of community and solidarity with the students. They also express hope that VGAHS and their own presence there help the students change themselves for the better. The administrators even tend to criticize society at large for its racism and the results that racism produces on the lives of East St. Louis people.

The administrators speak in their own way to the elements of the integrative model of liberation theology and critical pedagogy—that is, about the world of the students, but from a different perspective. Student and administrator voices join in expressing aspects of critique and possibility. The administrators adopt a discourse of critique as they address East St. Louis. Their voices adopt a discourse of possibility as they talk of hope and the changes they have seen in the lives of VGAHS students and in their own lives.

Their voices describe elements of community and commitment to their work with the poor and oppressed peoples of East St. Louis, two elements characteristic of the discourses of liberation theology and critical pedagogy. Thus, I present here the voices of the administrators representing (1) their experiences in East St. Louis, (2) a commitment to work with the poor and oppressed of East St. Louis, (3) the experience of community at VGAHS, (4) a sense of hope and change in the lives of their students, (5) changes in their own worlds and (6) the issue of the Catholic school identity of VGAHS.

The East St. Louis Experience

As George Reynolds responded to my questions about his experiences in years of living and working in East St. Louis, he observed how his own feelings of safety and security in the city have changed. Even the city itself deteriorated, he gained a sense of familiarity with it and a sense of security in it:

> I was very nervous about driving around town. I would come in and I would go to school. I didn't even think of cruising through the town because I knew, or at least I thought I knew from what I had read in the paper, what it was like. Which is really kind of funny, because now, six years later, I don't think twice about going anywhere in the city. You know the good and bad spots. You know how to look over your shoulder. You just become accustomed to it.

He went on to point out that his experiences in East St. Louis differ from how many people perceive the city to be, and he attributed a lot of these attitudes about East St. Louis to racism. He also noted that certain situations in East St. Louis are continually accepted because they are part of the daily lives of the African Americans who live there:

> On the one hand, the perception of everyone outside of ESL of what the city is and then the reality of what the city is are two different things. Just the fact that people live under the conditions they live in here—if they are all Black, it makes it okay. The fact that somebody lives on a dirt floor, that's wrong. But if it's a Black person, well people don't get upset. I don't know how many homes—the winter rolls through here, it gets pretty cold—people have their gas and electricity shut off. They do whatever they can to keep warm. These people are just trying to live and keep warm. I think if it were happening in a different area, with different people, there would be such a public outcry, that something should be done. But here, it's all right.

Attitudes and feelings towards East St. Louis have changed over the last few decades, white flight having caused it to become more and more an African American city. Reynolds linked the current condition of East St. Louis to racism and other people's refusal to become involved with an African American community:

> People get very territorial when you try to get them to become involved with ESL. People do not want to get involved in ESL, because of its short history over the last 25, 30 years. In 1960, it was an all-American city. You just couldn't heap enough praise on this community. Now nobody wants to touch it. Again, it goes back to racism. Racism is simply, as far as I am concerned, intolerance due to ignorance.

A search for a new job brought Sister Anne to East St. Louis. Responding to my question about how she had come to East St. Louis, Sister Anne told me how her preconceived ideas about both alternative schools and working with the poor had changed during her time in the city. Her experiences at VGAHS and living in East St. Louis have become significant parts of who she is now:

> I came to East St. Louis and interviewed for the job on Friday. I liked what I saw. I was attracted to it. I landed the job and said, "Yes, I'd like to take the job." I received permission and became the administrator of VG. It wasn't like I was dedicated to alternative schools or social justice or anything like that. However, once here, I really, really internalized for myself what this is all about. There was a whole lot of we're not evangelizing the poor, but are being evangelized by the poor. That was one of those pat phrases that you read about and you heard said in highest places. I sort of react, but when I was in my first year at VG that's what I felt.

As Brother Steven talked about living and working in East St. Louis, he expressed some of his own feelings about a sense of security for himself and for VGAHS. With some surprise, he noted that VGAHS has never been burglarized:

> I have never been threatened by anybody. They don't bother us. A kid was here a year ago and held up some gas station. Why didn't he come here? He could have tried to rip off this place. There's something about us. We are an oasis out there. They just kinda know that—don't touch us. We've never been broken into, once we got the bars and discouraged them. One try, that's all that I know of—one try.

Brother Steven also described how being a white person in East St. Louis adds to his own sense of security. He said he considers East St. Louis a secure place for the other whites affiliated with Church-sponsored works. At the same time, they are cautious in a prudent way:

> I walk around. I used to walk home from St. Joseph's park when I was in the choir at St. Joe's. That's more or less a mile, and we'd come back 9 or 9:30 at night even in winter. I think white people

> in East St. Louis are safer than the Black people. Either we're crazier and there's no sense doing anything or we're church people and you don't want to mess with them because that's some of the best stuff that's going in this city. Like the Sisters in the projects, these ladies have to be absolutely totally insane. I don't know that they even get threatened. Somebody might try to sell them some dope, that's happened a few times. They've never said anything about people pulling out guns or threatening to rape them or anything. They are cautious, but I don't think they are cautious to the point where they are shaking when they go in.

In regard to their own experiences in East St. Louis, George Reynolds, Sister Anne and Brother Steven suggest that life there is much different from how outsiders perceive it. Each feels a measure of security in East St. Louis, yet they understand the frustration that results from the poverty, violence and oppression among the people in the city.

A Commitment to Work with the Poor and Oppressed

A sense of a social contract with others to reach for a more just and equitable society is part of Reynolds' motivation for working at VGAHS. He contrasted life on both sides of the Mississippi River. He noted that many people in St. Louis simply refuse to notice the problems of East St. Louis. Some of them, in fact, see the people of East St. Louis as sub-human:

> It's as if they're still second-class citizens, actually sub-human, when you allow people to live in these conditions. Especially, too, when you look across the river at the skyline in St. Louis, and you see the buildings. You're standing right next to a burned out house and you see the arch and the downtown buildings. It's just a thirty-second drive across a bridge and it's a whole other world. People are comfortable with living that way, as if the people here do not even exist. That's what's really troubling.

A concern for the "other" partly explains Reynold's reasons for working in East St. Louis. Each person, he believes, has a social responsibility to others, in spite of what he reported about the people across the river:

> I'm not a saint, and I know people will demand a lot of things for their own communities. However, there are other communities or areas which are too easily forgotten. Part of the reason why I am here is because I think there is an overall call to do some kind of good for others. We're all socially responsible for each other. Am I my brother's keeper? Well I am thinking that the answer is yes. A lot of people don't agree with that, but the truth is there's an implicit social contract about living in society. Once you make the choice to live in the community, in a society, you have implicitly taken the obligation to work toward the betterment of that community and that's simply not happening here.

He continued our conversation by voicing rhetorical questions about the neglect of East St. Louis. He also described his own efforts to alleviate some of the problems there:

> Why is it so easy for you to just write off 40,000 people and say, "To hell with them"? What living is there in poverty and squalor? Through my own small efforts, I have made a little dent here and there, opening a few eyes. But we have a long way to go.

Sister Anne's work at VGAHS is part of her commitment as a nun following the duty of her order, the Daughters of Charity, to live out her vow of service to the poor:

> We talked about that [a preferential option for the poor] in my community because we'd take a fourth vow in service of the poor. We are supposed to be servants of the poor. That's why we need to keep examining ourselves on this point. We did a lot of talking about where we are working. There was this use of the phrase "the poor." We began to talk about different kinds of poor. I felt like what we were doing was justifying what we were already doing rather than trying to really analyze to see if we were doing what we had said we were supposed to do. Poor people in the U.S. are people who are under the poverty line. That's who we are supposed to mean when we say we serve the poor, and to try to change the meaning of the word "poor" is absurd. I kind of came on strong about that.

Part of Brother Steven's motivation for his involvement with VGAHS is his interests in the "working class," the "have-nots" and the poor. This motivation expresses less of a spirituality than a class identity, a solidarity with the students of VGAHS and his desire to associate with the "have-nots":

> I'm out of a laborer family. And I have never felt any desire at all to work among the haves. I've never dealt in a wealthy situation. The sum total of my teaching experience was at high schools which were strictly blue collar and middle class working. So I have avoided the schools of my religious community that are for the haves, thank God, because it would never work. If I had to be there, I am sure, my prejudices would shine through. I wouldn't get accepted at all. I couldn't handle it.

Brother Steven helped found VGAHS in response to a specific need for such a school as opposed to any "pure" desire for social justice. Still his work represents a commitment to those in need. He contrasted his motivation of responding to societal needs with the motives of social justice of Brother Harold, one of the other founders of VGAHS:

> For me, VG was just something to be done. There was a need and that was it. I think Brother Harold was more into social justice. Brother Harold had the feeling and basically in his own words, "Kids deserve an education and if the government won't provide it the citizens have an obligation to provide it." Therefore, we, because we are citizens, have an obligation to provide it because it's obvious that the government is not providing it. I think Brother Harold was more into that kind of a thing than into spiritual motives, saving souls or giving an example. Not that that's all not important, but that is important, what we were trying to do. We're just trying to say there's a need. Once we got here it became even more obvious and the longer we're here the worse it gets. Now it's unreal.

Each of the three administrators, then, associated their work at VGAHS with a commitment to help racial minorities and the poor oppressed by society. This commitment compels them to devote their energies and time to the VGAHS students and the people of East St. Louis.

The Experience of Community at VGAHS

Deliberate efforts to develop a community atmosphere take place at VGAHS. As George Reynolds described his history at VGAHS during our interview, he recalled how, as a teacher, he had felt a community spirit of care and concern for and with the students. He attributed this sense mostly to the small classes and his extensive personal interactions with the students. His job as the Executive Director of VGAHS requires less of this direct involvement. Yet he understands his own work and efforts as being part of the students' lives as they further their education:

> The small classes made being concerned for the students easier for me. You get to know your students very personally. You start a dialogue. I was able to find out what they needed to know, what they didn't know, what they needed. I then had to come up with some creative way to best impart that knowledge to them. I loved the classroom. Everyone was different. The world of the classroom is much preferred over being in the office because I was able to work directly with the kids. That's what our work is all about: providing the education, love to help them get their acts together, quit playing the victim, quit being victimized.

My questions during my interview with Sister Anne focused, at one point, on how VGAHS became a "caring community," since some students used these words in conversations at lunch or in the hallways. Her response suggested that VGAHS is a community at least partly because the teachers and staff want to be there:

> Tom: How would you categorize VG? Is it really a community? Is this really a caring community? In informal talks with some of the students, like in the hallways, they always say this is a place where they feel cared for. What makes it a caring community?
>
> Sister Anne: The people, the staff, the teachers, those who teach you are here because they want to be here. They're not here because they couldn't go somewhere else and make more money. Almost to a person, every one could do that if they chose to.

I continued the interview by asking Sister Anne about the deliberate efforts at VGAHS to developing a sense of community among the staff and the students. She explained that the Wednesday afternoon activities of sports, board games and cards, the birthday celebrations and the staff retreat all represent efforts to achieve and maintain a community:

> Tom: Are there deliberate efforts to make a community?
>
> Sister Anne: We do that. That's our Wednesday afternoon activity in the language you use to make community. We call it fellowship, because, I think I might have started it.
>
> Tom: Are there birthday celebrations?
>
> Sister Anne: Oh yes.
>
> Tom: I noticed on the calendar it says "staff retreat day." Is that an in-service day?
>
> Sister Anne: It's a get together day and sometimes we try to do some staff developmental kinds of things. We try to do some consciousness raising things among ourselves about whatever we think might be what we want to do that year. Not long range, not planned from any data that's been gathered or anything like that. But at a staff meeting, we say maybe, "What shall we do for the staff?" We have a meal together. Some time during the day we sit down and maybe spend an hour and a half in some serious discussion about some topic that we think is appropriate.

While I was focusing my conversation with Brother Steven on the history of VGAHS, he agreed that developing a community spirit with and among the students had always been a deliberate objective. He indicated that the number of students attending VGAHS at any one time would be small. The Downtown Campus, the original site of VGAHS, consists of two buildings, both former residences: one the former rectory for the priests of St. Adalbert's Parish and the other the former convent for the nuns who taught in the parish elementary school. VGAHS began here with a staff of three, a few students and $20,000, but the buildings lend themselves to the development of a community spirit. For example, classrooms were former bedrooms, living rooms, parlors and offices. Moreover, the concern for the students as persons who needed another chance at schooling built the community spirit of VGAHS. Brother Steven's own concern had originally focused on pre-high school students, but realizing that his and Brother Harold's experience lay with high schools, they shifted their focus to an alternative school to help young adults complete high school. This concern continues at VGAHS:

> I thought that would be really neat, to work with kids before they get buried under the system. But what's basically behind my thinking and the kernel of the idea was Marva Collins at West Side of Chicago. I was also concerned for kids who were buried before they even got into high school. They were trying to catch up, but they were so deep in the hole that catching up would have been virtually impossible. . . . So I wrote to the Bishop and told him that we were interested in opening this thing here and got documentation from our chapter, so he knew it was legit, and mentioned this building. I said, "And you know the former St. Adalbert Rectory, I think, would be a pretty neat place for what we're talking about." We're talking about eighteen kids and three staff members. You know, maybe we could work out something with the Diocese by way of rent and all that sort of thing. So eventually it all worked out. And we moved on in and opened up shop in '80. We will just do this with sixteen- to twenty-five-year-old students and see where it goes.

Brother Steven continued the conversation by explaining how the first students arrived at the school and how the early efforts had quickly become successful, with students earning high school diplomas. The acceptance by the community and those who came to VGAHS helped sustain the alternative school and Brother Steven's own role during his thirteen years at VGAHS:

> So, we got down here in August, had a couple meetings, got some fliers scattered around downtown, a couple of kids showed up. Nobody knew anything that was all going to go on, except that we were going to start this school. From there we went on and graduated one girl the first year. She was already within one year of graduating. The next year one more graduated. So, two years, two graduates. A great start, thank God. A lot of the success is in acceptance and we were accepted quickly by the students and the

> people in the neighborhood. I am probably more at ease here because I personally have also been accepted by the students and the people in the neighborhood.

Each of the three administrators understands that the VGAHS community experience has always been at the heart of its identity as an alternative school. They defined this community spirit in terms of the relationships between themselves, the other staff members, and the students. The size of the student body and the specific activities that take place promote the goal of developing a community atmosphere characterized by mutual concern among the students, teachers and administrators.

A Sense of Hope and Change at VGAHS

The administrators all expressed a sense of change and hope for VGAHS as an institution that must keep changing to fulfill an ongoing vision for itself as an alternative school. They also perceived VGAHS as an instrument for helping the students cope with change in their own lives and with instilling some realistic hope for a difference in those lives.

George Reynolds saw the hope and change for VGAHS as becoming part of the efforts of the larger community by collaborating with other agencies and institutions concerned for the people:

> I would like to see much more community interaction with the various agencies—for example with the day cares, Head Start, other literacy programs. There's not a whole lot of duplication of services but there is still some, and again, people are very territorial about their own program. I would like to see VG hook up, get a consortium or a coalition with the various agencies, where we start working and pooling our resources. Once, again, in numbers there's strength.

Reynolds articulated some of his hopes for VGAHS as an educational institution. These hopes might even involve a few changes at the school. In fact, he raised some questions with regard to how VGAHS responds to the needs of the community and the students. He felt that even the attitudes and assumptions of the teachers about who the students are and what their abilities are might require a change:

> I think we need to re-evaluate what we're doing in education. Again looking at the needs as the community changes, what are the present needs? What are the students' needs? I think, that to a large extent, since the staff is primarily white, we tend to victimize the students or look at that aspect. I think we make assumptions that aren't probably fair or totally accurate. I think, one of the assumptions we make unconsciously because of the fact we are dealing with dropouts is that they're not going to be astrophysicists. They're not going to be doctors or lawyers. Let's get them at least minimum skills so they can at least be self-sufficient so that they can hold some menial job. I don't think that's fair to the students because somebody has already put them in a category and said, "This is what you can do." All of a sudden you start tailoring your education toward that act.

One of his hopes is to see his school strengthen some academic programs in order to prepare some students for colleges or universities:

> I would like to see the school take on a stronger academic thrust rather than more of the job training vocational thrusts we have. Or at least have the two components working together. Again, not all the students are going to be one or the other. There may be some who prefer vocational work. Well, we can have a curriculum designed to get them into vocational training schools. But for those who want to pursue college, I think we need an academic program. That would provide them with the foundation that they could enter a four-year institution, if they wanted to.

He also mentioned that one of the ongoing concerns of VGAHS is the social needs of the students, especially in view of the fact that most of the young women students are single mothers:

> We are social workers too. In a sense that when you have 80, 90 percent of your female population as single teen mothers, things like day care, transportation and children's health, doctors' appointments, on down the line—those are very important concerns. Equally important, I think the health of their child is just as important as their getting an education, and to have something set up where you can accommodate both.

Concerning how VGAHS might effect change in the lives of the students, Sister Anne told the story of one student and expressed the hope that many similar changes take place in the lives of other students. Sister Anne felt that VGAHS provides the atmosphere for the students to change and gain some hope for themselves and their lives. She herself hopes that what happens at VGAHS might have a ripple effect on changing what happens in East St. Louis:

> We had a little girl come here. She has since dropped out. She lived right over there. I went once to her house—unbelievable, destitute. You could see by the way that she dressed when she came to school that she didn't have access to keeping her clothes clean. She would often be absent. There didn't seem to be any reason. She managed to continue and stay a quarter, came back the next quarter, and she would drop out or miss too many days. The next quarter would come and she'd want to be on the waiting list. She would come back. She began to talk. I got to know her and Ms. Frances took a little interest in her clothing. She loved to sew in Ms. Frances' class, and she began to make some clothes for herself and would wear them. Eventually she tried again to come. Eventually she became pregnant and had a baby causing her to drop out. We believe that the time she spent here was good and that she benefited from it. I say "we believe" because she knows that we care for her. She came to care for us somewhat. Maybe, that's just a little dabble, and who knows where the ripple goes and who knows what it has to do with sociological circumstances, racial tensions, East St. Louis, that whole business. Maybe it's just a tiny little bit, but we believe we were able to provide that little bit for her. And there are others. There are other stories pretty similar. That's what we believe. That's what we think we see. We provide an atmosphere in which they may change.

Brother Steven discussed some of his successful experiences with VGAHS students. One of his concerns is that he and VGAHS help the students succeed or make changes in their lives. Brother Steven described some of his struggles with the issue of where and how he might do the most good for his students:

> My feeling is that our reputation is okay. Here you get somebody that has gone nowhere. You hope that they are going somewhere.

> Not very far, but at least they are going somewhere. They had to stop and actually do an about-face and come back around. It is a very small number of students. Here I might teach twelve kids a day and turn around five. So the question is, "Where am I really doing the most good?" I happen to prefer to work with five and thirteen.

Brother Steven also noted that academic successes do not happen with every student, yet he firmly believes that what does happen at VGAHS is worth it for those students who undergo a change in their lives and gain a sense of hope. He described what the experiences at VGAHS are like during most quarters of the school year:

> I might see someone turn around, even though it is frustrating, because a lot of them don't turn around. Out of twenty-five kids that start here in a quarter, eighteen of them will maybe finish the quarter. Seven of them won't even finish. Of those seven, probably three or four will ask to come back and of those three or four most of them will also drop out a second time. Then each quarter there are a few Jody's who come in, you know, who were temporarily at least sidetracked. Maybe not a dead end but certainly going nowhere at the time. And all of a sudden it's like a whole new breath of life pops in. Some new ones come in. Willie was here three days and we haven't seen him since. He may come back again and he may not. Whatever we are doing was not what he was looking for, what he needed. Or maybe it had nothing to do with us at all. Maybe something else is in his life. You get a couple of other kids who go through. I don't consider what we are doing here wasted. It is just what is your philosophy? Is it helping a number or helping impact? Which is more important? I think in most of our schools the numbers game is more important than the turnaround.

George Reynolds' discussion of hope and change focused primarily on VGAHS as an institution and its need to develop other programs and services for its students and to cooperate more with other agencies in East St. Louis. Both Sister Anne and Brother Steven described their impressions of how VGAHS helps the students experience changes in their lives. They both believe that VGAHS helps its students develop a sense of hope and an inclination to think about new possibilities for themselves.

Changes in the Worlds of the Administrators

The three VGAHS administrators reported a sense of doing something worthwhile at VGAHS, which has an impact both on the students' lives and on those who live in East St. Louis. During our interviews, all three also reported changes in their lives and they explained how their own reflections and experiences moved them from a critical stance to a position of possibility and praxis. After reflecting on what should change in their lives, they tried to practice the solutions they had proposed to themselves. The history of VGAHS, as described by the administrators, also demonstrates this movement from a position of being critical to a position of possibility, a process of ongoing reflection on what is and what can be for the school. The decision to expand onto another campus and then the decision to merge back into one campus also demonstrate this movement from criticism to praxis: struggling to examine one's world, proposing solutions to improve it, and implementing these proposed solutions.

George Reynolds' world has experienced some changes as the result of his work at VGAHS. For one thing, his friends have reservations about that work. The fact that he has lived and continues to work in East St. Louis has lessened some of their prejudice, particularly in their becoming sensitive to his involvement with the African American community:

> Right now they just don't want to offend me, at least in my presence. I am sure when they're back in the locker room or wherever I'm not around, that it's business and conversations as usual. Otherwise, it's the small stuff. I think it's interesting at least through my work I have been able to affect people outside of ESL within my circle of friends, opened some eyes and hopefully made them a little more tolerant, reasonable people.

The theme of change in his own life and in the history of VGAHS recurred throughout my interview with Reynolds. He experienced a career change from chemist to teacher to chief administrator. As we have seen, his own hopes for VGAHS include changes both at the school and within the larger community. Another example appeared while he discussed the history of VGAHS and the change he has experienced as a part of this history, including the reasons some students choose to drop out of schooling:

> Well, we are starting our thirteenth year and the school has changed considerably since the day it opened. I think that's the problem with the inner city public schools. As society changed, they didn't. We have that flexibility in that adaptation, adaptability to change as the city changed. Even the city has changed since I have been here. For example, the students' reasons for dropping out of school have greatly changed. Before they were expelled or simply quit as dropouts, whereas today, you know, fear is cited more often than not as the reason.

George Reynolds went on to express the need for VGAHS to change continually in response to what the changes in society impose upon the students. He also acknowledged that some people are afraid to change and become comfortable with the status quo:

> I think the big thing, since we are an educational institution, is we really need to look at the education we're providing and that's what needs to change. It has changed, over the years, that we have to educate to the students—what will best help them move on in their lives. Because again, the climate changes. The needs change and the school is constantly changing and evolving. It's a dynamic program. There's always a tendency where people become comfortable and that, despite the fact that our whole claim to fame was our adaptability and our willingness to change. Because we've been here for so long, we're suddenly becoming established as traditional. It can be very hard to effect change within the school. Some people are just not ready for it.

Sister Anne told me how being at VGAHS has affected her life since she came to VGAHS for a job interview and to be part of her religious community in East St. Louis. She realized that working with the students has had a profound effect on how she now understands her world:

> I felt as though I was—and still do—feel as though I am, how should I say it, benefiting from being here in some deep psychological developmental and spiritual way from our clients. It seems as though that's the way it ought to be. Perhaps it should be

> reciprocal and perhaps it is, but for me the important thing is that I have learned and enveloped myself literally by being with these children. I call them "children." I think it is a habit. I know they are not children, but to me they're kinda like, I think of them as my children. I do benefit a great deal from being among them. I suppose I might say, they serve me every bit as much as I serve them. That's how I got here. That's why I am here.

Being at VGAHS also provides Sister Anne with a meaningful job and an active life in her later years. This life is a profound change after many years as principal, counselor and teacher in several large Catholic high schools:

> There's some superficial advantage for me, I think. Also that was not planned. I'm very conscious of it now and I'm realizing that it seems right to take advantage of it. I want to be active as long as I can. I hope I can be active in a little institution like VG in a much more effective way and more integrally to the system than I could be in a larger institution than this. In a great big high school, perhaps, I could be the record keeper or that kind of thing. But to be in the classroom, the way I am in the classroom with those children here—I wouldn't be able to do that for many more years, if I could do it now.

Brother Steven also told me how being at VGAHS has changed him. He focused on the experience of several religious congregations working together at VGAHS and the effects being at VGAHS might have on these congregations. He feels that the congregations' worlds have changed as the result of individual members becoming involved with the VGAHS students:

> My feeling is we're doing more for the religious than the religious is doing. I think the school must be doing more for the religious congregations represented here than the congregations are doing for here. If the congregations were mainly doing it for us and not getting more back, I don't know why God would be sending them here. Go down the line, any religious order that has worked here, I think, they've probably gotten a lot out of having somebody here.

More specifically in regard to the changes in himself, Brother Steven talked about his relationship to a culture different from his own:

> I really don't know and I question how much I have been enculturated. I don't think I have been enculturated that much. I think I am more alert to the culture and more sensitive to the culture but I don't think I really joined the culture. That's a weakness on my part to some extent. Though I must admit that there are so many problems with this culture that to join the culture and to buy into those problems strikes me as being crazy. Enculturation, not really. Contribution, I would say yes. I think I contributed a lot. Am I really into being one of the people? Should I be? If I do that then I couldn't do the other.

He has come to appreciate the "other" culture as good even though his dominant culture tends to construct the culture of the "other" as bad. The dominant culture both constructs and defines the culture of the "other" as bad and continually promulgates it as such. Brother Steven realized that he has altered his own understanding and definition of what is culturally good and has experienced the culture of the "other" as good in contradiction to what he formerly thought:

> I think right now that I am not afraid of the culture. I'm getting a little more appreciation of the amount of goodness that's there. It's very difficult. I think, we have our own ideas of what goodness is and that's stereotyped. It's too easy to say if it's different, it's not good. I'm getting better at realizing that there is other goodness besides what I conceive of as good. Some of the things I may be used to considering good really aren't all that good now that I have a different perspective. That's enlightening.

Each of the three administrators realize that their own lives have changed as the result of entering VGAHS and East St. Louis. Each has come to know these changes are also the effects of the students of VGAHS entering their worlds.

Catholic School Identity at VGAHS

Besides expressing the elements and themes of the liberation theology and critical pedagogy discourses, I found the Catholic school identity of VGAHS to be an issue for all three administrators. Until George

Reynolds became the chief administrator, VGAHS was on the official list of the Belleville diocese schools. Some of the teachers were distressed by his decision to withdraw from the list, but others were less concerned. In many informal conversations with the administrators and teachers, however, this issue—was VGAHS a Catholic school or not?—came up. Part of the issue involves the question of what makes a school Catholic. Even though VGAHS is not on the official list, it remains part of the Catholic Urban Ministries of East St. Louis and still receives funding and personnel support from several congregations of religious priests, brothers and sisters.

During my interviews with the administrators, I found their comments reflecting some of their own ambivalence about the identity of Catholic schools. Sister Anne stated emphatically that she does not work in a Catholic school in the way most people understand the expression "Catholic schools." She does believe, however, that VGAHS is concerned about the work of evangelization in terms of the Gospels and teachings of Jesus and that this concern just might be the main characteristic of Catholic schools.

> Tom: We have talked before about VG being a Catholic school or not. It seems like this identity varies with different people's perception of what a Catholic school is. How do you feel about it? Do you feel you work in a Catholic school, or would you say that you work in a Catholic environment?
>
> Sister Anne: I don't work in a Catholic school. That's to say that VG is a Catholic school is analogous to what I was just saying about working with the poor—who are the poor?—there is a generic poor. Catholic school in this country means something generic—big high schools with big buildings, faculties, athletics, etc.—like all those Catholic schools in any diocese, even those which I could name around here. Those are Catholic schools. When we say "Catholic school," we are not talking about us. We are small, we don't teach religion, we have almost all non-Catholics as students. In the other schools, you get a lot of Catholics. We are Catholic as I first talked about this with you: a Catholic school in the sense of teaching and helping others who need us. VG is not a Catholic school according to the way the Bishops want us to be. Was it in '73 that the Bishops wrote the great document which we talked about some time ago? We're not evangelizing, not in the

sense that I think the official church now talks about it.

Tom: But evangelizing in what sense then?

Sister Anne: Our evangelizing, I guess, is done unconsciously. If evangelizing is taken to mean emanating Gospel values and the teachings of Jesus—that is, if we want to take evangelization in that sense—then we are doing this. We are having some business here with integrity and sharing that with our clients and sharing what they give us. They are providing for us what we take from them and vice versa, in that big general sense of caring and sharing with each other. Our students grow in a sense, they not only grow academically but they also grow hoping that they or someone will change the situation they are now in. I'd like to believe this is true. I have no access to any standard to measure that point. We provide an atmosphere in which they may change.

George Reynolds acknowledged his own confusion about the identity of VGAHS as a Catholic school and why he decided to remove VGAHS from the Diocesan Directory. He said that the motivation for this decision was to achieve some clarity about the financial support of the school since one of his key roles as chief administrator is to seek money to support the school. He recalled how VGAHS had been identified for many years as a Marianist institution, since the initial funding and most of the personnel came from the Marianists. In time, however, the situation changed, with religious from other congregations joining the faculty and offering financial support. He indicated that the Diocese had not been contributing a lot of money directly to VGAHS but it was allowing VGAHS to use its buildings and properties. His remarks, as I said, reflect confusion over what makes a school Catholic. Does the source of financial support and personnel make a school Catholic, or is it the good works of teaching and helping others to grow and develop? Here are Reynolds' observations:

I'm a salesman half of the time, actually trying to raise money. We have no regular source of income. We're a free school. We have no source of income. We've got to beg for money. That's an unpleasant job. Most of the time, it's difficult. I think that another main concern is to identify and talk about the evolution of the identify of VG. Obviously in the beginning, it had a very strong identity as a Marianist work. However, we just have to have other people around. My own initial involvement here is because of my relationship with the Marianists. There are some individuals who still see VG as a Marianist Institution. However, we just happen to have a few Daughters of Charity and other religious around so is this still a Marianist work?

There are people who feel very strongly that this school is Catholic and it should be identified that way, while there are those who have other feelings about that it is not a Catholic school. . . . I think on the part of many that there is a bit of identity crisis at the school. Even among the staff, there are different views, radically different views as to what VG High School is or represents. Some of our history, how we were started indicates that VG wasn't just the Marianist Brothers, but also a Notre Dame nun. Now these three are actually referred to as the three co-founders, even by the two Marianists founders. They were provided with $20,000 seed money from St. Louis Province of the Marianists to start the school. However, VG was incorporated as simply a charitable and educational institution. This is where the identity crisis comes in that there's been such a strong Marianist involvement and presence physically, financially, and spiritually at the school but VG has never come out and said, "This is a Marianist Institution." It's like we support it to the hilt; however, we are not claiming it as a Marianist School.

I don't know why in the beginning it was set up that way, I have no idea. We use Diocesan property and buildings. But a very close relationship was set up with the Marianists and the diocese. It even reached the point—again, part of the confusion, even in a number of the Marianist newsletters and other literature—VG was implicitly and explicitly considered a Marianist Institution. At the same time we find ourselves listed in the Belleville Diocesan Directory as a Diocesan High School. These problems, when I assumed the position of executive director, going through the files and seeing this, I was confused as to just what we were. Of course, in becoming executive director, my primary concern was getting money for the school to keep the programs running. My first question was, "If we are a Marianist School, maybe we can garner a little more money from them. Or if we are going to be a Diocesan School, then perhaps we can garner more support from them."

> For example, the salaries have just been so substandard here compared to other Diocesan and Marianist schools. If we're going to be listed in directories and called a Diocesan School, I felt it only fair that our teachers receive Diocesan wages and benefits —like the Diocesan insurance. They get Diocesan retirement plans and, of course, suddenly you attach a dollar value to things. That changes things. We had a series of meetings. We had the Assistant Provincial. We met with the Vicar General of the Diocese and a number of the religious on staff who wished to participate in the meetings. We went through all of this, and looking at our articles of incorporation and charters and the bylaws I said, "I don't care what we are. My main concern is these kids. Providing education and helping them. It doesn't matter if we are private, public, Catholic, Jewish, whatever."
>
> This is what we need to do but let's define ourselves, and the consensus was "No, you are not a religious institution." In other words, I interpreted that as a sign that "We're not going to take you under our wing and provide 100% financial support." If that was not going to happen, since we do not have a regular source of income, and that when you are trying to solicit from those who have the money, particularly the corporations and foundations, you find that many of them do not like to donate to any religious institution. They don't want to get involved in supporting one religion or another. That would really tie my hands. If we were going to be a religious institution, but we were not going to be supported by the religious, it made it very difficult to solicit money. That's all I wanted—clarification. We have to go one way or another. We can't sit on the fence and I think that was what was happening in the past. We played both sides. For those who were interested in supporting religious institutions, we were a religious institution. For those who would not support religious institutions, we were not a religious institution. I couldn't play both sides of the fence. I wanted a well-defined one thing or another. I've got to know what we are so when we are getting money, this is it.

George Reynolds also expressed some concern over whether a Catholic school should offer religious instruction if the majority of the students are non-Catholic. Here, the issue of what it means to be a Catholic school gets raised in a different way. Reynolds does feel, however, that religious aspects are present at VGAHS, even if VGAHS is not legally defined as a religious institution:

> We're still in that process of identifying who we are. At least it has been set legally that we are legally not religiously affiliated. However, when you look at the institution, it's obvious that there is a very religious component here. I think, I'm not sure which is best. What makes it difficult for this to become a religious institution particularly a Catholic institution is that our student body is not Catholic. So the implications of if we were going to go ahead on our legal status and become a Catholic religious institution, we would be required to provide religious instruction, because that would be part of our mission as a Catholic institution. Yet, we're dealing with a non-Catholic student population. If we were in a Catholic area, that wouldn't be a problem. But I think the problem gets into that if once you define yourself as a Catholic institution then we are in the business of promoting Catholicism. I'm not sure that that would totally change the nature of the school. I'm not sure if this would have a direct effect on the student population. I am not sure how, but I think it would.

As one of the founders of VGAHS, Brother Steven believes he has always perceived VG not as a Marianist institution but as an institution with a Marianist spirit:

> I think VG has a Marianist spirit, but I don't consider it is a Marianist institution. I never did. One reason we chose not to have it as a Marianist institution is Harold and I figured, if we want to get out of here, we want to get out of here. We tell the Bishop, come May we're leaving. I could see us calling him up in February and saying, " Come May we are going to be leaving. We are not accomplishing what we thought we would accomplish and the buildings will go back to you. And we hope we are leaving it as good as it was when we got it." We felt that as religious we should be able to come in, but we also should be able to get out. That was a big part of the reason we are doing what we are doing. Our feeling was our main goal was to get VG started. At some point if we can get a lay group together to take it and run with it, fine. At that point, we are out of here. We'll go do something someplace else. As it turns out, I am sitting here. We're here and doing good work.

Brother Steven also recalled how other religious from other congregations came to VGAHS and how this was a blessing to both VGAHS and the religious congregations to which they belonged. More religious teach at VGAHS than at many other Catholic schools, however, the number of religious priests, brothers and sisters at a school do not necessarily make it Catholic. But, one might expect their presence to affect the spiritual lives of the students. The difference at VGAHS is clear to Brother Steven:

> We've been fortunate and unfortunate in having so many religious come. The financial argument says you will win. So if we can have skilled teachers with lots of experience and very idealistic and dedicated and pay them half the price or less, it's like we would be fools to say no. My feeling is what that really means is we're doing more for the religious than the religious is doing for us. When I say we, not the school not the Marianists, maybe the Marianists, too. But I think the school must be doing more for the religious congregations represented here than the congregations are doing for here. If the congregations were mainly doing it for us and not getting more back, I don't know why God would be sending them here. That's the only reason, I can figure why the good Lord keeps sending us new orders, new religious. It has been undoubtedly part of the reason we were able to expand. These congregations have to be getting something, because God knows that the Catholic church is not dumb. We may be a lot of things, but we are not dumb. They would not be having religious coming over here if they didn't feel they were getting something out of it. They certainly wouldn't have them come and pay their way. That's basically what happens.

Concerning the Catholic identity of VGAHS, Brother Steven concluded that VGAHS has more of the Catholic spirit than most other Catholic institutions. His remarks, however, focused on the practice of prayer and the religion classes as those elements that make a school Catholic. His comments raised again another issue of the identity of Catholic schools—the promulgation of Catholicism as an earthly institution or as a spirit of the Gospel:

> Here at VG, there is definitely a sense of community, Gospel values, maybe in one sense it's more Catholic than a Catholic

institution. Certainly, we're not institutionally Catholic. Oh no. Did I describe us as a Catholic school? Spirit-wise certainly, no doubt about it. Formally, not much. A little prayer at Thanksgiving dinner, the Christmas party. There are some times when teachers pray in their classes and I admire them for that. The kids are very respectful of that. If we do say a Lord's Prayer somewhere, most of them will join in. A couple might be giggling, but for the most part they go along with it. I was even tempted to ask whether anybody would be interested in a course on the Catholic Church. All we would do is talk about this is what the Catholic Church believes. This is what it is like, maybe go to a church service or two. I have never really done this and I don't know if it would fly or not, but it might. I could picture where four or five of our kids would say, " Hey, yeah, that's not too bad." There is no way that anybody could consider us institutional Catholic.

Now, if we are talking Catholic spirit, ecumenical spirit, yeah, there's no doubt about that, but those are much harder to define. Do we do anything specific of a religious nature? A lot depends on where the students are and the spirit of the staff. We had courses on world religion. I have taught courses in Scripture, very Catholic oriented. But I would also say, "This is where the Catholic Church stands on this. I know that from experience. This is where the other religions, the Protestants, stand on the kind of interpretation of the Bible. In your churches, this is probably what you would hear." Most of our kids probably don't go to church. Some do. In fact, probably more go to church than I would normally think. Some of them that I would never picture as going to church actually do. Virtually none of the students are Catholic. The Catholic mentality with all the symbolism and ritual, they just don't understand that. I keep waiting for a couple of kids to say, "Hey, why don't you invite me to your church sometime?"

Thus, the three administrators of VGAHS struggle with the issue of the identity of VGAHS as a Catholic school. Each of them expressed concerns that are part of the larger dialogue on the identity of Catholic schools. The issues that cause ambivalence about the Catholic school identity of VGAHS are similar to issues in other Catholic schools—for example, the number of religious sisters, brothers and priests teaching at a school; the ownership and financial support of the school and the religion classes and practices at a school.

Thus, even without an awareness of the critical discourses of liberation theology and critical pedagogy, the three administrators speak from their own perspectives on how the common elements of the integrative model of liberation theology and critical pedagogy operates in the lives of VGAHS students. They also understand VGAHS as a community, an alternative school, and a Catholic school that makes a difference in the worlds of their students. Their voices revealed lives that have changed as well as changes in their school. One can detect the elements of the integrative model of liberation theology and critical pedagogy as the administrators described their own world and proposed solutions for renewing this world. They reveal why they deliberately choose to live with a commitment and concern for the poor and the oppressed and to struggle toward developing a more humane community. Likewise, one can see hope in the interviews as they experience being members of the VGAHS community. One can also see how these elements of the liberation theology and critical pedagogy discourses are part of the larger dialogue about what makes a school Catholic. Can we not conclude that these common elements also underlie the evangelization that precedes a commitment to change in one's life and in the lives of other community members, and especially the poor and marginalized?

CHAPTER EIGHT

The Voices of the Teachers

> It is often through the mediation of teacher voice that the very nature of the schooling process is either sustained or challenged. The power of teacher voice to shape schooling according to the logic of emancipatory interests is inextricably related not only to a high degree of self-understanding, but also to the possibility for teachers to join together in a collective voice as part of a social movement dedicated to restructuring the ideological and material conditions both within and outside of schooling. Thus, we must understand the concept of teacher voice in terms of its own values, as well as in relation to the ways it functions to shape and mediate school and student voices.
>
> - Peter McLaren in *Life in Schools: An Introduction to Critical Pedagogy in the Foundations of Education* (1994, p. 228)

Most of my contact with the VGAHS teachers took place as I observed their classrooms. But I also observed them at their weekly faculty meetings, during lunch, while interacting with students individually and in groups, and over the three days of meetings I facilitated for them with a view toward reaching a consensus statement about which campus should remain open. I observed every teacher several times and formally interviewed all of them. Our interviews usually took place during a time when they had no class or before the school day, since some of them remained deeply involved with the students throughout the school day. In short, I had many informal conversations with each teacher during my time at VGAHS.

The teachers at VGAHS are white except for two. These two are African American women. One conducts the literacy program, and the other, a counselor from a social agency, helps teach the parenting class. But the literacy program operates to some degree independently of the high school routine and operation, even though this teacher participates in the faculty meetings.

I chose six teachers to represent the voices of the others. Of these six teachers, Brother Luke is the only one who lives in East St. Louis —at the local Marianist community, which occupies the former convent of St. Patrick's parish, adjacent to the VGAHS St. Patrick's Campus.

I began our interviews by asking the teachers about their histories of education involvement and how they had come to VGAHS. Each one offered comments and impressions about life in East St. Louis and about how these impressions have changed over the time they have worked there. They described how others, including friends and family members and fellow religious, react to them working in East St. Louis.

I coded the transcripts of the interviews with the teachers three months after coding those of the students and administrators. As with the students and administrators, I followed the integrative model of liberation theology and critical pedagogy in an etic and emic manner, identifying the same common elements of the discourses of liberation theology and critical pedagogy in the voices of the teachers. Thus, this chapter focuses on how the teachers articulated some of the elements of the integrative model as they took part in the unstructured interviews about the worlds of the students and their own.

I present the voices of the teachers as they describe (1) their perceptions of the world of the students, (2) their commitment to work with the poor and the oppressed, (3) the experience of community at VGAHS, (4) how VGAHS helps students make changes in their worlds and (5) how they have experienced change in their own worlds. Every one of these six teachers addressed each of these five aspects of the integrative model. To avoid over-saturation, however, I have included interviews of the three teachers most representative of the general perspectives exhibited by the others and to maintain a balance between religious and lay teachers.

The Teachers' Perceptions of the World of the Students

The teachers' perceptions of the students' world closely resembles how the students perceive their own world in East St. Louis, in a desolate environment that makes its own demands upon them as they face their own problems. The voices of the teachers, like those of the students, express a critical discourse in action as they describe the current student world and its problems, acknowledging that something is wrong in their world yet acknowledging that the students want to improve their world and make it more humane, just and equitable.

Sister Angela, a School Sister of Notre Dame, has been at VGAHS since 1982 and she was involved with VGAHS for the two summers before her arrival as a teacher. During the first summer, she taught in the summer school program and she spent the other summer helping with a variety of jobs like cleaning and cutting grass. She currently teaches three classes of Human Body and spends the other part of her day at a Women's Crisis Center in St. Louis, helping women prepare for the GED. Sister Angela described her perceptions of the world of the students and the many challenges this world presents to her school's goal of helping its students:

> I think that there's such a tremendous range of what can be done for the poor here. I see so many more things that can be done, so many. Like one thing I suggested on that evaluation sheet that I handed to Brother Steven this morning. We really need an outreach person. By that I simply mean, I think we could definitely use a person who would be able to go into the homes to help, to see what conditions there are. I more and more think we need somebody to be kind of a person called probation officer to our students. Many times you run into students who feel that they need clothing or food for a week. You probably saw that clothing room, which if I had more room, could be expanded. I saw students who needed glasses. Because of the Marianists we are able to provide glasses for our students.

Sister Angela further described how her perceptions of the world of the students influence the way she teaches her Human Body course. She focused on the home lives and eating habits of some of the students:

> I have to think more and more as I teach biology and science. I give them nutrition, everything from early childhood. Many of these students have not experienced a family life. Most of them come from a single-parent family. Some of them don't even know who their fathers are. You have the mother struggling to keep the family together. That means a mother can't always be at home with the children. The children are with a babysitter or some day

> care. The nutrition is generally poor insofar as when I'm going to be talking about the digestive system and along with talking about the digestive system we talk about food. You'll find out when I mention different vegetables, some of them haven't even heard of the vegetables. That is not a priority with them at all. Fresh fruit, I think, is nonexistent for many of them. They can't afford it.

She reported that she is continually overwhelmed by the living situations of some of the students and she wondered if she would have the stamina to live in the same kind of world. She was moved by what they do experience and how they continue to come to VGAHS with the hope of making a difference in their own lives:

> Generally speaking I think our students here are good and they're really trying. If I had to experience what they experience, I could not go to bed at night and feel safe and secure. And I've already heard the stories of some of them living with crack in their homes. It's something I've never experienced. Some of them don't feel safe in their homes and live in constant fear. One thinks about all they have to do. It's real thought provoking. I often think, "What would I do if I were them?"

Timothy O'Fallon is a young man who had taught at VGAHS for one year as part of a Jesuit Volunteer Program. He had worked as an admissions counselor and college representative for a college in upstate New York before coming to VGAHS. This is his first experience as a teacher. O'Fallon taught Human Body and English and coordinated the physical activities for Wednesday afternoons. As a newcomer to both East St. Louis and teaching, O'Fallon noted how his own expectations differed from his actual VGAHS experiences:

> I was expecting a lot worse and I was expecting people with a lot of anger. But because of the circumstances in which they live, their lives aren't great. There's a lot about their lives that is not good; it's not easy but they still come. Some of them still come every day and still do the work and are interested for some reason in being here. You know we're a voluntary program. You know whether they want to be or someone else wants them to be, they're here and they're learning as opposed to standing on the street.

I continued our conversation by asking O'Fallon to share some of his impressions of the students of VGAHS, individually and collectively:

> Individually, it varies a lot, there are some very mature students here, there are some immature students here, there are some students who are truly adults because they've had to be, they've grown fast. And there are some students who have children and responsibility but are still very immature. They're still only sixteen and seventeen years old. And they still should be somewhat immature, sixteen-seventeen-year-olds who should be enjoying what their peers enjoy across the country. They can be a little bit immature, but it's funny that they still have somewhat of an adult life in a sense, with a child, having to pay bills and things like that. It's a big chore. Collectively, again, I think, there's a reason for most of them being here so on the whole, they do try to do their work and they do try to be responsible students to the extent that they can be. But they're not used to doing a lot of work from public schools or wherever they came from. So it's hard for them to get back in the swing of things and they don't think much is expected of them. I find if you have patience, if you clearly define what is expected of them, even if the expectations are high, they'll come in and say "Oh, we can't do that." But they do, they do it.

Judy Frances has spent her life as a teacher and was in her fourth year at VGAHS. Before, she spent eight years teaching at Assumption High, the Catholic high school in East St. Louis, which closed several years ago. Before that, she had taught for many years in the St. Louis public schools. During our interview, she expressed her frustration as a teacher in the public schools, and how she had been rejuvenated by teaching at Assumption. Our conversation then turned to her experiences at VGAHS in contrast to her experiences at Assumption:

> Tom: And yet you sense a difference between the students at Assumption and the students here. So in one sense do you feel more effective as a teacher here?
>
> Ms. Frances: It's just a different kind of structure. I felt we were very effective at Assumption. We just had a lot more battles to

> overcome. Partly because of numbers. You can certainly do a much better job with twelve in a history class than you can with thirty-seven, especially when thirty of them don't want to be there.

Our conversation then focused on VGAHS. Ms. Frances focused her responses on its students, noting that she often has hopes for her students earning their high school diploma and experiencing some changes in their lives. She also has those days when she wonders if there is any hope of making a difference in their lives:

> Tom: What's VG like? Or how do you react when people say that's an alternative school, that's not a real school?
>
> Ms. Frances [after a long pause]: I don't get that, I get more of "Oh that's for dropouts. Well what kind of kids are they?" I get a lot more of that. "What kind of kids?" rather than "What kind of school?"
>
> Tom: How do you answer?
>
> Ms. Frances: Well, they're just kids who have had some problems and are coming back to school. A lot of them are on probation. A lot of them dropped out because of pregnancy and wanted to get their education. And very often they say, "Are there many Blacks?" [Chuckle.] Yeah, there are Blacks.
>
> Tom: Do they ever say, "Well that's the way those people are?" Or does it reinforce some peoples' beliefs about Blacks?
>
> Ms. Frances: I think so. I get some of that. I have an aunt who is a very dedicated Catholic and she gives us money from time to time so when I go to visit, she usually is pretty interested in the school and one of her big questions is, "Do you ever think there will be progress? Do you ever think there's really hope for them?" Because she only knows, of course, what she reads in newspapers, and I think she gets discouraged.
>
> Tom: And you think there is hope?
>
> Ms. Frances: Some days.

Tom: And other days?

Ms. Frances: Other days, I wonder.

Sister Angela perceived the world of the students as characterized with a variety of needs, the result of poverty. She struggles to formulate ways she and VGAHS can continue to help her students in their living situations. Timothy O'Fallon described the world of the students similarly. He described his students as young but assuming adult responsibilities as they attempted to further their schooling in spite of adverse educational experiences before VGAHS. Judy Frances saw the world of the students as heavily influenced by race and living conditions in East St. Louis. All three teachers criticized the world of the students conducive to poverty and hostile to education. But each also expressed hope for their students. Thus, the teachers addressed the world of the students from a critical point of view as well as from a perspective of possibility for changing their world.

A Commitment to Work with the Poor and Oppressed

The discourses of liberation theology and critical pedagogy start with a concern for the poor and oppressed, a concern which evolves into a solidarity with the poor and oppressed. A deliberate commitment to work with the poor formed part of the motive for each teacher's work at VGAHS.

Sister Elaine, a vibrant and enthusiastic person, had been at VGAHS for six years after several years of teaching in rural and inner-city Catholic elementary schools. She had also been the principal of a Catholic elementary school. Sister Elaine and Brother Steven currently work at the Family Center at the former Downtown Campus of VGAHS. During our interview, she expressed a commitment to working with teenagers and with the poor:

> I am interested in working with older, not younger kids, but kids at the age that we have here, teenagers instead of a younger age group. I had been working in St. Louis, an area around the projects. I was interested in working with poor kids, because I felt they offered a lot. They have a lot of energy.

Sister Elaine went on to describe how her work at VGAHS reflects her desire to work with the poor and share her talents with others. She understands this motivation as part of her own commitment as a religious sister:

> Tom: Being with the poor is a conscious part of your motivation?
>
> Sister Elaine: Yes. I don't think at the beginning of my religious life it was, but I think my upbringing, my parents and my family background was very good. There's much love. I have had a lot given to me. I believe that God has given me certain talents that I need to share with individuals who are, maybe, not as blessed financially as I am, educationally as well. I'm really living my faith with what I do being here. My needs of sharing with others are satisfied here as a person, as a Catholic, as a religious.

Brother Luke is a native of East St. Louis and most of his family continues to live in the area. Besides teaching in high schools in Texas, Canada, Chicago and St. Louis, he had spent twenty-three years teaching English at Assumption High School. When it closed, he, like Judy Frances, came to VGAHS. He taught at VGAHS until his death in September of 1995. He understood his work at VGAHS as a continuation of his presence among and commitment to working with the African American community of East St. Louis, as well as being near his own family:

> The opportunity of staying in the city and going down to VG seemed a very enticing proposal. I came down and visited and liked the place, especially the small classes. So I knew right away that there wouldn't be any stress as an English teacher, having to carry a briefcase full of papers home every night, then stay up till three or four o'clock every morning, correcting papers as I had done for twenty-three years at Assumption. It seemed much easier, much more relaxed, less stressful. It seemed like a good deal to me, being in the city with the type of people we taught at Assumption, Blacks in particular. I felt very comfortable with them and being around them. Teaching at VG still gave me an opportunity to get involved with like wakes and weddings and things of that kind of former students or parents of students that I had taught ten years or more ago, whose families I knew quite well, children of students I had taught. So all of these things combined and, given a choice, made it rather appealing.

A willingness to work with young people was part of Brother Luke's motivation for teaching at VGAHS. During our interview, he noted that working with young people helps keep him feeling young:

> I have taught in Texas, Canada, Chicago and St. Louis. Kids are kids. I don't think there's too much basic difference between whether they're white or Black. That's one thing. Staying with kids helps me feel young. I think that I have something to offer not only to the school but constantly to the Church in the area as well.

After raising her family, Lois Day went to college to earn her bachelor's and master's degrees in education. The only place she has taught is VGAHS. She started in 1983, the fourth teacher and the first layperson on the staff. She was planning to retire at the end of the school year (1992-93), when the two campuses planned to merge. Ms. Day had come to VGAHS looking for a job. Even though none had been advertised, she wanted to be part of what VGAHS was attempting to do for young people in East St. Louis:

> I came right here. I started here in September 1983. The reason I came here is because at that time, I didn't want to take a job away from anyone, because I didn't need to work. But I wanted to work. I saw an article in *The Messenger* about the school and because my maiden name was Gray, it caught my eye. They didn't advertise for help. I just called up and told them my credentials. I pestered Brother Harold until he hired me. I figured that was a sign. I believe in signs: same name, seeing the article, graduating at the right time and all that stuff. I figured I was meant to come here.

I asked Ms. Day if part of this wanting to work at VGAHS included a concern for helping the poor. She replied that she had always had some interest in the African American community as she became more aware of their situation in our country and wanted to reduce racist attitudes and practices. She talked about the books she had read as well as becoming acutely aware of African Americans in society:

> Tom: Was any part of your motivation then or now helping, working with the poor?

> Ms. Day: Yes. My mother was always very liberal, I guess. She would tell us these stories about when she had worked for the railroad and had taken trips while she working, before she was married. I don't know why this story has always stuck in my head, but she had gone to Memphis and they sat, she and the girl she was with, in the back of the bus. The bus driver, she said she was very shy, was very embarrassed, came back and told her she couldn't sit back there. That was for the colored. She never did think that was fair. That's why she told us the story. The first time I saw a Black person driving a bus was after I was married in 1948 and I went to San Francisco. I was really amazed that I saw a Black bus driver. At that time there were no Blacks driving public buses. Blacks were not visible. I was very aware of all the problems in the '60s. I'm a reader. I read everything I can get my hands on. When all the trouble started with civil rights, I read all the autobiographies on all the Black people. Reading all those books made you really want to help them get ahead. That was one of the reasons.

Ms. Day expressed no fears about working in East St. Louis, and she has concluded that many white people base such fears on prejudice:

> Also I was not afraid to come down to ESL. Most people won't even come near the place, but I had to walk three or four blocks. I got off on Main Street and I had to walk over to Broadway. I would do that every morning for two years and nobody ever bothered me. I was familiar with the streets. I never had any fear coming down. A lot of people would never even come near the place.

Sister Elaine, Brother Luke and Lois Day acknowledged that part of their motivation and reason for being at VGAHS is to associate with the people of East St. Louis and help the young people there to improve their lives. Their commitment to the poor and oppressed takes the form of working with young African Americans in the depressed community of East St. Louis. The other teachers at VGAHS echoed this commitment.

An Experience of Community at VGAHS

The development of a community spirit among the teachers and students can promote the process of learning and change in students' lives. This community is one way the VGAHS teachers demonstrate their commitment to the poor and oppressed beyond being simply teachers. Timothy O'Fallon described the community atmosphere of VGAHS in terms of a safe environment where people care for each other. Recall that the students expressed this same impression, which encouraged them to accept responsibility for their own behavior and learning:

> Tom: What are your impressions of the overall dynamics of VG?
>
> O'Fallon: I think it's a real good environment for the students. The fact that it's small, and the fact that the way the school is set up and the rules of the school are supposed to make them take responsibility for their actions, make them take responsibility for lives as students here, I think that's real positive. In most schools the rules are set up, not so they'll take responsibility but so they expect punishment for their actions. I think pretty much the rules are set up here so they take responsibility. I think that it creates a safe, a fairly safe, structured environment in the middle of their somewhat chaotic lives. I think a lot of them enjoy coming to school here because it is a place where they can maybe be a little bit immature or maybe have a little fun with their friends or maybe do a little bit of work and not get busted on the corner. So I think it's a safe environment. I think people who are here care about students; you don't see a lack of caring by the teachers.

O'Fallon went on to describe his own struggles, as a newcomer to VGAHS and a beginning teacher, with his role as a member of this community:

> It's a tough balance and being a young person, being a first-time teacher, being unfamiliar with the material that I'm teaching and being unfamiliar with the culture, it's been difficult for me to strike a balance with all of that. In terms of classroom management, in terms of my personal relationship with students, I'm still working on that, trying to figure out where I am with all that.

As a native of East St. Louis, Brother Luke knows that the VGAHS students are in some ways typical of the people of this city, who he has always found to be frank and generous. These two characteristics contribute to the community spirit at VGAHS, to how students relate to each other, and to how teachers relate to the students:

> The students of ESL, the people are basically, there are several characteristics about them. One, they are very frank. They'll tell you exactly what's on their mind. Sometimes their language isn't more than just criticizing. That's the way it was. They tell you what they think. Secondly, they're extremely generous. Literally, they'll give you the shirt off their back. I think those two characteristics are still pretty outstanding for the people here.
>
> Tom: Do you find those characteristics exist in students here?
>
> Brother Luke: Very much so. You help kids. Particularly, the girls, they talk about anything and everybody and whether a teacher is present or whether males are present. It doesn't bother them at all. The groups of students here are small enough so that you almost have to be a family, fit in, and trust each other. In a family all things and topics come up and they give each other all kinds of advice. Here you even feel very comfortable doing that as a teacher.

Brother Luke further went on to describe how the structures and dynamics of VGAHS also foster the development of community as opposed to a more traditional school setting:

> Tom: How would you characterize VG as a school, say to Assumption or other places you taught?
>
> Brother Luke: Well, they both have different advantages. There are advantages I guess to the traditional school. The faculties, I think, are very similar. The students individually in small groups are very similar. You'll find many students who will work. Some of them are there to pass the time. Some of them are there because their parents want them to be there. Students at VG are quite a bit more independent. They're not relying so much on parental support, parental background. Because of their own situations, they're more independent. The reasons they left the traditional school are able to help them here. Whether it's large-size classes or teachers talking over their heads or not teaching but just trying to maintain

> order. The atmosphere here is more Christian than maybe in some Catholic schools. Definitely more Christian. You're more concerned about the individual. And here because the rooms are so small, the classes by necessity are small, you have to learn to live with each other, with the idiosyncrasies or habits or what not. If not, you'd go up the wall in a very short time. There's a lot of give on the part of the students and faculty.

The attitudes and dispositions of the teachers, wanting to help the students in whatever ways possible, also contribute to the community spirit. Brother Luke noted that the teachers work at VGAHS because they want to, not simply to have a job. They perceive their work as more than a job and VGAHS as a place to help and care for others:

> I think every teacher here is truly concerned about the welfare of each student here. That goes a long way with the extra time they're willing to put in with meetings and with tutoring or class work. I don't find the same true in many other high schools. Other high schools, you've got an eight-to-four job and that's it. You're assigned extracurricular supervision and things like that. Here, it's pretty much voluntary. You volunteer for things because you see a need, the things that bring the students and the faculty, I think, much closer.

Sister Angela echoed Brother Luke's sentiments with regard to the concern the teachers show for the students beyond simply teaching:

> Our teachers are interested first of all in the student and helping the student, and secondly in teaching subject matter. But more and more, I am convinced you need to try to build up the self-esteem of each individual and let them know that you're really interested in them.

She also contrasted her experiences at VGAHS with those as a teacher at another high school, and she noted that VGAHS is a community in the way that teachers and students interact and the way teachers show their concern:

> I would characterize VG as being very loving and accepting and understanding of the community of our students. I think teaching

> here at VG, we are more aware of the needs of the student because so much here at VG we're doing more than just teaching. At Rosary High School, we taught. Here we are more concerned primarily with what happens within the classroom, but definitely what happens outside the classroom.

All of the teachers reported that they considered a concern for the students an important part of being a teacher at VGAHS. They also acknowledged that this concern helps maintain a community spirit at their school. Timothy O'Fallon noted that this concern promotes a safe and caring environment for the students different from the one in which they spend much of their time outside of school. Both Brother Luke and Sister Angela noted that the teachers' concern for their students extends far beyond teaching content. They also contrasted their experiences as teachers at VGAHS with their former teaching experiences in Catholic high schools. They observed that the classroom sizes and atmosphere at VGAHS help them nurture this concern for the students. Thus, the teachers, like their students, experience a unique community at their alternative school.

VGAHS Helps Students Change Their Worlds

VGAHS exists to help young people complete their high school education, but it also helps them in other ways. It helps them change their world. These changes, of course, vary with the individual situations and histories of the students, but the experience of change in one's world and one's self-perception is an important element of the discourses of liberation theology and critical pedagogy. This change results when one moves from a position of critique to a position of possibility as the consequence of gaining hope.

Sister Elaine believes she sees a sense of hope in East St. Louis despite the city's image. She experiences this hope with her students as they effect changes in their worlds:

> From working here for the last six, seven years, there's something here that's hopeful. There's something here that's good. People, the kids, the ones who want to do something are the good part of it. My reaction to ESL is in no way as fearful or as negative as what other people see. You mention ESL anywhere and people go fifteen miles out of their way to go around the city instead of going through it. Bad things happen. There's lots of drugs, lots of

> violence and we have to be worried about it. We have to know that it is not a safe place all the time. We can't take chances that we could take at other places.

Sister Elaine described how she conducts herself in East St. Louis, using common sense about what she does and where she goes, but always with respect for the students and people of the city. She believes that this respect for the people helps them feel differently about their own world. I asked Sister Elaine to address specifically how VGAHS might help students change their worlds. VGAHS may not, she said, cause big changes, but it does have an effect on the students and how they perceive themselves and their worlds:

> Tom: Do you think the student experiences here help transform them and their vision?
>
> Sister Elaine: I've learned in working with the poor, this translates into working with anyone here, that if I were to begin with the intention to change something, it doesn't work like that. It is big changes with society, with a lot of people, which are needed. But even I have learned working with the kids during the day, that if they experience you as a positive person and that person gives them some hope or listens to them, that's their connection with God. For some kids, that's all you need to do. Like a couple of our kids, Ricardo was just here for a day or so. I'm not going to change his life. I probably won't see him again. By the time he gets done with a class for fifty minutes for a couple days, he knew that if he were going to put the time in, we would be here to help him achieve that. He's got a reference and it's not my fault that he decided not to keep on coming here.

At times, Sister Elaine sees herself as an instrument of change for some of her students. At other times, she fails to sense any change but continues to work with that person:

> I believe I should tell the kids that they are able to do something. I guess that's education. I try to encourage the girls, "You can do it on your own most of the time." And the same thing with the guys, the gangs that hang out. They mean something by themselves, in order that they can believe in themselves and believe in their

> gifts, in order that they will succeed. There are people that you have to just work with longer than the time you're able to. I guess that you express some of your values to them. And they say, "That makes a little bit of sense. Maybe I should work that this way." There is also a frustration that goes with it, because there are people you have worked with but they probably still hold a grudge, and you can't do anything to change them. You try and try and try to help them to be successful in some other way.

Brother Luke characterized VGAHS as a Christian school in the way that the teachers respect the students, help them complete their degrees, and assist them any other way they can:

> I think we are an extremely Christian school. I don't think we go out of our way to find out what religion, if any, the kids belong to. But there is a very definite Christian attitude of respect for one another, respect for the property of one another and of being really concerned about a person. It's not just an artificial surface. The kids have no hesitation to ask, "I have to get to the doctor. Can you run me to the doctor?" Or, "I have to go here. Will you take me?" In other schools, there'd be a great reluctance on the part of staff members to do that. Here, it is pretty well accepted that if the staff member has the time and what not, they'll bend over backwards to do that type of thing. We have kids here, for example, who cannot honestly afford transportation. They don't have the money to take a bus. We do the best we can to provide money to get them a bus pass, and encourage them to get to school if it's at all possible. And many of them are a little bit embarrassed or ashamed to ask for a bus pass. They'll walk. When the weather changes they might stay home for a day or two until staff finds out that the reason is lack of transportation. We'll find funds, find money to get them a bus pass to tide them over until they're able to work out something.

Judy Frances shared several examples from her government, American history and sewing classes, of incidents when students changed and gained knowledge about themselves. One of her own hopes is to help her students apply subject matter and new knowledge to achieve change. Ms. Frances described her American history class as a vehicle for helping students to read and understand words, then think and discuss these words and concepts, then apply them to their own experiences:

> In American History class, we generally read out loud. And I just let them volunteer. And sometimes they're sort of reluctant and they don't read. But generally they sort of fight over who's going to read. So we just take volunteers or if I get a lot of argument, I say okay, we'll just go around the table. And we stop and we just talk when they have a question or when I have something I want to emphasize or when they're done reading a certain section. Then I just ask questions and they take notes, and I say, "Well if no one knows this word, we better make this number one," and they write it down and we talk about it. And that's really pretty much the way History goes. And then I do supplement it with Black Americans whenever they fit in. And I work current events in when they'll fit in. Like right now we're doing cults, the old religious revival back in the 1600s and so I'm trying to bring in modern day cults and of course the Ku Klux Klan always comes up then.

She went on to describe her Government class in which she tries to achieve the same goals:

> In Government class this quarter, we did a pretty good project on the elections where they each picked a couple issues and presented both candidates' sides of the issues, told what the current situation was and then evaluated each side's proposals as to whether they would or wouldn't work, could or couldn't be done, based on their knowledge of how government functions. That way they had to work in their knowledge of how our government works and then finally which solution they thought would be the better of the two. I thought they did a good job. I think they learned quite bit that way.
>
> Tom: They related some of that to their own experiences?
>
> Ms. Frances: Not as much as I hoped.

She also recorded her occasional frustration with the student reactions to those concepts that force them beyond their own experiences, knowledge and self-interests.

Tom: Do you find that especially with history, government, and geography, the students' sense of anything beyond themselves is very limited?

Ms. Frances: Very, very. I suppose it depends on their background too, but generally they have a difficult time with maps, with anything a little bit abstract even. Unless they've traveled quite a bit, like Janet was in the service, her dad was in the military so she has been all over, and she has a much better sense of that. But for most of them, anything out of East St. Louis is foreign. And their normal response, even in a current events class, is "Well who cares? Why does the United States do anything for the rest of the world? Who cares about those people, when there are so many people here in trouble?" And it's real hard to get them to think that whatever happens in the world also affects this country. They can't visualize that at all. They don't really seem interested in problems other people have other than their own. In American History, I always stress the Native American and a few of them eventually say, "Well they're as bad off as we are. They have problems too." And one day, not long ago, a student said, "You know there's things on TV where they showed a special about people going hungry." And she said, "They showed this one white woman that didn't have enough money to feed her kids." She said, "Would that be true?"

Judy Frances then turned her attention to her sewing classes, which are far different in structure and content than her social studies courses. The students there gain a sense of accomplishment and satisfaction in what they produce. The students in these classes are both young men and young women, and they make a variety of items, from clothes to stuffed animals:

I think the sewing classes are real good classes in terms of what you can teach them, because it's fun. It's not a lecture, recording everything. But it's real easy there to watch them develop their reasoning, their thinking, their following instructions. I always work as much math in as possible, like they have to measure a button to know what size button hole, and to read fractions to them is just beyond them. They always just say, "Oh I was never any good at fractions." And then they'll sit, and sometimes they'll

> sit a day and a half before they figure out that they are going to have to read that tape measure. But I think it's good for them to have a class like that where they can accomplish and they feel really proud of what they can do. It's motivational because they can work at their own rate.

Ms. Frances told me she feels at home at VGAHS and feels supported by the other teachers as she works in her own way to help her students. In addition to her classes, Ms. Frances also coordinates the lunch program, including the menu planning, the shopping, and the lunch preparation, with students helping to set up, serve, and clean up:

> I just feel like this is a place where I belong, and when I come here it's just home. When that changes, I won't be around. I won't work with people I can't get along with.

Each of the teachers believes that what happens at VGAHS both helps the students earn their high school diplomas and helps them change the way they perceive themselves and their worlds. Sister Elaine said she felt that the atmosphere of VGAHS and her own efforts are instrumental in helping students towards these goals. Brother Luke noted that the teachers willingly help the students in any way possible. Judy Frances described what she covers and the pedagogies she uses to help students change perspective on their worlds and themselves.

Changes in the World of the Teachers

Working in an alternative school with the young men and women of East St. Louis would naturally change the world of the teachers, and they all agreed that they have experienced changes in their understanding of themselves as teachers and as persons. Sister Angela described how her experiences at VGAHS had heightened her awareness of African Americans and how this change had led to changes in her teaching methods and her perceptions of herself as a teacher:

> I did not have too much experience with Black people because I taught out at North County at Rosary High School and there were very few Blacks there at that time. I got to know the students here quickly. At the very beginning, I had a hard time trying to understand them. I guess many times I didn't want to ask them to repeat what they said. After awhile, I got to know them and now I

> think the students here are easy to understand.

Sister Angela continued by reflecting further upon her experience at VGAHS and comparing it with her former teaching experiences. Teaching at VGAHS has caused her to change some of her own teaching methods, gain an awareness of students who had been unsuccessful in regular schooling and gain an awareness of economic and social differences in their schooling:

> The experience of teaching here is—wow!—definitely different than before. Basically, I think the experience is, first of all, the subject matter itself is different. The reason is many of our students find it very difficult, especially reading. The vocabulary for many of our students is very poor. Therefore, it's difficult to actually read and comprehend some of the material. Here, when I teach, I actually have them read and I read. Wherever I taught before coming here, the reading basically was considered homework. Here, the students find homework very difficult. In fact, to get students to do homework is a real challenge. Previously my students were basically high school kids, teenagers from a stable home, where Mom and Dad are in the home, where they do not have to struggle for survival like the students have to struggle for survival here. Many of our students here are mothers. At Rosary when I was there, only one student was a mother. One student in all the years I was at Rosary! Here this is a common thing. I think the whole situation is totally different.

Sister Angela told a story about the crucifix with the body of a Black Jesus on her classroom wall. The story reminds her about how her own consciousness of her students as being different from herself has changed during her time at VGAHS. She has developed an awareness of the students as "the other" in terms of race and realizes that she needs to be sensitive to her own use of language and symbols that might affect her students negatively:

> See that crucifix on the wall? Let me tell you the story behind it. I used to have a crucifix with a white Jesus, and one of my students came in one day and said, "You have a white Jesus on that crucifix!" I thought, I never realized that, my white mentality, but he did. It really meant something to them. I had a white Jesus and

> not a Black Jesus. I went home and asked the nuns if anybody had a Black Jesus. One of the nuns gave me this crucifix and I've had it there ever since.

Timothy O'Fallon has already experienced a sense of change in his life, after only a year at VGAHS. His own interests and concerns for social justice and in sharing part of his talents with others are what compelled him to become a Jesuit volunteer in East St. Louis:

> There are a couple of different areas of emphasis in Jesuit volunteer programs and two of those relate directly, I think, to VG. One of them is social justice and that is true of most of the work sites of the Jesuit volunteer program, and the other is a simple lifestyle. I try and give these students a chance to have the types of things I grew up with, which are good role models and people who care, which maybe they don't get at home or at other places. The other thing is the simple lifestyle of the people of this community. So those are two of the things that brought me to VG.

O'Fallon had learned a lot about what it means to be as poor as the young men and women of East St. Louis. This new cultural awareness influences his way of teaching and interacting with the students:

> Tom: Do you think your experience here with the students has taught you something about the African American culture as well as the culture of poverty?
>
> O'Fallon: Yeah, I think I learn more about it every day. You know, it's funny. I don't know if you interviewed Jamil or not. He's an interesting case, in his culture because he speaks aloud, he's a church goer, and he's used to saying "Amen, Alleluia." He's used to saying something all the time either to reiterate or just part of his culture is speaking aloud. At first that was hard for me in terms of trying to handle a classroom, but we've kind of come to sort of an agreement where he catches himself when he knows he's being really loud, I will say something or I'll let somebody let him know if this is destructive to the class. That's part of the culture. There's a lot of other things that I probably won't be able to articulate until I have more experience. I think there's a lot that's seeping in that I haven't processed yet.

He went on to discuss his memories of his first day at VGAHS and he observed that as the days go by, his teaching style and his interactions with students improve:

> Another thing that happened on my first day was that I prepared for what I thought would be about two days worth of teaching and [chuckle] I used up that material in about twenty minutes in the first class. For about a half an hour I sat there and kind of danced and entertained. So from that point, I really started to over prepare and make sure that I had enough material. And one of the highlights is getting to the point where I don't have to do that, where I feel comfortable enough with the students and the material to prepare just enough and know that there is going to be some interaction and some question and some filler and some joking around.

Some of what he learned about East St. Louis O'Fallon gained from his conversations with students. At times, he was surprised about the information the students gave him about their own lives and their city:

> I asked the students one of the first days I was here, what they liked and disliked most about East St. Louis, and I was really surprised about the number that wrote "What I like about East St. Louis." They all stated the drawbacks, you know, the police never come, there are gangs everywhere, drugs and violence everywhere. But they also, all said without exception it's a nice place, my family is here, or it's a nice place because I have good friends here, it's a nice place to live in. My assumption coming in was it was bad, and I couldn't imagine that anyone could ever live, have any remote idea of happiness in this desolate violent, terrible place.

O'Fallon's ideas about East St. Louis have changed since his arrival. As our conversation continued, he described how he has dealt with his feelings as a young white man entering into the African American culture of East St. Louis, an experience different from anything he had previously known:

> Tom: Do you see in yourself some uncomfortableness with coming over to East St. Louis, being in East St. Louis, and being in a

> culture other than your own?
>
> O'Fallon: Yes, I do. I feel pretty comfortable over here and I didn't at first. I did feel uncomfortable with the culture in terms of being white versus being in a Black environment. I didn't feel terribly uncomfortable with that. But I did feel uncomfortable with the city because of the reputation of the city. And I don't feel as bad, I don't feel as scared because I feel a part of the community, I feel a part of what's good about the community. That includes VG, the people downstairs who are doing their work, all different groups, all different people, you know our neighborhood which seems like a real nice neighborhood, where people come together, where people make a point of keeping the neighborhood clean and intact.

Lois Day shared a lot of her own feelings about changes in her own life over her ten years at VGAHS. At the time of our interview, she was looking forward to retiring. She expressed a different perspective on the students than the other teachers, and she seemed less hopeful about her efforts as a teacher. She felt unsure about her effectiveness with the students in regard to exciting them about reading and thinking about life, even though this had been one of her goals:

> Going to school was a great release in life. That's why I feel so bad around here that I can't stimulate any of the students to reach that. I shouldn't feel so bad. I don't have maybe one or two who are really what I call, I don't know, an intellectual, somebody who had that great desire, that longing to know everything there is in the world and to conquer everything. I guess it isn't given to everyone. That's what I would like to give to people. Because I didn't give it to my children. I don't know who I am to give it to anyone. I don't know that I have really stimulated anyone. If I could just turn one into a reader, that would satisfy me, but I have not been able to do that. Some of the girls have gone on to sewing. I really haven't gotten much beyond that. It's sad and I don't know whether they just aren't bright or whether they need to be stimulated. I know that you can teach yourself by just reading and get an education by yourself. I don't think I have had that much success. I am more of a pessimist whereas everybody else here is an optimist. Even though I can't get into them or close to

> them, anything that they want done, I'll do it, patching on their clothes, any favors.

She went on to say she has struggled to understand the young men and women of VGAHS. She realizes that her own cultural experiences as expressed in her values differ from those of her students, but she expressed reluctance to change her judgments of some of the student behavior, even though she might not react as strongly as she used to:

> The students here do have multiple problems. It's just like they draw them in as students. I swear they are a magnet. They get out of one problem and then they get into another. I don't know why that is, but they are happy. They're very good natured, most of them. They drag their feet, some of them do, when it comes to learning. That's a problem I have with them. I don't know whether that's inherent. I have a very strict moral code and the first couple of years I was here every time a girl would get pregnant, I would really have a fit. I would just be shocked. Now, I don't even think about it any more. I think it's their way of life. What are you going to do? The government or somebody has to come in and change it. I don't want to get into the morality of it. That isn't something you can impose on someone.

Ms. Day expressed some retrospective surprise over how long she had stayed at VGAHS because she felt her feelings and approaches to the students to be so different from those the other teachers profess:

> All the other staff is more open than I am. I'm a very closed person. I'm not a person you can get close to. I live more in my head than I do in my body, which is my problem. I am really surprised that Brother Harold let me stay all these years. Without the spirit of the other teachers, I wouldn't have stayed here this long I guess. There was always an atmosphere here among the teachers, where it was family among the teachers. There was never any criticism. It was a very free-going group here, at least as far as the teachers go.

I continued our conversation by focusing on her own sense of being surprised she had remained at VGAHS so long. She noted how she had changed during those years in terms of losing patience and hope about making any difference in the lives of others. She also recognized that she has a sense of needing some spiritual or inspirational revival in her own life:

> Tom: You were talking about you're surprise at being here so long.
>
> Ms. Day: Yes and also sometimes things get to me and I lose my temper. Lately I have been doing too much. I think it's just age. When I started here I was fifty-six and I didn't think I'd ever want to quit. I just wanted to keep working. I guess age catches up with you and you figure well, it's time to quit. I don't have the patience any more. Mostly because I don't see any answers to any problems. I used to be very inspired. I always went to great lengths. As my husband said, "You can't change the world. Stop worrying about it." I always had that idea. I always figured that one person could make a difference, but I am jaded with age. I do think I need some inspiration myself. Yes, I know my spirit is down when I really get these ideas. You need to feel alive, with an inner spirit.

The teachers at VGAHS acknowledge that they experienced changes in their own worlds as the result of their work at VGAHS. These changes included new perspectives on and knowledge about people of a different race and culture. They also changed their perspectives about themselves as teachers and persons concerned about helping others. Sister Angela has found a new awareness about African Americans and a sensitivity to their religious expressions. Timothy O'Fallon has gained a new awareness of himself as a teacher, of his students, of East St. Louis, and of how the students and people of East St. Louis experience being poor. Lois Day has undergone a change in her own thinking about the students and her own hopes for making a difference in the lives of others. Her comments convey more pessimism and fatalism than the other teachers and she admitted that she feels burnt out after all her years at VGAHS. But for the most part, the changes have helped the teachers understand and react positively to a culture far different from theirs and to people far different from themselves.

Summary

The administrators and the teachers of VGAHS spoke to the various elements of the integrative model of liberation theology and critical pedagogy. They did so from the perspective of people who see what happens to their students and what happens to themselves. The teachers and administrators see East St. Louis as a victim of racism. They expressed a commitment to the poor and oppressed young people of the city. They also described how they experienced community at VGAHS and expressed the realization that the students undergo changes in their lives at VGAHS. They generally affirmed a sense of hope that they can help guide their students through these changes. Also, each teacher and administrator had noticed changes in how they perceived themselves and their own worlds.

The administrators and teachers at VGAHS pursue their work out of a commitment to the poor and oppressed. They understand that VGAHS should help the students change their worlds and senses of self. They believe that their work helps students become critical of their situations and hopeful about their lives.

The VGAHS administrators and teachers all expressed a commitment to the students. They all hope their own presence represents a means of helping the students move criticism toward some sense of possibility. Both teachers and administrators understand that the work of VGAHS extends beyond simply teaching classes and bestowing high school diplomas. They also hope their students can improve and develop their self-concepts and confidence. The community experience at VGAHS is an important nontraditional aspect of the school. Both teachers and administrators, while at home and secure in East St. Louis, criticize what happens in the city and perceive the situation there as the result of racism in the surrounding areas.

For the most part, the administrators and teachers focused on individuals, including both the students and themselves, making successful changes in the community spirit of VGAHS. But these changes remain for now on the individual level. A sense of a political consciousness or a larger community consciousness so far eludes the students and the experiences of the VGAHS administrators and teachers. An awareness of the critical discourses of liberation theology and critical pedagogy could help the teachers and administrators instill this critical and political consciousness. The teachers and administrators appear to need more awareness of the experiences and histories of the students from the perspectives of class, race and sexual identity formation and to understand how the dominant culture constructs these perspectives within the African American culture of East St. Louis. The administrators and teachers need to explore ways to influence and change

the larger community and to associate t
political and racial issues of East St. Lou
many negative images of the city the domi
to construct and maintain.

The teachers and administrators do not
language of liberation theology and critical pedagogy, however,
express some elements of these two critical discourses as developed in the integrative model. They explained how they had experienced some aspects of this integrative model in their own lives, and how they had perceived the students experiencing aspects of the model.

Their voices contribute to an understanding of what happens at VGAHS from the perspective of the integrative model of liberation theology and critical pedagogy. These voices clarify how critical discourses can enter the dialogue about the identity of Catholic schools, albeit in a tension between a Gospel spirit and a Catholic institution. These voices characterize both elements of the discourses of liberation theology and critical pedagogy in practice and an array of elements that make a school Catholic. These interviews mark a starting point for understanding how the discourses of liberation theology and critical pedagogy can provide lenses for examining not only what occurs in other schools, including other Catholic schools and public and private schools, but also how one can use these critical discourses to evaluate schooling practices.

[illegible]

Chapter Nine

Reflections

> Catholic education has left a lasting imprint on your community, from the days of St. Elizabeth Ann Seton to the present. I am confident that all of you understand the importance of continuing, indeed of expanding, that eminent tradition of Catholic education, in your parishes, your high schools, your colleges and universities. Catholic schools, historically and as a matter of duty, have made a substantial contribution to society by giving special attention to economically disadvantaged segments of society. I hope that you will continue to look for ways of ensuring the continuation of this essential service, despite the financial burdens it entails. Catholic education serves the future of all Americans by teaching and communicating the very virtues on which American democracy rests.
>
> - John Paul II in Baltimore, October 8, 1995

In these words, Pope John Paul II exhorted American Catholics to continue their commitment to Catholic schools, and specifically to those schools that accord the economically disadvantaged segments of society special attention. Vincent Gray Alternative High School is one example of a school carrying out this mission. In presenting the qualitative research in the preceding chapters, I demonstrated how the discourses of liberation theology and critical pedagogy can describe advantageous alternative practices of schooling. Ideally, this understanding will affect the practices of Catholic and public schools, and lead to improved schools for all students—but particularly, for those students marginalized by the dominant culture on the basis of race, class and gender. Ideally, this collection of interviews expresses clearly enough for application some of the common elements of the discourses of liberation theology and critical pedagogy—the central thesis being that they can influence practices in Catholic schools as they struggle to understand their own identity in serving those segments of society characterized as new immigrants or the economically disadvantaged.

This concern for the poor is, to repeat, the focus and goal of the Catholic Bishops and other contemporary American religious communities as well. At their national meeting in November 1995, the Catholic Bishops echoed their concerns of the economic pastoral letter of 1985, "Economic Justice for All." In this updated pastoral letter, "A Decade after 'Economic Justice for All': Continuing Principles, Changing Context, New Challenges" (Origins, 1995), the Bishops state that "the Catholic community must continue to speak for poor children and working families" amid the reality that "there is still much poverty and not enough economic opportunity for all our people" (p. 390). This call for economic justice is clearly not just "a response to the Scripture" but also "a requirement of Catholic teaching" (p. 390).

The challenge in this pastoral letter raises the issue of Catholic school identity in relation to the discourses of liberation theology and critical pedagogy. Furthermore, the Bishops challenge and urge "Catholic educational institutions to redouble their efforts to share our teaching, to help their students develop concern for the poor and for justice, and to contribute to the common good by their research and educational activities" (p. 392). Here again VGAHS provides an example of a school concerned for the poor and for justice, and in turn, the educational activities at VGAHS can lead other Catholic educational institutions toward this same concern.

My research at VGAHS focused on the voices of students, alumni, teachers and administrators there. Collectively these voices comprise a symphonic expression illustrating how an integrative model of liberation theology and critical pedagogy can lead to an understanding of the educational practices at Vincent Gray Alternative High School. Throughout this discussion, I resisted a reified approach to the discourses of liberation theology and critical pedagogy. By utilizing an integrative model of the common elements and themes of these two critical discourses to show how students, administrators and teachers at VGAHS articulate them, I illustrated how educators can conclude that liberation theology and critical pedagogy discourse can reconstruct schooling practices in Catholic and public schools. Thus, I offer an example of critical theory and practice in a liberation theology context.

For example, both of these critical discourses advocate the importance of developing a community spirit within schools. Each encourages helping students develop both a language of critique and a language of possibility about their own living situations. These two critical discourses also provide educators with a language for evaluating pedagogical practices at other school sites. These two critical discourses can also help Catholic schools respond to the contemporary challenges of the Pope and the Bishops to develop a concern for the poor and disadvantaged.

A Symphony of Voices

As I reflected upon the voices of the students, teachers and administrators of VGAHS, I realized that they are more a symphony than a cacophony in that I heard harmonious elements of liberation theology and critical pedagogy discourses. I began Chapter Six by recalling how the students in a public speaking class gave new meaning to the poems of Langston Hughes as they related some of his poems to their own experiences. These students, along with administrators and teachers, now foster an understanding of how the discourses of liberation theology and critical pedagogy describe practices at VGAHS and encourage VGAHS to develop in light of these discourses. Hence, VGAHS serves as a model to other Catholic schools as they struggle to serve the poor and oppressed.

I consider these voices a symphony because, even though each voice is unique, each articulated the central elements and themes of these two critical discourses interwoven with the other voices like motifs of a classical symphony. Moreover, the voices are like the symphony orchestra in that, while each instrument makes its own unique sound, all the sounds together produce the harmony.

The voices of the eight students, six current and two graduates, used in this qualitative study may resemble the voices and express the general experiences of the other VGAHS students. The interviews with these students gave life to what I had already learned about the discourses of liberation theology and critical pedagogy. The combination of these eight student voices and my knowledge of these two critical discourses prompted the development of the integrative model.

The six current students fairly represent the many themes in the lives of other young men and women in our schools or of those who have opted out of school—a pregnant teenager, a single mother or father, a former drug addict, an alcoholic—all experiences in the lives of young people fully expressed in other educational qualitative studies—in, for example, the works of Wehlage, Rutter, Smith, Lesko, and Fernandez (1989); Page and Valli (1990) and McLaughlin and Tierney (1993). The two graduates as young adults exemplify the struggles of those new parents trying to raise a family in a community not far different from the one they knew, and the struggle to keep their dreams about their careers, work and personal relationships alive and renewed.

These students, speaking to the different elements of the integrative model of liberation theology and critical pedagogy presented in Chapter Four, demonstrated both a willingness to criticize their worlds and lives and a willingness to imagine some possibilities for change. Their voices also expressed how VGAHS has encouraged their reflections, decisions and practices in their lives in East St. Louis. These students talked about experiencing change in their self-identities and a sense of community at VGAHS. Their voices sounded tones of hope for a better world and realistic hopes for themselves in such a world. But they also know that their hopes for changes in themselves and in their worlds must be recursive and ongoing. Each one vowed to remember their dreams while realizing that each one's life, in Langston Hughes's phrasing, "ain't been no crystal stair."

The voices of the administrators and the teachers also touched on elements of the integrative model of the liberation theology and critical pedagogy discourses. They explained how they perceived the world and experiences of the students from their perspectives as white, college-educated adults. But the administrators and teachers moved beyond student experiences at VGAHS to discuss their own experiences and the changes that have occurred in their lives. These voices echo some of the passions and interests of other teachers and administrators concerned with the empowerment of students, social justice and social change as reflected in such other studies as Wehlage et al. (1989); Casey (1993); Kreisberg (1992); Miller (1990); and McLaughlin and Tierney (1993).

The administrators' criticism of what is happening in East St. Louis: neglect born of racism. They also explained how they have changed their preconceptions of East St. Louis after living and working there. They all expressed a personal commitment to the poor and oppressed. They also remarked on the spirit of community at VGAHS between and among the students and the teachers. They expressed specific administrative concerns in regard to VGAHS as an institution struggling with its own identity and vision. Finally, the administrators also described the changes in their lives during their years at VGAHS, as they adjusted their ideas about schooling and the culture of African Americans in East St. Louis.

The six teachers interviewed for this book described their students: East St. Louis residents enjoying little success in former schooling experiences. As they spoke, they adopted the language of critique when describing the community and the lives of their students, as well as a language of possibility and hope for those students and their city. Like the administrators, the teachers work at VGAHS in East St. Louis because of their commitment to the poor and oppressed. Everyone I met freely acknowledged the remarkable community at VGAHS. The teachers believe that VGAHS helps students change their lives. Finally, the teachers, too, have experienced changes in their lives, having entered into the world of their students.

Each of the interviewees expressed aspects of the integrative model of the two discourses in their own ways and from their own identities and histories. Yet one heard the harmony in their voices as they described their current world and its problems, and as they discussed their own lives in the city of East St. Louis. Their voices tell us that something is indeed wrong there and the cause is not necessarily internal. They all voiced a desire to improve their lives.

In the interviews of the students, administrators and teachers, one can discern a methodology, proposed in the integrative model of liberation theology and critical pedagogy, for changing one's world, a methodology expressed as moving from a critical position to a position of possibility. The students, administrators and teachers spoke of possible solutions for transforming the world and they spoke of implementing the solutions.

The students, administrators and teachers expressed other common elements of the integrative model: the experience of community at VGAHS; a hope for changes in how students see themselves; a commitment among the teachers and administrators to the poor and oppressed; a feeling of victimization among the students stemming from the dominant culture and their former schooling experiences; an expressed need for continual reflection and the realization that worthwhile change must be ongoing and recursive.

While expressing common elements of the critical discourses of liberation theology and critical pedagogy, all the voices also expressed the qualities and dynamic characteristics of Catholic education. Catholic schools have traditionally demonstrated a community and justice and for making the world a more humane and caring place. All Catholic educators know that this commitment to change in others begins with them and they must share it with students and colleagues. The common elements in the discourses of liberation theology and critical pedagogy operate in the process and dynamics of Catholic education. All Catholic educators see their schools as faith communities with a view toward making the world more humane, just and caring. One finds harmony in the common elements of liberation theology, critical pedagogy, and the essential identity of the Catholic school. The challenge is to hear and respond to this harmony.

What Might Be Happening at VGAHS

It is time now to propose how this integrative model of liberation theology and critical pedagogy discourses might benefit VGAHS as well as other schools, both public and Catholic.

Inasmuch as the students, administrators and teachers articulate the elements of the integrative model of liberation theology and critical pedagogy implicitly, I can only begin to imagine what could be happening at VGAHS if the administrators and teachers there became familiar with critical theory, and specifically, the discourses of liberation theology and critical pedagogy. Some of the religious sisters and brothers who work at VGAHS know something about liberation theology, and they consciously express this awareness in their desire to exercise a "preferential option for the poor" as part of their personal commitment to a ministry at VGAHS and in East St. Louis.

But thorough grounding in both liberation theology and critical pedagogy could benefit the administrators and teachers as they struggle to understand the identity of VGAHS as a Catholic school and formulate a vision for VGAHS. These discourses provide a language of both critique and possibility already expressed to some degree in the mission of VGAHS and in the ways with which it is practiced there. The language of these discourses could help the administrators and teachers develop policies that encourage both a habit of criticism and a sense of the possible in each student at VGAHS. These two discourses could help to create an atmosphere and a curriculum that speaks directly to the development of an identity of the students as African Americans and to their struggles and political role as residents committed to changing the oppressed realities for African Americans in East St. Louis. The formation of a critical consciousness could begin to guide the vision and curricular practices of VGAHS, but it needs to be accepted by both teachers and students. Marcia Moraes (1992) observed that "if students are able to critically interrogate their experiences and those of other students, they will be able to understand how social relations are historically shaped by discourses of class, race, and gender" (p. 131). Consequently, the critical discourses of liberation theology and critical pedagogy could help VGAHS become more politically active and more involved with the larger community and thus effect changes within the larger community.

Many good things already happen at VGAHS, but even the established community spirit there could develop and begin to reach out to include other persons in the larger community. This happens now in a small way in the classes on parenting which parents bring their children to an extended period one day a week. But VGAHS students, administrators and teachers could involve themselves more in community projects in their own neighborhoods or the VGAHS neighborhood.

The dilemma of being a community unto itself is shared by other schools that serve at-risk students. Wehlage et al. (1989) recommended a sense of membership for these students and reciprocal relationships with their teachers. Wehlage and his colleagues considered this membership important "for those students who have histories of school failure and who lack the support of strong homes and communities outside the school" (p. 133). Epstein (1992) also advocated a strong community experience characterized as "intimate and caring: devoid of the deficit model, filled with life and intellectual stimulation" as a necessary aspect for alternative schools dealing with dropouts (p. 64). VGAHS has become a caring, supportive community for the students, teachers and administrators, an experience of community affirmed by each interviewee.

Wehlage et al. (1989) further recommended that schools for at-risk students serve as both communities of support and developers of community partnerships. VGAHS, while continuing to be a supportive community, needs to explore ways to develop both community partnerships and more community involvement with the larger community of East St. Louis.

While the students, administrators and teachers articulated the common elements of liberation theology and critical pedagogy set forth in the integrative model, if they were to become consciously alert to the language and concepts of these two discourses, they could together consciously apply them in daily classes, the weekly all-school meetings and the staff meetings. These discourses could guide administrators and teachers making decisions about which courses to adopt, about the content of courses and about the pedagogies practiced in the classes. For example, a shift away from a school-teacher-centered curriculum and gaining credits could take VGAHS toward a student-centered curriculum with the focus on critique and possibility, and on implementing the solutions needed to foster change in their lives. In short, the two critical discourses could provide a language for talking about the progress of students as administrators and teachers currently discuss that progress in their weekly staff meetings.

Wehlage et al. (1989) addressed similar concerns as they focused on the need to restructure what happens in schools and the role of the teachers in schools that serve at-risk students. They stated that

> School programs must develop inventive ways to meet the needs and problems of their students. In general, the educators we studied recognized that a continued diet of more of the same curriculum and teaching was unlikely to engage at-risk students who had a history of failure. . . . In general, our findings suggest the need for substantial changes in the structure of schools if they are to respond to the diversity of students. . . . Reforms in teaching, curriculum and social relations between adults and students are needed before at-risk students are likely to be retained to graduation and to succeed in their quest for achievement. These changes, if broadly implemented, would require substantial restructuring of schools and a redefinition of teaching roles (pp. 26-27).

With a conscious awareness of the discourses of liberation theology and critical pedagogy, the students, administrators and teachers of VGAHS could challenge the dominant culture's understanding of what defines a school, what makes a school Catholic, and what knowledge is important in a curriculum leading to a high school diploma. Such efforts could encourage the dominant culture to change preconceived notions and prejudices about Catholic schools, alternative schools, African Americans and East St. Louis.

Some Caveats

This qualitative study focused on VGAHS and, being dependent upon an understanding of Catholic education as critical theory and practice in a liberation theology context, is, however, limited in several ways. In choosing the two critical discourses of liberation theology and critical pedagogy, I realize that other critical discourses and ideologies are also applicable to understanding Catholic school practices. I also present and develop the discourses of critical pedagogy and liberation theology as I understand them, and I have appropriated from these discourses those elements best suited to my analysis. Meanwhile, I appropriated concepts, elements and themes from these two discourses as I constructed the integrative model and the language the model uses.

Also, the liberation theologians and the critical pedagogists whose work I rely on are only a few among many. The works of other liberation theologians—including those among Latin American women, among developing nations besides Latin American countries and among African Americans could foster further understanding of the experiences of administrators, teachers and students at schools located in neighborhoods similar to those of East St. Louis. Likewise, the works of other critical educators and the ongoing dialogue between critical pedagogy and contemporary postmodernism and postcolonialism could also promote the study of what happens in public, Catholic and alternative schools.

My limited understanding of postmodernism impeded to some extent my understanding of truth and the world. I exemplify the hopes of modernism with a view of a world becoming a more just and humane community. I also believe in the value of an individual commitment to and effort toward this ideal. An integrative model, the structure I used for understanding what happens at VGAHS in relation to liberation theology and critical pedagogy appears to be a reification of these two discourses, and I realize that an integrative model can also limit the breadth of these two discourses.

I have chosen to emphasize the positive aspects of life at VGAHS, and I declined to include signs of resistant behavior in some students. In my data analysis, the students who might have complicated the components of the integrative model are absent. Nor have I focused on such other issues in the voices of the students, teachers and administrators as identity construction, gender and class, which also relate to these two critical discourses. All of those not fully explored here await further development.

The data used in this study comes selectively from the large compendium I accumulated at VGAHS. Still, my time at VGAHS could have been longer—a year, two years, a career—to increase its value as ethnography. I believe my stay there was long enough for me to understand what happens there.

Finally, I chose which interviews to include as well as what extracts from those interviews I would present. The students and alumni I interviewed were suggested by the two principals. The voices of other students and alumni and some students who never earned their high school diplomas might have sounded different notes. One could develop this study by including more dissident, dissonant voices. Such voices might either affirm or negate some of the associations I found with elements of the two discourses as expressed in the integrative model of liberation theology and critical pedagogy.

Looking Forward

I worked to ensure that the voices I present in this book truly represent each person interviewed and that this profile of VGAHS will help others to understand how to apply the two critical discourses to Catholic schools. VGAHS, I think, provides a useful example of these two critical discourses in practice.

Further, I am convinced that what I have presented here demonstrates that the discourses of liberation theology and critical pedagogy can indeed guide what happens and what could happen in both public and Catholic schools. Critical pedagogy and liberation theology are more than just academic constructs existing in a reified manner. They provide a realistic way of understanding and evaluating school practices. These discourses can emerge as forces from college textbooks and theology tomes to influence the experiences of the poor and marginalized here and in developing nations. One can see the value of these discourses as applied to education both in the descriptions of the VGAHS students, administrators and teachers and as they are authenticated in their day-to-day experiences.

My representation of these experiences can help other educators toward a conviction that the discourses of liberation theology and critical pedagogy promote an understanding of schooling beneficial to the discussion of reforming and restructuring all schooling practices, not just the practices at alternative or Catholic schools. I also set out to increase an awareness and understanding of the two discourses among those who see these discourses shrouded in an inaccessible, esoteric language. I have illustrated them in familiar terms and in the naive responses of students, administrators and teachers.

As I write, the two critical discourses continue to contribute to the discussion and current development of curriculum theory. Their themes and elements continually appear in the work of educational scholars addressing curriculum. For example, Slattery (1995) shows how a "postmodern vision of curriculum as theological text is emerging" (p. 67) and he encourages teachers "to be prophets and create a fresh new vision of curriculum as theological text" (p. 85). Both liberation theology and critical pedagogy play key roles in understanding curriculum in a postmodern sense. Purpel (1989), utilizing critical theory, developed the prophetic tradition of the Hebrew scriptures, liberation theology and creation theology as the foundation for developing a religious and moral framework for public education. He, too, sees educators as prophets urging us past the trivialization of education. Noddings (1992) echoed the theme of caring and community as part of the curriculum and structures of schooling.

Pinar et al. (1995) sees the role of critical theory, critical pedagogy and theology in understanding curriculum, both historically and concurrently, "as a provocation to reflect on and to think critically about ourselves, our families, our schools" (p. 848). After a lengthy treatment of critical pedagogy and of understanding the curriculum as a political text, they state that "an essential aspect of the project to understand the curriculum is to understand that the curriculum is also a moral and ethical project, grounded theologically" (p. 637).

The two critical discourses add little to the technical manuals for curriculum guides and classroom practices. As Moraes (1992) stated, "[T]eaching does not mean following in a technical manner. What is important is that all of us who are named 'teachers' must think about what we do, why we teach, and whether or not we want to continue avoiding our political and ethical responsibilities or culpabilities as educators" (p. 134). The discourses of liberation theology and critical pedagogy challenge administrators and teachers to reflect on and to struggle with what happens with students in our schools and classrooms. They can fashion their practices from the perspective of liberation theology and critical pedagogy so as to provide more equitable experiences for all students, not just the successful and those of the dominant culture.

The students, administrators and teachers of VGAHS demonstrate that the discourses of liberation theology and critical pedagogy provide a set of postulates for articulating the purposes of a school and for constructing and evaluating its practices. These two discourses can also guide schools in their struggle to answer such questions as What makes you a "school of excellence"? or What makes you an "effective school"? or What makes you a Catholic school? These critical discourses both provide a language to help schools articulate their identity and help schools develop and propound their philosophies, mission statements and visions. The discourses encourage educators to dream new dreams, break down the walls and dispel the shadows—to give life once again to dreams of a democratic, just and equitable schooling for all of our young people.

This study of VGAHS also advances the use of qualitative research into educational practices, and it contributes to the development of qualitative research literature and to the ongoing discussion of qualitative research as a method well suited for the study of education. It also provides an example of theory and practice in my own experiences of integrating qualitative research with my research experiences at and with a school site.

Eisner (1991) enumerated six features of a qualitative study: (1) a field focus, (2) the use of self as an instrument, (3) an interpretive character, (4) the use of expressive language and the presence of a voice in the text, (5) attention to particulars and (6) believability deriving from coherence, insight and instrumental utility (pp. 32-39). This study, I suggest, embodies each of these features. The focus is both on the theory of the liberation theology and critical pedagogy discourses and on how these two critical discourses helped me make sense of what happens at Vincent Gray Alternative High School. The study includes the voices of the students, administrators and teachers on the site and my own voice as I analyze and interpret their voices from the perspective of the two critical discourses.

LeCompte and Preissle (1993) suggested that qualitative research is "generated by curiosity about people in both everyday and extraordinary situations; it leads to investigations of the most complex of social phenomena. The word 'ethnography' literally means 'writing about people'; in our minds, there is no more intriguing task" (p. 356). My curiosity about the relationship between the discourses of liberation theology and critical pedagogy led me to wonder if and how these discourses were present at a school. My experience in Catholic schools encouraged me to wonder what shape or practices a Catholic school would have if it were committed to some aspects of these two critical discourses. My curiosity about an alternative school in East St. Louis led me to examine the everyday lives of the students, administrators and teachers at Vincent Gray Alternative High School. My curiosity gave me the chance to cross some borders for a few weeks and become acquainted with some of the most extraordinary people I have met, in a most extraordinary school. This study emerged from my curiosities, but this book is really the work of the students, administrators and teachers of Vincent Gray Alternative High School.

Bibliography

Aronowitz, Stanley. (1993). Paulo Friere's radical democratic humanism. In Peter McLaren & Peter Leonard (Eds.), *Paulo Friere: A critical encounter* (pp. 8–24). New York: Routledge.

Aronowitz, Stanley & Giroux, Henry A. (1991). *Postmodern education: Politics, culture, and social criticism*. Minneapolis: University of Minnesota Press.

Augsburger, David. (February, 1994). "Diversity and variety: Creativity and spirituality or competition and conflict?" Paper presented at the Annual Convention of the National Organization for the Continuing Education of Roman Catholic Clergy, San Diego, CA.

Bennett, Kathleen P. & LeCompte, Margaret D. (1990). *The way schools work: A sociological analysis of education*. New York: Longman.

Benson, Peter L., Yeager, Robert J., Wood, Philip K., Guerra, Michael J., & Manno, Bruno V. (1986). *Catholic high schools: Their impact on low-income students*. Washington, DC: National Catholic Education Association.

Beutow, Harold A. (1970). *Of singular benefit: The story of Catholic education in the United States*. New York: Macmillan.

Beutow, Harold A. (1988). *The Catholic school: Its roots, identity, and future*. New York: Crossroads.

Black Catholic Bishops of the United States. (1984). *What we have seen and heard*. Cincinnati: St. Anthony Messenger Press.

Boff, Clodovis. (1987). *Theology and praxis*. Maryknoll: Orbis Books.

Boff, Leonardo. (1991a). *Faith on the edge*. Maryknoll: Orbis Books.

Boff, Leonardo. (1991b). *New evangelization: Good news to the poor*. Maryknoll: Orbis Books.

Boff, Leonardo & Boff, Clodovis. (1984). *Salvation and liberation*. Maryknoll: Orbis Books.

Boff, Leonardo & Boff, Clodovis. (1989). *Introducing liberation theology*. Maryknoll: Orbis Books.

Boyer, Ernest L. (1983). *High school: A report on secondary education in America.* New York: Harper & Row.

Brigham, Frederick H., Jr. (1990). *United States Catholic elementary and secondary schools 1989–90.* Washington, DC: National Catholic Education Association.

Brigham, Frederick H., Jr. (1995). *United States Catholic elementary and secondary schools 1994–95.* Washington, DC: National Catholic Education Association.

Bryk, Anthony S. & Holland, Peter B. (October, 1982). The implications of Greeley's latest research. *Momentum*, pp. 8–11.

Bryk, Anthony S., Holland, Peter B., Lee, Valerie E., & Carriedo, Reuben A. (1984). *Effective Catholic schools: An exploration.* Washington, DC: National Catholic Education Association.

Bryk, Anthony S., Lee, Valerie E., & Holland, Peter B. (1993). *Catholic schools and the common good.* Cambridge: Harvard University Press.

Burns, James A. (1912a). *The growth and development of the Catholic school system in the United States.* New York: Benziger Brothers.

Burns, James A. (1912b). *The principles, origins and establishment of the Catholic school system in the United States*. New York: Benziger Brothers.

Burns, James A. (1917). *Catholic education: A study of conditions.* New York: Longmans, Green and Co.

Burns, James A. & Kohlbrenner, Bernard. (1937). *A history of Catholic education in the United States*. New York: Benziger Brothers.

Carlson, Dennis. (1992). *Teachers and crisis: Urban school reform and teachers' work culture*. New York: Routledge.

Carroll, Lewis. (1871/1941). *Through the looking glass and what Alice found there.* New York: The Heritage Press.

Casey, Kathleen. (1993). *I answer with my life: Life histories of women teachers working for social change.* New York: Routledge.

Castelli, Jim. (September, 1995). Vatican II: 30 years on the road from Rome. *U.S. Catholic*, pp. 6–13,

Chopp, Rebecca S. (1989). *The praxis of suffering.* Maryknoll: Orbis Books.

Chrobot, Leonard F. (February, 1994). "The sociology of cultural diversity." Paper presented at the Annual Convention of the

National Organization for the Continuing Education of Roman Catholic Clergy, San Diego, CA.

Cincinnati Enquirer. (March 11, 1991) Ethnic diversity increasing, census shows. March 11, p. 1.

Coleman, James S. & Hoffer, Thomas. (1987). *Public and private high schools: The impact of communities.* New York: Basic Books, Inc.

Coleman, James S., Hoffer, Thomas, & Kilgore, Sally. (1982). *High school achievement: Public, Catholic, and private schools compared.* New York: Basic Books, Inc.

Congregation for Catholic Education. (1977). *The Catholic school.* Boston: Daughters of St. Paul.

Congregation for Catholic Education. (1982). *Lay Catholics in schools: Witnesses to faith.* Washington, DC: United States Catholic Conference.

Congregation for Catholic Education. (1988). *The religious dimension of education in a Catholic school.* Boston: St. Paul Books & Media.

Convey, John J. (1992). *Catholic schools make a difference: Twenty-five years of research.* Washington, DC: National Catholic Education Association.

Convey, John J. (September, 1994). "Priorities for research on Catholic schools." A paper presented at the research symposium: "Catholic schools: A tradition of excellence–a future with hope," The University of Dayton.

Coward, Geoffrey. (1989). Review of *Schooling as a ritual performance. Educational Studies,* 20, 138–141.

Declaration on Christian education. (1965) Boston: St. Paul's Books & Media.

Dolan, Jay P. (1992). *The American Catholic experience: A history from colonial times to the present.* Notre Dame: University of Notre Dame Press.

Dolan, Jay P. (February, 1994). "The one or the many: Cultural diversity and the rage for order in American Catholic history." Paper presented at the Annual Convention of the National Organization for the Continuing Education of Roman Catholic Clergy, San Diego, CA.

Dreyfous, Leslie. (November 26 ,1995). A literary portrait of a deprived America. *Dayton Daily News,* Section A, p. 19.

Eckhoff, Mary Ann (April, 1992). "The national congress on Catholic schools for the 21st century." Paper presented at the National

Catholic Educational Association Convention, St. Louis, MO.

The economy pastoral ten years later (November 23, 1995). *Origins*, 25, 23, 389–393.

Eisner, Elliot W. (1991). *The enlightened eye: Qualitative inquiry and the enhancement of educational practice.* New York: Macmillan Publishing Company.

Epstein, Kitty Kelly. (1992). Case studies in dropping out and dropping back in. *Journal of Education,* 174, 55–65.

Estrada, Kelly & McLaren, Peter. (1993). A dialogue on multiculturalism and democratic culture. *Educational Researcher,* 22, 3, pp. 27–33.

Finn, Chester E. (September 20, 1993). The return of the dinosaurs. *National Review.*

Freire, Paulo. (1985). *The politics of education*. New York: Bergin & Garvey.

Freire, Paulo. (1989). *Pedagogy of the oppressed.* New York: Continuum.

Freire, Paulo. (1990). *Education for critical consciousness*. New York: Continuum.

Freire, Paulo. (1993). *Pedagogy of the city.* New York: Continuum.

Freire, Paulo. (1994). *Pedagogy of hope: Reliving* Pedagogy of the Oppressed. New York: Continuum

Freire, Paulo & Faundez, Antonio. (1989). *Learning to question: A pedagogy of liberation.* New York: Continuum.

Freire, Paulo & Macedo, Donaldo. (1987). *Literacy: reading the word and the world.* Massachusetts: Bergin & Garvey Publishers, Inc.

Gadotti, Moacir. (1994). *Reading Paulo Freire: His life and work.* New York: State University of New York Press.

Giroux, Henry A. (1979). Toward a new sociology of curriculum. *Educational Leadership,* 37, 248–253.

Giroux, Henry A. (1980). Critical theory and rationality in citizenship education. *Curriculum Inquiry,* 10, 329–366.

Giroux, Henry A. (1981a). *Ideology, culture, and the process of schooling.* Philadelphia: Temple University Press.

Giroux, Henry A. (1981b). Resistance and the paradox of educational reform. *Interchange on Educational Policy,* 12, 3–26.

Giroux, Henry A. (1983). *Theory and resistance in education: A pedagogy for the opposition.* New York: Bergin & Garvey.

Giroux, Henry A. (1988a). *Schooling and the struggle for public life:*

Critical pedagogy in the modern age. Minneapolis: University of Minnesota Press.

Giroux, Henry A. (1988b). *Teachers as intellectuals: Toward a critical pedagogy of learning*. Massachusetts: Bergin & Garvey Publishers, Inc.

Giroux, Henry A. (Ed.). (1991). *Postmodernism, feminism, and cultural politics*. New York: State University of New York Press.

Giroux, Henry A. (1992). *Border crossings: Cultural workers and the politics of education.* New York: Routledge, Chapman and Hall, Inc.

Giroux, Henry A. (1993). *Living dangerously: Multiculturalism and the politics of difference.* New York: Peter Lang.

Giroux, Henry A. & McLaren, Peter. (Eds.). (1989). *Critical pedagogy, the state and cultural struggle.* New York: State University of New York Press.

Giroux, Henry A. & McLaren, Peter. (Eds.). (1994). *Between borders: Pedagogy and the politics of cultural studies.* New York: Routledge.

Goodman, Jesse. (1992). *Elementary schooling for critical democracy.* Albany: State University of New York Press.

Greeley, Andrew M. (1982). *Catholic high schools and minority students.* New Brunswick: Transition Books.

Grimes, Charlotte. (1984, January 29). Giving dropouts an alternative. *St. Louis Post Dispatch,* Section J, pp. 1, 7.

Guerra, Michael J. (1991). *Lighting new fires: Catholic schooling in America 25 years after Vatican II.* Washington, DC: National Catholic Education Association.

Guerra, Michael J., Donahue, Michael J., & Benson, Peter L. (1990). *The heart of the matter: Effects of Catholic high schools on student values, beliefs and behaviors.* Washington, DC: National Catholic Education Association.

Guerra, Michael J., Haney, Regina, & Kealey, Robert J. (1992). *Executive summary: Catholic schools for the 21st century.* Washington, DC: National Catholic Educational Association.

Gutierrez, Gustavo. (1988). *A theology of liberation.* Maryknoll: Orbis Books.

Gutierrez, Gustavo. (1990). *The power of the poor in history.* Maryknoll: Orbis Books.

Gutierrez, Gustavo. (1991). *The God of life.* Maryknoll: Orbis Books.

Harkins, William. (February, 1987). "Higher expectations" in the Catholic inner city high school. *Momentum*, pp. 14–16.

Hennelly, Alfred T. (Ed.). (1990). *Liberation theology: A documentary history.* Maryknoll: Orbis Books.

Hoatson, Robert M. (April, 1992). "Serving the poor—Exploring the options." Paper presented at the National Catholic Educational Association Convention, St. Louis, MO.

Hoatson, Robert M. (April, 1993). "Catholic education: Good news for the poor but." Paper presented at the National Catholic Educational Association Convention, New Orleans, LA.

Hughes, Langston. (1932). *The dream keeper and other poems.* New York: Alfred A. Knopf, Inc.

Hughes, William A. (May, 1986). The implications for episcopal leadership. *Momentum*, pp. 7–8.

Jimenez, Ricardo. (May, 1986). Educating Hispanics–assessment and recommendations. *Momentum*, pp. 9–10.

John Paul II. (October 11, 1995). Once again the United States is called to be a welcoming society. *L'osservtore Romano, pp.* 3, 6.

John Paul II. (October 11, 1995). Religious education should look to the Catechism as sure guide. *L'osservatore Romano,* p. 13.

John Paul II. (October 11, 1995). Sometimes witnessing to Christ means challenging your culture. *L'osservatore Romano,* pp. 11, 13.

John Paul II. (October 11, 1995). Your power has responsibilities. *L'osservtore Romano.* pp. 1, 15.

Kavanaugh, John F. (April, 1992). "Option for the poor: An invitation to religious educators." Paper presented at the National Catholic Education Association Convention, St. Louis, MO.

Keely, Charles. (1989). The Catholic church and the integration of immigrants. *Migration World,* 17, 5, 30–33.

Kelly, Francis D. (Ed.). (1991). *What makes a school Catholic?* Washington, DC: National Catholic Education Association.

Kozol, Jonathan. (1991). *Savage inequalities: Children in America's schools.* New York: Crown Publishers, Inc.

Kozol, Jonathan. (1995). *Amazing grace: The lives of children and the conscience of a nation.* New York: Crown Publishers, Inc.

Kreisberg, Seth. (1992). *Transforming power: Domination, empowerment, and education.* Albany: State University of New York Press.

Lankshear, Colin. (1989). Rituals and revelations [Review of *Schooling as a ritual performance*]. *Journal of Education,* 171, 132–149.

LeCompte, Margaret & Preissle, Judith. (1993). *Ethnography and qualitative design in educational research.* San Diego: Academic Press, Inc.

Lesko, Nancy. (1983). *Ritual resolution of ideological tensions in a parochial high school.* American Educational Research Association, Montreal, Canada. (ERIC Document Reproduction Service No. ED 231 725)

Lesko, Nancy. (1986). Individualism and community: ritual discourse in a parochial high school. *Anthropology & Education Quarterly,* 17, 25–39.

Lesko, Nancy. (1988a). *Symbolizing society: Stories, rites and structure in a Catholic high school.* Lewes, England: Falmer Press.

Lesko, Nancy. (1988b). "We're leading America": The changing organization and form of high school cheerleading. *Theory and Research in Social Education,* 4, 263–278.

Lincoln, Yvonna S. (1995). In search of students' voices. *Theory into Practice,* 34, 88–93.

Lyke, James P. (1992). Catholic schools: The lifeblood of evangelization. In Michael Guerra, Regina Haney, & Robert J. Kealey, *Executive summary: Catholic schools for the 21st century* (pp. 47–48). Washington, DC: National Catholic Educational Association.

Manno, Bruno V. (October, 1982). An update on the Coleman study. *Momentum,* pp. 4–7.

Manno, Bruno V. (December, 1985). Catholic schools: Countering the stereotypes and serving minority interests. *Momentum,* pp. 58–59.

Mayock, Louise. (1979). "The influence of the Second Vatican Council on the American Catholic school." Doctoral dissertation. University of Pennsylvania.

Mayock, Louise & Glatthorn, Allan. (December, 1980) NCEA and the development of the post-conciliar Catholic school. *Momentum,* pp. 7–9, 47.

McCarthy, Colman. (April 3, 1992). Gray students are geniuses of a particular kind. *National Catholic Reporter,* p. 19.

McDermott, Edwin J. (1986). *Distinctive qualities of the Catholic school.* Washington, DC: National Catholic Educational Association.

McLaren, Peter. (1986). Review article–"Postmodernity and the death of a politics: A Brazilian perspective." *Educational Theory,* 36, 389–401.

McLaren, Peter. (1986a). Making Catholics: The ritual production of conformity in a Catholic junior high school. *Journal of Education,* 168, 55–77.

McLaren, Peter. (1986b). *Schooling as a ritual performance.* Boston: Routledge & Kegan Paul.

McLaren, Peter. (1987). The anthropological roots of pedagogy: The teacher as liminal servant. *Anthropology and Humanism Quarterly,* 12, pp. 75–85.

McLaren, Peter. (1989). *Life in schools: An introduction to critical pedagogy in the foundations of education.* New York: Longman.

McLaren, Peter. (1991a). Critical pedagogy: Constructing an arch of social dreaming and a doorway to hope. *Journal of Education,* 173, 1, pp. 9–34.

McLaren, Peter. (1991b). Critical pedagogy, multiculturalism, and the politics of risk and resistance: A response to Kelly and Portelli. *Journal of Education,* 173, 3, pp. 29–59.

McLaren, Peter. (1991c). Field relations and the discourse of the other: collaboration in our own ruin. In William B. Shaffir, & Robert A. Stebbins, (Eds.), *Experiencing fieldwork: An inside view of qualitative research* (pp. 131–163). Newbury Park: Sage Publications.

McLaren, Peter. (1992). Collisions with otherness: "Traveling" theory, post-colonial criticism, and the politics of ethnographic practice–the mission of the wounded ethnographer. *Qualitative Studies in Education,* 5, 77–92.

McLaren, Peter. (1993). Multiculturalism and the postmodern critique: Towards a pedagogy of resistance and transformation. *Cultural Studies,* 7, 118–146.

McLaren, Peter. (1994). *Life in schools: An introduction to critical pedagogy in the foundations of education,* 2nd ed. New York: Longman.

McLaren, Peter. (1995). *Critical pedagogy and predatory culture: Oppositional politics in a postmodern era.* New York: Routledge.

McLaren, Peter & Tadeu da Silva, Tomaz. (1993). Decentering pedagogy: Critical literacy, resistance and the politics of memory. In Peter McLaren, & Peter Leonard, (Eds.), *Paulo Freire: A critical encounter* (pp. 47–89) New York: Routledge.

McLaren, Peter & Lankshear, Colin. (1994). *Politics of liberation: Paths from Freire.* New York: Routledge.

McLaren, Peter & Leonard, Peter. (Eds.). (1993). *Paulo Freire: A critical encounter.* New York: Routledge.

McLaughlin, Daniel & Tierney, William G. (Eds.). (1993). *Naming silenced lives: Personal narratives and processes of educational change.* New York: Routledge.

Medcalf, John. (June 24, 1995). A prophet's lesson. *The Tablet,* pp. 801–802.

Meyers, John F. (April/May, 1994). A dramatic renewal (1974–1986). *Momentum,* pp. 60–64.

Middeke, Rafe. (1981). The Vincent Gray Alternative High School: One year old. (Original source unknown—photocopy from files of Vincent Gray Alternative High School).

Miller, Janet L. (1990). *Creating spaces and finding voices: Teachers collaborating for empowerment.* Albany: State University of New York Press.

Moraes, Marcia. (1992). Review of *Paulo Freire: A critical encounter. Journal of Education,* 174 , 128–135.

Morrison, Toni. (1987). *Beloved.* New York: Penguin Books.

National Commission on Excellence in Education. (1983). *A nation at risk: The imperative for educational reform.* Washington, DC: U.S. Department of Education.

National Conference of Catholic Bishops. (1972). *To teach as Jesus did.* Washington, DC: United States Catholic Conference.

National Conference of Catholic Bishops. (1976). *Teach them.* Washington, DC: United States Catholic Conference.

National Conference of Catholic Bishops. (1990). *In support of Catholic elementary and secondary schools.* Washington, DC: United States Catholic Conference.

National Congress on Catholic Schools. (1991) Summary of beliefs and direction statements. In *Momentum,* April/May 1995, pp. 10–11.

Noddings, Nel. (1992). *The challenge to care in schools: An alternative approach to education.* New York: Teachers College Press.

Obidinski, Eugene. (1984). Parochial school foundations of Buffalo's Polonia. *Urban Education,* 18, 4, 438–451.

O'Gorman, Robert T. (1987) *Catholic identity and Catholic education in the United States since 1790.* Nashville: Scarritt.

Ohio Catholic Conference of Bishops. (1990). *Catholic schools: Heritage and legacy.* Ohio Catholic Conference.

Oldenski, Thomas. (1994). "Liberation theology and critical pedagogy: Theory and practice at an alternative school site." Doctoral dissertation, Miami University, Oxford, Ohio.

Oldenski, Thomas. (Summer, 1995). An experience of crossing borders: Voices of administrators and teachers at an alternative high school. *EnText*, 71–90.

Oldenski, Thomas. (1995). Critical pedagogy: A union of liberation theology and feminist ethic of risk? *Journal of Curriculum Discourse and Dialogue*, Fall 1994/Spring 1995, 69–76.

Page, Reba & Valli, Linda. (Eds.). (1990). *Curriculum differentiation: Interpretive studies in U.S. secondary schools*. Albany: State University of New York Press.

Perko, F. Michael. (1990). Education and the social sciences [Review of *Symbolizing society: Stories, rites and structure in a Catholic high school*]. *Educational Studies*, 21, 98–103.

Perry, Margaret. (1976). *Silence to the drums: A survey of the literature of the Harlem Renaissance*. Westport: Greenwood Press.

Phan, Peter C. (February, 1994) "Cultural diversity: A blessing or a curse for theology and spirituality?" Paper presented at the Annual Convention of the National Organization for the Continuing Education of Roman Catholic Clergy, San Diego, CA.

Pinar, William F., Reynolds, William M., Slattery, Patrick, & Taubman, Peter M. (1995). *Understanding curriculum: An introduction to the study of historical and contemporary curriculum discourses*. New York: Peter Lang.

Purpel, David E. (1988). Review of *Schooling as a ritual performance*. *Educational Theory*, 38, 155–163.

Purpel, David E. (1989). *The moral and spiritual crisis in education*. Massachusetts: Bergin & Garvey Publishers, Inc.

Quantz, Richard A. (1992). On critical ethnography (with some postmodern considerations). In Margaret D. Le Compte, Wendy L. Millroy, & Judith Preissle (Eds.) *The handbook of qualitative research in education* (pp. 447–505). San Diego: Academic Press, Inc.

Quantz, Richard A. & O'Connor, Terence W. (1988). Writing critical ethnography: Dialogue, multivoicedness, and carnival in cultural texts. *Educational Theory*, 38, 1, 95–109.

Reck, Carleen. (1991). Catholic identity. In *The Catholic identity of Catholic schools*. Washington, DC: National Catholic Educational Association, pp. 21–38.

Rice, Patricia. (May 25, 1992). An alternative to poverty: Vincent Gray High School in East St. Louis gives dropouts another chance. *St. Louis Post-Dispatch,* section D, pp. 1, 6.

Rodriguez, Domingo. (February, 1994). "One church, but not one happy family." Paper presented at the Annual Convention of the National Organization for the Continuing Education of Roman Catholic Clergy. San Diego, CA.

Roman Synod. (1971) *Justicè in the world.* In Michael Walsh & Brian Davies (Eds.) (1991), *Proclaiming justice and peace: Papal documents from Rerum Novarum through Centesimus Annus.* Mystic, CT: Twenty-Third Publications, pp. 268–283.

Ryan, Francis. (Fall, 1992). The first to opt out: Historical snapshots of Catholic schooling in America. *Educational Horizons,* 53–64.

Schumacher, Sally & McMillan, James H. (1993). *Research in education: A conceptual introduction,* 3rd ed. New York: HarperCollins College Publishers.

Scott, Karla. (June 10, 1981). Vincent Gray provides alternative for drop outs. *East St. Louis News,* Section 3, p. 1.

Segundo, Juan Luis. (1976). *The liberation of theology.* Maryknoll: Orbis Books.

Segundo, Juan Luis. (1992). *The liberation of dogma.* Maryknoll: Orbis Books.

Shimabukuro, Gini. (1993). "Profile of an ideal Catholic school teacher: Content analysis of Roman and American documents, 1965 to 1990." Doctoral dissertation, University of San Francisco, California.

Shimabukuro, Gini. (August/September, 1994). In search of identity. *Momentum,* pp. 23–26.

Shor, Ira. (1993). Education is politics: Paulo Freire's critical pedagogy. In Peter McLaren & Paul Leonard (Eds.), *Paulo Freire: A critical encounter* (pp. 25–35). New York: Routledge.

Shor, Ira & Freire, Paulo. (1987). *A pedagogy for liberation: Dialogues on transforming education.* New York: Bergin & Garvey.

Slattery, Patrick. (1995). *Curriculum development in the postmodern era.* New York: Garland Publishing, Inc.

Slaughter, Dianna T. & Johnson, Deborah J. (1988). *Visible now: Blacks in private schools.* New York: Greenwood Press.

Sleeter, Christine E. & McLaren, Peter L. (Eds.). (1995). *Multicultural education, critical pedagogy, and the politics of difference.* New York: State University of New York Press.

Smith, Pamela K. (1989). "In search of forms and practices for democratic education." Doctoral dissertation, Miami University, Oxford, Ohio.

Spring, Joel. (1991). *American education: An introduction to social and political aspects.* New York: Longman.

Svoboda, Melannie. (November 11, 1995). The eight beatitudes of writing. *America,* 173, 15, 23–24.

Taylor, Mark Kline. (1990). *Remembering Esperanza: A cultural-political theology for north American praxis.* Maryknoll: Orbis Books.

Torres, Carlos Alberto. (1993). From the pedagogy of the oppressed to a luta continua: The political pedagogy of Paulo Freire. In Peter McLaren & Peter Leonard (Eds.), *Paulo Friere: A critical encounter* (pp. 119–145). New York: Routledge.

Traviss, Mary Peter. (1989). *Doctoral dissertations on Catholic schools, K-12 1976–1987.* Washington, DC: National Catholic Education Association.

Tway, Eileen. (1988). The resource center: The whats and wherefores of schooling [Review of *Schooling as a ritual performance*]. *Language Arts,* 65, 503–504.

Vincent Gray Alternative High School. (1981). *An introduction to Vincent Gray High School.*

Vincent Gray Alternative High School. (1992). Student handbook.

Vladimiroff, Christine. (May, 1986). Choosing life—not survival. *Momentum,* pp. 15–16.

Wagner, Jean. (1973). *Black poets of the United States: From Paul Laurence Dunbar to Langston Hughes.* Chicago: University of Illinois Press.

Waldon, Clarence R. (February/March, 1994). The inner-city school: Pastoral gift or burden? *Momentum,* pp. 20–22.

Watson-Gegeo, Karen-Ann. (1987). Review of *Schooling as a ritual performance. Harvard Educational Review,* 57, 222–224.

Wehlage, Gary G., Rutter, Robert A., Smith, Gregory A., Lesko, Nancy, & Fernandez, Ricardo R. (1989). *Reducing the risk: Schools as communities of support.* Philadelphia: The Falmer Press.

Welch, Sharon D. (1985). *Communities of resistance and solidarity.* Maryknoll: Orbis Books.

Welch, Sharon D. (1990). *A feminist ethic of risk.* Minneapolis: Fortress Press.

Willis, Paul. (1977). *Learning to labour: How working class kids get working class jobs.* Westmead: Saxon House.

Yeager, Robert J., Benson, Peter L., Guerra, Michael J., & Manno, Bruno V. (1985). *The Catholic high school: A national portrait.* Washington, DC: National Catholic Education Association.

Yearwood, Lori Teresa. (January 25, 1993). Dropouts climb educational mountain. *St. Louis Post-Dispatch*, Section A, pp. 1, 6.

Yelvington, Rube. (1990). *East St. Louis the way it is 1990.* Mascoutah, IL: Top's Books.

Index

Made in the USA
Middletown, DE
22 August 2021

46621450R00149